Ivory Tower and Industrial Innovation

INNOVATION *and* TECHNOLOGY *in the* WORLD ECONOMY

Editors

MARTIN KENNEY
University of California, Davis/Berkeley
Round Table on the International Economy

BRUCE KOGUT
Wharton School, University of Pennsylvania

Other titles in the series

Ivory Tower and Industrial Innovation

*University-Industry Technology Transfer Before and
After the Bayh-Dole Act in the United States*

DAVID C. MOWERY, RICHARD R. NELSON,
BHAVEN N. SAMPAT, *and* ARVIDS A. ZIEDONIS

Stanford Business Books

An Imprint of Stanford University Press
Stanford, California   2004

Stanford University Press
Stanford, California

√© 2004 by the Board of Trustees of the Leland Stanford Junior
University. All rights reserved.

Printed in the United States of America
On acid-free, archival-quality paper

Library of Congress Cataloging-in-Publication Data

Ivory tower and industrial innovation : university-industry
technology transfer before and after the Bayh-Dole Act in
the United States / David C. Mowery . . . [et al.].
    p. cm. — (Innovation and technology in the world economy)
  ISBN 0-8047-4920-5 (cloth : alk. paper)
1. Technology transfer—United States.   2. Academic-industrial
collaboration—United States.   I. Mowery, David C. II. Series.
T174.3 I96 2004
338.973'06—dc22

                                                2003025632

Typeset by G&S Typesetters, Inc. in 10/12.5 Electra

Original Printing 2004

Last figure below indicates year of this printing:
13   12   11   10   09   08   07   06   05   04

CONTENTS

TABLES AND FIGURES

ACKNOWLEDGMENTS

We are indebted to the staffs of the technology licensing offices of Columbia University, Stanford University, and the University of California for invaluable assistance with the collection and analysis of these data. Our access to the data at the University of California was made possible through the support of Jay Stowsky and Suzanne Quick from the Office of the President of the University of California. Kathryn Ku of Stanford University made the data from Stanford's Office of Technology Licensing available to us for research use. The research on the Columbia University data underpinning this paper also benefited from the efforts of Michael Crow, Holly Raider, and Annetine Gelijns of Columbia University. Michael Barnes and Lynn Fissell of the University of California assisted in the collection and analysis of the University of California data, and the research on the Stanford data benefited from the assistance of Sandra Bradford. Special thanks to Michael Barnes for the use of his university patenting data and to Adam Jaffe of Brandeis University, Bronwyn Hall of UC Berkeley, and Manuel Trajtenberg of Tel Aviv University and the NBER for making the NBER–Case Western Reserve patent data available to us. We thank the staffs at the archives of Columbia University, MIT, the National Research Council, and the Smithsonian Institution for access to their records. In addition, we are indebted to W. Stevenson Bacon for access to the Research Corporation's archives and discussions about its patent management activities.

Bronwyn Hall, Scott Stern, Rosemarie Ziedonis, Josh Lerner, Stephen Cameron, Rebecca Henderson, David Roessner, Scott Shane, Ken Leonard, Frank Lichtenberg, Adam Jaffe, and seminar participants at UC Berkeley, Columbia University, the University of Pennsylvania, the University of Maryland, the University of Reading, and the Federal Reserve Bank of Philadelphia gave us many helpful comments on earlier versions of much of the research contained in this volume. We are especially indebted to Nathan Rosenberg of Stanford University, who contributed to portions of Chapter 2 and who played a central role in the early stages of the research project that produced this volume.

Support for this research was provided by the Andrew W. Mellon Foundation; the Alfred P. Sloan Foundation; the California Policy Seminar; the UC President's Industry-University Cooperative Research Program; the Office of the Provost at Columbia University; the Division of Research at the Harvard Business School; the Institute of Innovation, Organization, and Management at the Haas School of Business, UC Berkeley; and the Mack Center of the Wharton School at the University of Pennsylvania.

Ivory Tower and Industrial Innovation

1

Introduction: The Ivory Tower
and Industrial Innovation

This monograph deals with the relationship between U.S. universities and industrial innovation, focusing in particular on the role of patenting and licensing of academic inventions in supporting "technology transfer" between universities and industry. The role of universities in industrial innovation and economic growth has received considerable fanfare in recent years, as U.S. universities have expanded their patenting and licensing activities since the early 1980s. Many observers have attributed this expanded patenting and licensing to the Bayh-Dole Act of 1980, although little hard evidence has been provided in support of this conclusion. Nor has much evidence been produced to support the argument that patenting and licensing of university inventions are necessary to support the transfer to industry and commercial development of these inventions. Other, more critical accounts of the Bayh-Dole Act have suggested that the growth in academic patenting and licensing has changed the "research culture" of U.S. universities, leading to increased secrecy, less sharing of research results, and a shift in the focus of academic research away from fundamental to more applied topics.

The evidence presented in this volume suggests that the Bayh-Dole Act was one of several factors that contributed to the growth of patenting and licensing by U.S. universities during the 1980s and 1990s. The Act provided a strong congressional endorsement for academic institutions' involvement in patenting and licensing research discoveries and simplified the formerly complex administrative processes through which U.S. universities gained title to the intellectual property resulting from publicly funded research. Even without the Bayh-Dole Act, however, we believe that university patenting would have grown significantly during the 1980s and 1990s. As we point out below, many

2   U.S. universities were active patenters and licensors long before the passage of the Bayh-Dole Act, and they expanded these activities during the 1970s and early 1980s in response to advances in biomedical research and changes in the legal treatment of patents on life forms. It is likely that these and other universities with less experience in patenting and licensing would have initiated or expanded these activities even in the absence of the Bayh-Dole Act. Indeed, U.S. research universities were an important source of support for the passage of the Act in 1980, as we note in Chapter 5. Nonetheless, there is little doubt that U.S. universities now are more heavily and directly involved in patenting and licensing of research results than at any previous time in their history.

The Bayh-Dole Act was motivated by the belief that university patenting would spur and facilitate the transfer of university discoveries to industry for commercial development. Although the evidence on this point presented in this volume is at best suggestive rather than definitive, it indicates that research results and knowledge flow between universities and industry (and we stress the two-way nature of this flow) through publications by academic researchers, conference presentations, faculty consulting, and the movement of personnel between universities and industry, to name but a few channels. Before and since the Bayh-Dole Act, much of the interaction between universities and industry has not involved patenting and licensing.

In some cases, university patenting may indeed aid technology transfer, but in many cases patenting of an invention by a university is not necessary to support the transfer and commercialization of an invention. In these cases, patents may produce income for the university (although most patents yield little licensing income), while creating some risk that restrictive licensing policies can limit the diffusion and use of an invention or related knowledge. Indeed, in some fields of research, patenting and licensing could limit the operation of other channels of mutual influence and interaction.

In short, the issues raised by university patenting and licensing are complex, and the course of action that is likely to yield the greatest public benefit (the overriding goal of Bayh-Dole) varies among inventions and fields of technology. Nevertheless, for the foreseeable future, U.S. universities (and, it seems, more and more non-U.S. universities) will be patenting more intensively. A key challenge for policy concerns the appropriate design of licensing policies for universities engaged in patenting of inventions financed with public funds to ensure that publicly funded research yields the greatest possible societal benefit.

The growth in U.S. university patenting and licensing has been concentrated in a relatively narrow set of research fields, notably the biomedical sciences and some areas of engineering. It is unlikely, therefore, that increased patenting and licensing have altered the "culture" of academic research throughout U.S. universities, simply because these activities have focused on relatively few academic disciplines. Even within the fields where licensing and patenting are concentrated, however, there is little evidence of a significant shift in the focus or output of academic research, although the available evidence on this point is limited and is likely to indicate any such shift only well after the fact.

Another factor behind the growth of university patenting is the extension of definitions of "patentable material" into the realm of science. Since scientific research in many fields relies heavily on a relatively liberal exchange of materials and other intellectual artifacts, greater assertion of private property rights over these artifacts and materials potentially could increase the transactions costs of scientific research and impede progress. But this extension of the realm of the patentable reflects developments in a much broader set of policies and institutions (notably, in the U.S. Patent and Trademark Office) than university patent and licensing policies or the Bayh-Dole Act.

ORGANIZATION OF THE VOLUME

Although the Bayh-Dole Act and its effects are central issues in the chapters that follow, our examination of the Act's origins and consequences requires a broader consideration of the historical evolution of university-industry relations and technology transfer in the United States, which we undertake in Chapters 2–4. American universities have made significant contributions to technological innovation in industry for well over a century. The Morrill Act of 1862 was emblematic of an American commitment that universities should serve the democracy and its citizens. Research at university agricultural experimentation stations provided the scientific base for the hybrid corn revolution of the 1930s and the postwar years and played a central role in developing hybrid seed varieties tailored to the particular conditions of individual states. But U.S. universities' contributions to the development of the American economy went well beyond agriculture. Edwin Armstrong's work at Columbia University laid the basis for vacuum tube–based amplification of electronic signals, a key contribution to the development of modern radio technology. Much of the early work in developing computers and lasers, as well as the Internet, was performed in universities. And universities played leading roles in the development of a number of important pharmaceuticals.

These historic contributions of U.S. universities to industrial innovation were made through a diverse array of channels of interaction, all of which

4   continue to figure prominently in university-industry knowledge exchange
and technology transfer. Although a number of U.S. universities did pursue
patents in the pre-1980 period (see Chapters 3 and 4), many university contributions to technical advance did not rely on patenting of the university discoveries. One particularly important factor supporting the development of research links and two-way flows of knowledge and technology between U.S.
universities and industry throughout the twentieth century is the structure of
the U.S. university system, which differs in important ways from those of other
industrial economies. We discuss this issue in more detail in Chapter 2.

Chapter 3 analyzes the debates of the 1920s and 1930s over the role of university patenting and licensing by way of highlighting the remarkable similarities, as well as some important contrasts, between these debates and those
over the Bayh-Dole Act in the late 1970s. Through much of the twentieth century U.S. universities were ambivalent about direct involvement in patenting
and licensing. In part, this ambivalence reflected concerns that any appearance of profiteering at public expense would be politically embarrassing. As a
result, a number of leading research universities limited faculty patenting, primarily in the biomedical arena, for much of the pre-1970 period. Even where
such leading research universities as MIT encouraged patenting by faculty,
they avoided direct involvement in the management of these patents and associated licenses.

Indeed, concern over the effects of direct university involvement in patent
management was one motive for University of California professor Frederick
Cottrell's founding of the Research Corporation in 1912 to manage patenting
and licensing for academic institutions. As we point out in Chapter 4, many
U.S. research universities "outsourced" these activities to the Research Corporation or other patent management organizations during the postwar
era. The corporation's growth and eventual eclipse by universities' independent management of patenting and licensing during the 1970s reflect many of
the same challenges that contemporary university technology licensing managers face.

Chapter 5 describes the political origins and passage of the Bayh-Dole Act,
and Chapters 6 and 7 analyze previously unexamined data dealing with the
Act's effects on patenting and licensing by U.S. universities. Chapter 6 focuses
on three leading research universities, and Chapter 7 examines broader national trends in university patenting and licensing before and after the Bayh-
Dole Act. Our quantitative analyses shed light on the effects of Bayh-Dole but
do not address the validity of a key premise of the Bayh-Dole Act, the importance of patenting for the commercialization of individual university inventions. In order to examine this issue, Chapter 8 presents detailed case studies
of five university inventions that highlight the diversity of circumstances that

influence the process of technology transfer and commercialization. Like the surveys of industrial managers that are discussed in Chapter 2, our case studies reveal substantial contrasts among fields of research and innovation in the role of patents and licenses. Moreover, these cases suggest considerable heterogeneity among inventions within the biomedical field. The final chapter summarizes our findings and discusses their implications for further research.

WHAT HAVE WE LEARNED?

Although a number of U.S. universities were patenting and licensing faculty inventions during much of the twentieth century, academic patenting and licensing are not the primary channels for technology transfer and knowledge exchange with industry. Surveys of industry R&D managers during the 1980s and 1990s consistently suggest that patents and licenses are less important than other channels for knowledge flow and interaction with university researchers (for example, faculty publications or conference presentations) in all fields, including the biomedical sciences.

The passage of the Bayh-Dole Act in 1980 coincided with several other developments of great importance for the growth in U.S. university patenting and licensing. The U.S. Supreme Court affirmed the validity of patents on life forms in the same year, and the 1970s and 1980s were a period of significant scientific advances in biomedical research (much of which was supported by the U.S. National Institutes of Health) that proved to have considerable potential for industrial applications. Indeed, two large research universities that had long been active patenters and licensors (Stanford University and the University of California system) shifted their patent and license portfolios in favor of biomedical inventions before the passage of the Bayh-Dole Act, and a leading post-1980 "entrant" into patenting, Columbia University, filed an application for its most lucrative single licensed invention, also in the biomedical field, before the Act's passage.

Passage of the Bayh-Dole Act was followed by increased patenting at both of the "experienced" institutional patenters in our dataset and a decline in the share of these patents finding industrial licensees, consistent with a shift toward patenting less significant inventions in the immediate aftermath of the Act's passage. But overall, there is no evidence at any of these three leading research universities that the frequency of citations by other patents to their post-1980 patents (widely interpreted as a measure of the economic or technological "importance" of a patent) declined significantly by comparison with nonacademic patents. These universities' patents were more heavily cited on average than nonacademic patents before as well as after the Bayh-Dole Act.

6   Before and after the Bayh-Dole Act, the licensing revenues of the experienced academic patenters were dominated by a very small number of "home run" inventions, most of which were biomedical inventions. This characterization also accurately describes the 1985–95 licensing revenues of Columbia University, which had much less historical experience in patenting and licensing. The unpredictable and infrequent appearance of such "home runs" means that many U.S. universities active in patenting and licensing of faculty inventions have found these activities to be unprofitable. Although income is only one of several motives for pursuing these technology transfer activities, it figures prominently among the reasons for entry by many universities into patenting and licensing after 1980. Moreover, greater institutional experience in managing patenting and licensing may not increase the probability that such a "home run" will be discovered by a university's faculty or other researchers and be disclosed to its licensing office.

The effects of the Bayh-Dole Act on the patenting activities of experienced academic patenters thus were more modest than many assessments suggest. Nevertheless, the Bayh-Dole Act facilitated the entry into patenting of a number of institutions with little experience in managing patenting and licensing activities. These novice patenters did indeed receive less heavily cited patents initially, but by the end of the 1980s their patents were cited no less intensively than those assigned to "experienced" academic patenters and (like the patents assigned to "experienced" universities) were more heavily cited than nonacademic patents in the same classes.

As we noted earlier, the case studies in Chapter 8 seek to examine an important assumption animating the drafting and passage of the Bayh-Dole Act, viz., the belief that patenting was both necessary and sufficient to facilitate the transfer to industry and commercial development of university inventions. The case studies indicate that the processes of knowledge exchange and technology transfer are complex, and the channels through which these processes operate most effectively differ significantly among different fields of technology. Moreover, these processes also require a strong "relational" component for their smooth operation — as we note in Chapters 4 and 8, centralization in university licensing operations historically has been difficult, because of the need for frequent interaction between licensing professionals and the faculty inventors.

Another set of assumptions underpinning the design of the Bayh-Dole Act dealt with the characteristics of the intellectual property for which universities would seek patent protection. The Act saw patented intellectual property as a key enabling factor in the process of technology development — without clear property rights on intellectual property, commercial developers would not make the investments necessary to bring these inventions to the market. But a portion of the growth in university patenting since 1980 appears to involve an extension of patents to cover inputs to science, rather than technological arti-facts that are candidates for commercial development. The supporters of Bayh-Dole devoted little consideration to any negative effects of university patenting and licensing on "open science," partly because the growth of patenting in scientific, as opposed to technological, fields was not apparent in the early 1980s.

These and other developments, however, underscore the need to place the Bayh-Dole Act in context. The growth of university patenting is in part a response to the extension during the 1980s and 1990s of intellectual prop-erty rights to cover new types of artifacts (for example, research tools) and the willingness of the U.S. Patent and Trademark Office to grant broad claims that may affect a much broader set of future "prospects" for development of a given technology. The Bayh-Dole Act was not itself responsible for this exten-sion, but its effects cannot be understood without considering these broader developments.

Another reason for keeping this broader context in the foreground of any evaluation of Bayh-Dole's effects is the recent enthusiasm among other industrial-economy governments for adopting policies for university technol-ogy transfer that closely resemble the Bayh-Dole Act. Other governments' em-ulation of the Bayh-Dole Act is motivated by their desire to increase and en-hance research collaboration and technology transfer between their national university systems and industry. But these "reforms" overlook the long history of university-industry collaboration and technology transfer in the United States that predates the Bayh-Dole Act. Especially in the absence of broader structural reforms in their national university systems, emulation of Bayh-Dole is likely to accomplish little and could well prove to be counterproductive.

Our overall verdict on the Bayh-Dole Act thus is a mixed one. Much of the post-1980 upsurge in university patenting and licensing, we believe, would have occurred without the Act and reflects broader developments in federal policy and academic research. This increase in patenting and licensing, how-ever, is concentrated in a few fields of academic research, and any "cultural impacts" associated with such expanded patenting and licensing therefore are also relatively localized within U.S. research universities. At the same time, any evidence of significantly detrimental effects on the norms or direction of academic research, disclosure of results, conflicts of interest, and the like will take time to emerge, and such evidence will be apparent only after any dam-age has occurred. The Act's emphasis on patenting and licensing as a critically important vehicle for the transfer to industry of academic inventions lacked a strong evidentiary foundation at the time of its passage, and evidence on the

8   role of patenting and licensing as indispensable components of technology transfer remains mixed. U.S. universities have long collaborated with industry in applied and fundamental research, and channels other than patenting have been critical to this collaboration. Nonetheless, patenting per se is less critical to any assessment of the Act's effects on public welfare than are the types of licensing policies adopted by universities. Finally, any encouragement from the Bayh-Dole Act for greater patenting of scientific, as opposed to technological, artifacts remains an issue for concern.

As we point out in our concluding chapter, U.S. universities have enjoyed a charmed political life during most of the post-1940 era, benefiting from a surge in federal financial support for academic research that was rooted in key public missions, such as national defense and public health. Federal support for U.S. academic research grew in parallel with the rise of U.S. research universities to their current positions of international preeminence. The remarkable postwar advance of U.S. research universities to global research leadership from positions of parity in some fields of research and laggards in many others reflects the reliance of federal support for university research on principles of interinstitutional competition and autonomy. As they face a new century of challenges and opportunities, it is essential for the preservation of their preeminence that U.S. research universities maintain their historic commitment to the free flow of knowledge and to research in the service of the global public interest. As denizens of universities, we are confident that robust debate and discussion can only contribute to the pursuit of these goals.

2

HISTORICAL OVERVIEW: AMERICAN UNIVERSITIES AND TECHNICAL PROGRESS IN INDUSTRY

In the opening chapters of this monograph, we consider the contributions of universities to technical progress in industry and the role of patenting in these contributions during the 1890–1980 period.[1] This chapter focuses on the role of American universities in industrial innovation prior to and immediately after World War II; Chapters 3 and 4 examine aspects of U.S. universities' patenting activities during the pre-1980 period. We also seek in this chapter to present a broader perspective on the nature of the contributions by U.S. universities to industrial innovation, the channels through which these contributions have been realized, and the factors that have encouraged these contributions.

DISTINCTIVE STRUCTURAL CHARACTERISTICS OF U.S. HIGHER EDUCATION

Their focus on training for farmers and workers, along with research oriented to regional economic development, differentiated American land-grant universities from European universities of the late nineteenth and early twentieth centuries. U.S. public universities, especially those established under the terms of the Morrill Act, affected the direction of the academic research enterprise during this period to a greater extent than the private Ivy League institutions. These characteristics were anticipated in Alexis de Tocqueville's discussion of attitudes toward science in the young republic:

> In America the purely practical part of science is admirably understood and careful attention is paid to the theoretical portion, which is immediately requisite to application. On this head, the Americans always display a clear, free, original, and

inventive power of mind. But hardly any one in the United States devotes himself to the essentially theoretical and abstract portion of human knowledge. (1990, vol. 2, p. 42)

Rather than focusing on the "essentially theoretical and abstract portion of human knowledge," de Tocqueville argued that "science" in the young republic concerned itself with applications:

> Every new method which leads by a shorter road to wealth, every machine which spares labor, every instrument which diminishes the cost of production, every discovery which facilitates pleasure or augments them, seems [to such people] to be the grandest effort of the human intellect. It is chiefly from these motives that a democratic people addicts itself to scientific pursuits . . . In a community thus organized, it may easily be conceived that the human mind may be led insensibly to the neglect of theory; and that it is urged, on the contrary, with unparalleled energy, to the applications of science, or at least to that portion of theoretical science which is necessary to those who make such applications. (1990, vol. 2, p. 45)

This utilitarian orientation to science influenced the research and other activities of American universities. British visitors (and at least a few U.S. observers, including Flexner [1930] and Veblen [1918]) disdained the "vocationalism" of the nineteenth- and early-twentieth-century American higher educational system. Long before their British and other European counterparts, U.S. universities assumed responsibility for teaching and research in fields such as agriculture and mining; commercial subjects such as accounting, finance, marketing, and management; and an ever-widening swath of subjects in civil, mechanical, electrical, chemical, aeronautical, and other engineering disciplines.

There were a number of reasons for the "practical" orientation of U.S. universities. In contrast to most European systems of higher education before and after 1945, the American university system has always lacked any centralized control. Although the Morrill Acts of 1862 and 1890 provided federal support for the establishment of the land-grant universities, administrative oversight of these institutions, as well as primary responsibility for their operating budgets, remained under the control of state governments in the United States.[2] Throughout the twentieth century, U.S. universities retained great autonomy in their administrative policies.

The U.S. university system also was much less oriented to training graduates for governmental service than were the university systems of Germany, France, or Japan. Although some "finishing" and religious preparatory schools such as Harvard and Yale originally were modeled on European institutions, many U.S. universities and colleges chose their missions and research agenda on the basis of the special needs of their local environment. One consequence of this approach was that the funding and enrollment of these schools became heavily dependent on the mores and needs of the local community.[3] And as de Tocqueville indicated, these mores tended strongly to the practical. Partly because of these utilitarian motives, as well as the demand by many communities for colleges or universities, the United States developed a higher education "system" that was larger than those of contemporary European nations. As Trow (1979) points out,

> America had established 9 colleges by the time of the Revolution, when 2 — Oxford and Cambridge — were enough for the much larger and wealthier mother country. The United States entered the Civil War with about 250 colleges, of which over 180 still survive. Even more striking is the record of failure: between the American Revolution and the Civil War perhaps as many as 700 colleges were started and failed. By 1880 England was doing very well with 4 universities for a population of 23 million, while the single state of Ohio, with a population of 3 million, already boasted 37 institutions of higher learning . . . By 1910 we had nearly a thousand colleges and universities with a third of a million students — at a time when the 16 universities of France enrolled altogether about forty thousand students, a number nearly equaled by the faculty members of the American institutions. (pp. 271–72)

Not surprisingly, the U.S. higher education system enrolled a larger fraction of the eighteen-to-twenty-two-year-old population than those of any European nations throughout the 1900–1945 period. According to Geiger (1986), roughly 12 percent of this age group was enrolled in U.S. universities and colleges as early as 1928, a sharp increase from 8 percent in 1920. Although the fraction of this age group enrolled in colleges and universities probably declined during the Great Depression, Graham and Diamond (1997, p. 24) estimate that the share reached 12 percent once again by 1940, three times the 4 percent of Europeans in this age cohort enrolled in colleges and universities in the same year. Not until the 1960s did European enrollment rates exceed 10 percent of the relevant age cohorts, by which time U.S. enrollment rates within this group were reaching 50 percent (Burn et al., 1971).

The Morrill Act of 1862 was rooted in these American views about the role of university research and teaching. The Act's intent was eminently practical, inasmuch as it was dedicated to the support of agriculture and the mechanical arts by encouraging the establishment of state-controlled universities whose long-term prosperity and success depended on their responsiveness to the demands of the local community. But private universities also depended on local support throughout much of the nineteenth and twentieth centuries for their sustenance and growth. Their dependence on local sources of financial and political support, combined with the lack of centralized control or

12   stipulations concerning curriculum, meant that U.S. universities generally were quick to introduce new courses or disciplines into their curricula in response to community demands. Ben-David (1968) contrasted this dependence on local sources of support with the situation in most European university systems through much of the twentieth century, arguing that

> For the European civil servant in charge of the matter, the problem of financing universities posed itself in the form of how to spend as little as possible given an established set of objectives and a scale of priorities. The American university president, however, had to ask himself how to increase income by convincing a variety of donors about the importance of the university and by finding new markets and extending existing ones for its services. For the university president the range of objectives and the scale of priorities were not regarded as given. It was one of his tasks to watch for circumstances justifying their change, and to push for changes if recognized as necessary or useful. This entrepreneurial leadership, the only one suited to the age of organized and rapidly changing research and training, was also adopted by the state universities. (p. 36)

A primary activity of early American universities was the provision of vocational skills for a wide range of professions of concern to local economies. In many cases, training was combined with research concerned with the problems of local industry. For example, the University of Akron supplied skilled personnel for the local rubber industry, became well known for research in the processing of rubber, and subsequently achieved distinction in the field of polymer chemistry. Land-grant colleges combined training with research on the needs of the local agricultural community — the Babcock test for measuring the butterfat content of milk was developed by an agricultural research chemist at the University of Wisconsin. Introduced in 1890, the test provided a new and reliable method to determine the adulteration of milk, a matter of no small consequence in a state of dairy farms.

Public universities also developed new degree programs to address local vocational and economic interests. After World War I, U.S. colleges of engineering at public universities offered undergraduate degrees in a bewildering array of specialized engineering subjects; at the University of Illinois, this included architectural engineering, ceramic engineering, mining engineering, municipal and sanitary engineering, railway civil engineering, railway electrical engineering, and railway mechanical engineering. An observer noted that during this period, "Nearly every industry and government agency in Illinois had its own department at the state university in Urbana-Champaign" (Levine, 1986).

On occasion, university research on problems of industry involved large-scale, long-run commitments to the solution of a particular problem. One of the most important such projects was conducted at the Mines Experiment Station of the University of Minnesota, beginning before World War I and continuing through the early 1960s. This long-term applied research project addressed the consequences of the gradual exhaustion of the high-yielding iron ores in the Mesabi Range. As the supply of these ores declined, researchers focused on ores of lower iron content, specifically the abundant deposits of low-quality taconite ore. Although it did not rely on new scientific knowledge, the solution to innumerable engineering and processing problems associated with taconite extraction and refinement required decades of experimentation at the Mines Experiment Station (Davis, 1964).

A final characteristic of the U.S. higher education system that distinguished it from those of other industrial economies throughout the twentieth century was the emergence of a unified national market for faculty at U.S. research universities. The departmental structure of most U.S. universities and colleges and the emergence of strong disciplinary degree programs and societies by the late nineteenth century meant that faculty qualifications were established on the basis of their contributions to disciplinary research rather than their contributions to a specific institution.[4] This interinstitutional mobility, combined with the strong competition among U.S. universities for prestige, resources, and students, meant that faculty moved among universities, especially the most prestigious public and private research universities, more frequently than was true of faculty in other national systems of higher education. Such mobility provided a powerful mechanism for the diffusion of new ideas, curricula, and research approaches among U.S. universities that was less highly developed in other national systems of higher education.

Throughout the twentieth century, the U.S. system of higher education has been distinguished from those of other industrial economies by its large scale, the high level of autonomy enjoyed by individual universities and colleges, the dependence by these institutions on local sources of financial and political support, and the strong competition among universities and colleges for funds, prestige, faculty, and students. These structural characteristics of U.S. higher education created powerful incentives for university researchers and administrators to establish close relationships with industry. They also motivated university researchers to seek commercial applications for university-developed inventions, regardless of the presence or absence of formal patent protection. Finally, the large scale and vocational orientation of many U.S. universities, combined with the conduct of research within these universities, created an effective channel for the rapid dissemination of new research findings into industrial practice — the movement of graduates into industrial employment.

14 THE INSTITUTIONALIZATION OF ENGINEERING
AND APPLIED SCIENCES

The orientation of U.S. university research toward the resolution of "practical" problems of concern to local industry can be illustrated by a selective discussion of the contributions of U.S. university research to the institutionalization of new disciplines in engineering and the applied sciences. Among other things, these disciplines provided a systematic basis for research and training that provided intellectual links among the individuals and universities engaged in such activities.

During the early twentieth century, fields such as chemical engineering, electrical engineering, and aeronautical engineering became established in American universities. Each of these fields developed programs of graduate studies with certified professional credentials, professional organizations, and associated journals. These new disciplines and professions both reflected and solidified new connections between American universities and a variety of American industries. Growth in these new disciplines and training programs in American universities responded to increased use of university-trained engineers and scientists in industry, especially the rise of industrial research in the chemical and electrical equipment industries in the early years of the twentieth century (see Hounshell and Smith, 1988; Mowery, 1981; Noble, 1977; Reich 1985).

Engineering education hardly existed in the United States before the Civil War. Many schools offered vocational engineering education, but systemic training of professional engineers was nearly unknown until the latter part of the century. Although the first U.S. engineering college, Rensselaer Polytechnic Institute (RPI), was founded in 1824, the U.S. Military Academy at West Point, founded in 1802, trained many of the first professional engineers in the United States. Graduates of West Point made major contributions to the vast construction enterprises associated with the building of an extensive, ultimately transcontinental, railroad system beginning in the 1830s. The needs of the railroad, telegraph, and, later, an expanding succession of new products and industries increased the demand for engineers. In response, new schools such as MIT (1865) and Stevens Institute of Technology (1871) were established, and engineering courses were introduced into the curricula of older universities. Here again the American experience in higher education differed from that of Europe. In Great Britain, France, and Germany, engineering subjects often were taught at separate institutions; but these subjects were introduced at an early date into elite U.S. universities. Yale introduced courses in mechanical engineering in 1863, and Columbia University opened its School of Mines in 1864 (Grayson, 1977).

Electrical Engineering

The response of the American higher education system to the emergence of electricity-based industries was swift. Although many historians cite 1882, when Edison opened the New York City Pearl Street generation station, as the year the U.S. electric equipment and generation industries were founded, in fact crude versions of the telephone and electric light had already been introduced by 1882, and the demand for well-trained electrical engineers was growing rapidly. Firms such as General Electric and Westinghouse had limited success in training their own employees in this new field.

U.S. universities responded rapidly to this new demand for engineering training. MIT introduced its first course in electrical engineering in 1882. Cornell introduced a course in electrical engineering in 1883 and awarded the first doctorate in the subject as early as 1885. By the 1890s, "schools like MIT had become the chief suppliers of electrical engineers" in the United States (Wildes and Lindgren, 1985). In contrast to the research of such industrial pioneers as Edison, Westinghouse, and Bell, university-based research and education in the emergent discipline of electrical engineering defined a community of technically trained professionals with well-developed links among universities and between universities and industry. Throughout the twentieth century, U.S. schools of engineering provided the research in engineering and applied science on which the electrical industries were based.

University research in electrical engineering and physics generated more than research advances and trained graduates. The establishment of new companies by university professors intent upon commercializing their research findings has occasionally been portrayed as a uniquely post–World War II development, but this practice has ample earlier precedents. The Federal Company of Palo Alto, California, was founded by Stanford University faculty and became an important supplier of radio equipment during World War I (Bryson, 1984). The klystron, a thermionic tube for generating and amplifying microwave signals for high-frequency communication systems, was the subject of a 1937 agreement between Hal and Sigurd Varian, inventors of the klystron, and the Stanford Physics Department. Stanford University provided the Varians with access to laboratory space, faculty, and a $100 annual allowance for materials. In exchange, Stanford received a one-half interest in any patents, an arrangement that yielded handsome returns for the university.

The development of electrical engineering within American higher education responded to a national need, the emerging electricity-based industries, in contrast to the more provincial needs that had motivated many previous university researchers. Training electrical engineers became the responsibility of public and private U.S. universities, whose training activities strengthened

16   and supported a fertile interface between university research and technical advance in industry. Throughout the twentieth century, university research also contributed to industrial innovation through the establishment of consulting relationships with industry and the occasional foundation of firms by faculty.

Chemical Engineering

Another illustration of the critical role of U.S. university research in engineering is the emergence of the discipline of chemical engineering in the United States in the early twentieth century. The development of this discipline was associated to a striking degree with a single institution: MIT (see Servos, 1980). The discipline of chemical engineering was created to address the challenges resulting from the fact that the knowledge generated by major scientific breakthroughs in chemistry provided little or no guidance for the manufacture of new products on a commercial scale. Chemical engineering is *not* applied chemistry and cannot be adequately characterized as the industrial application of scientific knowledge generated in the chemical laboratory. Rather, it involves a merger of chemistry and mechanical engineering, that is, the application of mechanical engineering to the large-scale manufacture of chemical products (see Furter, 1980).

The complexities of this transition from laboratory to commercial production help explain the gap of several or many years that separates the discovery under laboratory conditions of many important new chemical entities from their commercial production. An entirely new methodology, one distinct from chemistry, was developed to manage the transition from test tubes to a manufacturing operation for which output was measured in tons rather than ounces. This new methodology exploited the concept of "unit operations," a term coined by Arthur D. Little at MIT in 1915. Unit operations provided the basis for a rigorous approach to large-scale chemical manufacturing and thus may be taken to mark the origins of chemical engineering as a unique discipline.[5] Unit operations also provided the basis for the systematic, quantitative instruction of future practitioners — in other words, a form of generic knowledge that could be taught at universities.

Arthur D. Little, Warren Lewis, and other faculty encouraged the development of collaborative relationships with U.S. industry that involved research and teaching, the exchange of students in cooperative education, and the foundation at MIT of the school of chemical engineering practice. Organized research in chemical engineering developed in parallel at MIT and in industry and was especially influenced by the symbiotic relationship between engineers at Standard Oil of New Jersey and MIT faculty who worked to codify, advance, and disseminate the key tenets of the emergent discipline.[6]

Much of the collaboration during this period combined joint development of these new practices in academic and industrial laboratories with relatively widespread dissemination, particularly through teaching and textbooks. The Standard Oil refinery in Baton Rouge, Louisiana, also played a key role as an unofficial external laboratory and employer of a great many of the MIT graduates and (as consultants) a number of the faculty at MIT in the school of chemical engineering. In many respects, this collaboration culminated in the development of fluidized bed catalysis in 1941. Research conducted at MIT complemented research done in the Baton Rouge refinery; although patents were an important output of this research activity, the university had no direct role in managing or licensing this intellectual property.

The key to this style of collaboration was personnel exchange between MIT and industry through faculty consulting, faculty rotations to and from industry, and placement of graduates. Personnel exchange brought expertise from MIT to industry and transferred practical knowledge from industry to academia, where it was refined and codified, supporting the development of a broader engineering discipline. As in many other areas of engineering or scientific research, access by faculty to industrial facilities was important, as the scale and type of equipment in industry often were unavailable within the university. The industrial collaborators obtained the ownership of or were assigned the intellectual property resulting from collaboration, and a great deal, although not all, of the results of the research by academics in the industrial context was published.

Aeronautical Engineering

The contribution of American higher educational institutions to the progress of aircraft design before World War II is another example of the production by universities of information of great economic value to the development of a new industry. An excellent illustration of university engineering research that yielded valuable design data and techniques for the acquisition of new knowledge was the propeller tests conducted at Stanford University by W. F. Durand and E. P. Lesley from 1916 to 1926 (Vincenti, 1990, chap. 1 and p. 137). Extensive experimental testing was necessary because of the absence of a body of scientific knowledge that would permit a more direct determination of the optimal design of a propeller, given the fact that "the propeller operates in combination with both engine and airframe . . . and it must be compatible with the power-output characteristics of the former and the flight requirements of the latter" (Vincenti, 1990, p. 141). The method of experimental parameter variation was necessary because a useful quantitative theory did not exist. Vincenti points out that the Stanford experiments accomplished more than just data collection but something other than science. Instead, they contributed to the development of a specialized methodology that could not be directly deduced from scientific principles, albeit one that was consistent with those principles.[7]

The Stanford experiments led to a better understanding of aircraft design by producing a form of generic knowledge that lies at the heart of the modern discipline of aeronautical engineering.[8] The Stanford experiments made important contributions to American aircraft design in the 1930s, most notably in the emergence of the DC-3 in the second half of the decade. But the great success of the DC-3 also owed a large debt to another educational institution, the California Institute of Technology. Cal Tech's Guggenheim Aeronautical Laboratory, funded by the Guggenheim Foundation, performed research that was decisive to the commercial success of Douglas Aircraft, located in nearby Santa Monica. The technical breakthroughs associated with the DC-3 and its predecessors, such as durable and reliable components, and the aircraft's increased passenger capacity, which lowered its seat-mile operating costs, were largely the product of the Cal Tech research program, highlighted by their use of multicellular construction and the exhaustive wind tunnel testing of the DC-1 and DC-2.

Computer Science and Engineering

Computers are among the most remarkable technical contributions of American universities in the last half of the twentieth century. Important development work on computers had been performed in Europe (Alan Turing in Great Britain and Konrad Zuse in Germany were among the pioneers), but the emergence of electronic, digital computers was largely the product of wartime research and development activities conducted at American universities. This research was concentrated in schools of engineering and transformed a logical possibility into a technical reality. University-based research created a new discipline, computer science, which was influenced by the historical development of disciplines such as electrical engineering and physics but nurtured its own research methodology.

The first fully operational electronic digital computer, the Electronic Numerical Integrator and Computer (ENIAC), was built at the Moore School of Electrical Engineering at the University of Pennsylvania during 1943–46 under the direction of Presper Eckert and John Mauchly. Eckert and Mauchly's work drew on research at other American universities, particularly work by

John Atanasoff, a mathematician and physicist at Iowa State University, and Vannevar Bush, an electrical engineer at MIT.

Atanasoff's device was designed for the solution of systems of linear equations, although he appears to have given a good deal of thought to the possibility of a general-purpose electronic digital computer. But Atanasoff's machine never became operational and existed only in crude prototype form (see Stern, 1981). Another important predecessor of the ENIAC was the differential analyzer developed at MIT by Vannevar Bush and his associates. Consistent with our discussion above of the practical motivations for much of the engineering research at MIT and other U.S. universities during this period, Bush's work grew out of problems associated with the transient stability of electric power transmission in interconnected, large-scale electric power networks.

The Moore School's construction of a differential analyzer in 1939 led to a close relationship between the school and the U.S. Army's Ballistics Research Laboratory at the Aberdeen Proving Ground. The army financed the ENIAC project in order to develop equipment to calculate solutions to ballistics problems more rapidly. By the time the ENIAC was ready for testing in 1945, the war had ended, but the intercession of John Von Neumann preserved the ENIAC for eventual use in the extensive calculations on the design of a hydrogen bomb (Stern, 1981, p. 62).

How should the university research that led to the postwar emergence of the digital electronic computer be categorized? The early participants were trained in engineering, mathematics, and physics. Mauchly and Bush taught and performed their research in schools of engineering. Atanasoff taught physics and mathematics at Iowa State. Howard Aiken, who conducted research on computers at Harvard during World War II, was a mathematician who had previously worked in engineering.[9] But their research is difficult to place in the conventional R&D boxes of "basic research," "applied research," or "development." Although the term "computer science" is common enough in university curricula today, the discipline, if it is indeed a science rather than engineering, is a distinctly different kind of science. It is certainly not a natural science but may be appropriately regarded, in Herbert Simon's apt phrase, as a "science of the artificial" (Simon, 1969, p. xi). Much of the research in computer science, after all, resembles engineering in that it deals with the design and construction of artifacts, or machines.

The Applied and Engineering Sciences in U.S. Universities

Simon's appellation also applies to other engineering disciplines developed within U.S. universities. These "sciences of the artificial" consist of purposive, goal-directed activities. Their explicit design orientation excludes them from

20 the usual definition of basic research, which involves a quest for fundamental understanding. In the traditional natural sciences, such a quest has often been identified with research with no immediate concern with practical applications. But much research in the applied sciences and engineering is quite basic, since it involves a search for fundamental understanding. Most of the research in the medical sciences is undertaken with specific practical applications in view. Medical studies of carcinogenic processes necessarily involve research into fundamental aspects of cell biology. All of these lines of inquiry were classed by the late Donald Stokes (1997) as research in "Pasteur's Quadrant," defined as research that seeks to understand the fundamental physical, biological, or chemical processes that underpin specific problems, solutions, or applications.

This selective review of the development of a number of important engineering disciplines suggests that engineering education in the United States has consistently attempted to provide reference points for inquiry into the details of practical problems. At the same time, however, university research has provided an intellectual framework for training professional decision-makers, as Herbert Simon (1969) reminds us:

> The intellectual activity that produces material artifacts is no different fundamentally from the one that prescribes remedies for a sick patient or the one that devises a new sales plan for a company or a social welfare policy for a state. Design, so construed, is the core of all professional training; it is the principal mark that distinguishes the professions from the sciences. Schools of engineering, as well as schools of architecture, business, education, law, and medicine, are all centrally concerned with the process of design. (pp. 55–56)

A number of other academic disciplines resemble engineering in their orientation to specific useful goals, such as the improvements in agricultural productivity that are the focus of much research in the life sciences in schools of agriculture. Statistics, surely one of the most useful of disciplines, is another example of such a discipline that achieved curricular and department status in the United States long before it did so in Europe. And consistent with our earlier discussion of their role in promoting research of interest to their regions, among the most important institutions in the early development of statistics were Iowa State University and North Carolina State University, both of which applied statistics to the analysis of agricultural yields and prices.

By the start of World War II, the applied sciences and engineering disciplines were well established within U.S. higher education, especially at the land-grant universities, which accounted for a large share of American university research. The presence of the engineering disciplines and the applied

sciences extended but did not replace the longer-standing tradition in American universities of research and education in the service of local industry and
agriculture.

The Medical Sciences

The medical sciences exhibit a similar pattern of basic research oriented to
practical ends. Although U.S. universities' basic research capabilities in the
medical sciences emerged only after World War II, the 1910 report by Abra-
ham Flexner, *Medical Education in the United States and Canada,* began the
processes that greatly expanded the role of biomedical research within American medical schools. Flexner argued that medical students needed better
training in the natural sciences, that medical schools should undertake basic
biomedical research, and that these schools should strengthen their affiliations
with teaching hospitals. This combination of teaching, research, and medical
practice is the hallmark of the American academic medical centers that have
made significant contributions to technical progress in medicine since 1945.

Research on the causes of human illness has much in common with research in the applied physical sciences and engineering disciplines. Much
of it aims for deep understanding of fundamental scientific principles, but
it is motivated by the very practical objective of relieving humans of the
scourge of disease. This characterization of motives and results accurately
characterizes the work of Koch and Pasteur in the nineteenth century that
identified bacteria as the cause of many human illnesses, as well as fields such
as endocrinology, neurology, and biochemistry that emerged in the late nineteenth and early twentieth centuries.[10] Although most of the fundamental research in these fields was dominated by European research centers until
World War II, American medical schools enhanced their research capabilities
in these fields during the 1920s and 1930s. The great expansion in federal funding of research at U.S. academic medical centers that began after 1945 built on
the institutional research capability that had been created in the preceding
four decades.

THE IMPACT OF WORLD WAR II ON FEDERAL
FUNDING OF ACADEMIC RESEARCH

Our discussion thus far has emphasized the distinctive structure of the U.S.
higher education system throughout the late nineteenth and twentieth centuries and the contrasts between this structure and those of other industrial nations. In this section, we discuss the dramatic changes in the financing of U.S.

academic research that occurred in the space of less than a decade in the mid-twentieth century. These shifts in the sources of funding for U.S. academic research created a research infrastructure in U.S. higher education whose scale and other features also contrasted with those of other industrial economies.

War preparations and the U.S. entry into World War II in December 1941 transformed federal R&D programs and priorities. Overall federal R&D expenditures (in 1996 dollars) soared from $784.9 million in 1940 to a peak of $12.4 billion in 1945, including an increase from $279.2 million to $4 billion (1996 dollars) in Defense Department R&D spending. The success and the organizational structure of the massive federal wartime R&D program yielded several important legacies. The successful completion of the Manhattan Project, whose research budget in the peak years 1944 and 1945 substantially exceeded that of the Department of Defense, created a research and weapons production complex that ushered in the age of truly "big science." Ironically, the Manhattan Project's success in creating weapons of unprecedented destructive power contributed to rosy postwar perceptions of the constructive possibilities of large-scale science for the advance of societal welfare.[11]

Far smaller in financial terms, but highly significant as an institutional innovation, was the Office of Scientific Research and Development (OSRD), a civilian agency directed by Vannevar Bush that relied on research contracts with private firms and universities. The largest single recipient of OSRD grants and contracts during wartime (and the inventor of institutional overhead) was MIT, with seventy-five contracts for a total of more than $886 million (1996 dollars). The largest corporate recipient of OSRD funds, Western Electric, accounted for only $130 million (1996 dollars) (Pursell, 1979, p. 364). The contractual arrangements developed by OSRD during the Second World War allowed the OSRD to tap the broad array of academic and industrial R&D capabilities that had developed during the interwar period. Members of the scientific community were called upon to recommend and to guide, as well as to participate in, scientific research with military payoffs.

The OSRD and other wartime programs transformed the scale and sources of funding for academic research in the United States. Indeed, the postwar federal presence within academic research funding assumed a shape that differed dramatically from that envisioned by one of the most famous and influential figures in U.S. science policy during this century, Vannevar Bush. In response to a request that he had solicited from President Franklin D. Roosevelt, Bush drafted the famous 1945 report on postwar federal science policy, *Science: The Endless Frontier*. Anticipating the analysis of later economists, Bush argued that basic research was the ultimate source of economic growth and advocated the creation of a single federal agency charged with responsibility for funding basic research in all defense and nondefense areas, including health. The complexities of postwar domestic politics, as well as Bush's resistance to congressional oversight of his proposed agency, ultimately doomed his proposal. Rather than a civilian agency overseeing all of federal science policy and funding, various mission agencies, including the military and the National Institutes of Health (NIH), assumed major roles in supporting basic and applied research. By 1953, more than 86 percent of federal R&D spending (5 percent of which supported academic research) was controlled by the Defense Department and the Atomic Energy Commission.

THE POSTWAR STRUCTURE OF FEDERAL
SUPPORT FOR ACADEMIC R&D

The transformation of the postwar U.S. research system expanded and transformed the role of publicly funded research in U.S. universities. Although Bush's recommendations of a single federal funding agency for basic research were not implemented and his advocacy of institutional, rather than project, funding also was ignored, U.S. universities enjoyed significant increases in federal R&D support during this period. From an estimated level of less than $150 million in 1935–36, federal support for university research (excluding Federally Funded Research and Development Centers [FFRDCs] at universities and colleges) grew to more than $2.1 billion in 1960 and nearly $14 billion in 1995 (Table 2.1; all amounts in 1996 dollars). Federal funding of academic research, which amounted to no more than 25 percent of total academic research support in the mid-1930s, by 1960 accounted for more than 60 percent of the total.

The overall academic research enterprise increased almost six-fold in constant dollars between 1935 and 1960 and more than doubled again by 1965 (see Table 2.1). In 1953, less than a third of all U.S. basic research was performed in universities and FFRDCs at universities and colleges. By 1995, however, these institutions performed 60 percent of U.S. basic research (National Science Foundation, 1996).[12] Increased federal support for university research transformed major U.S. universities into worldwide centers for the performance of scientific research, a characterization that applied to only a few U.S. universities in a limited number of fields during the prewar years.

In addition to financing an expanded academic research enterprise, federal support for graduate education and university facilities, especially after the 1958 *Sputnik* "crisis," enlarged the pool of scientific personnel and supported the acquisition of the physical equipment and facilities essential to the performance of high-quality research. In the case of computer science, federal

TABLE 2.1

Federal Support for Academic R&D, 1935 and 1960 –2000
(millions of 1996 dollars)

Year	Total academic R&D ($)	Federally supported R&D ($)	Federal share of total academic research funding
1935	575	138	24%
1960	3,418	2,143	63
1965	7,333	5,338	73
1970	9,453	6,668	71
1975	9,939	6,671	67
1980	11,575	7,817	68
1985	14,120	8,828	63
1990	19,551	11,570	59
1995	22,827	13,726	60
2000	27,379	15,932	58

SOURCES: Data for 1935, National Resources Committee (1938); data for 1960 and after, National Science Foundation (2001).

support for university purchases of large mainframe computers was indispensable to the institutionalization of a new academic discipline in U.S. universities. Federal programs also increased financial aid for students in higher education during the late 1950s.[13] By funding both university education and research, the federal government strengthened the university commitment to research and reinforced the link between research and teaching. The combination of research and teaching in higher education has been carried much further in the United States than elsewhere. In much of Europe and Japan, for example, a larger fraction of research is carried out in specialized research institutes not connected directly with higher education and in government-operated laboratories.[14]

Although the historically unprecedented federal investment in academic research helped propel American universities to international preeminence in basic research and graduate education, the bulk of federal funding of academic research was predicated on the expectation that the research would yield practical benefits for federal agency missions. The National Science Foundation (NSF) was established in 1950 to fulfill the Bush vision of federal support for basic research that sooner or later would yield social benefits. But the NSF has never accounted for even a fifth of federal support for university research during the postwar period. Instead, agencies concerned with two key postwar federal missions, defense and public health, have dominated federal support for academic research.

The Department of Defense and two other agencies with significant defense-related responsibilities, the National Aeronautics and Space Administration (NASA) and the Atomic Energy Commission (AEC; later the Department of Energy), accounted for more than 80 percent of federal support for academic research in 1954, a share that dropped below 30 percent of the total after 1970 (see Table 2.2). During the 1953–60 period, the NIH provided roughly a third of total federal academic research funding, and since 1960 NIH funding of university research has substantially increased. By the early twenty-first century, the NIH accounted for more than 60 percent of federally funded university research.

This enormous postwar federal investment in academic biomedical research forged stronger links between basic science and clinical applications in U.S. biomedical research. By combining scientific research with clinical practice, the U.S. academic medical center has been able to link science and innovation to a remarkable degree, enabling the rapid collection by scientists of feedback from practitioners in the development of new medical devices and procedures, facilitating clinical tests of new pharmaceuticals, and contributing powerfully to innovations in both pharmaceuticals and medical devices. The combination of science and clinical applications in one institution is unusual — as Henderson, Orsenigo, and Pisano (1999) and Gelijns and Rosenberg (1999) point out, most western European medical institutions emphasize clinical practice and applications more heavily than scientific research. In contrast, U.S. universities and academic research facilities have maintained an important presence in the R, as well as the D, of R&D throughout the postwar period.

The mission orientation of the major federal funders of academic research is reflected in the distribution of research funding among fields of science and engineering. By 1989, for example, more than half of academic research in

TABLE 2.2

Funding of U.S. Academic Research by Federal Agencies, 1954–2001

Year	Share of federal research funds for academic R&D originating within particular agencies						
	NIH	NSF	DOD	NASA	DOE	USDA	Other
1954	n/a	1.3%	51.0%	n/a	32.5%	5.2%	10.0%
1971	36.7%	16.2	12.8	8.2%	5.7	4.4	16.0
1976	46.4	17.1	9.4	4.7	5.7	4.7	12.0
1981	47.0	15.7	12.8	3.8	6.7	5.4	11.0
1986	49.4	15.1	16.7	3.9	5.3	4.2	8.4
1991	54.3	14.1	11.3	5.2	6.1	3.8	13.7
1996	55.3	14.5	12.1	5.5	5.0	3.1	4.5
2001	60.5	14.9	8.7	4.4	4.0	2.8	4.7

SOURCE: National Science Board (2002). Data for 2001 are based on preliminary NSF estimates.

26   science and engineering was in the life sciences. Much of the research funded by these agencies is appropriately defined as basic research, in that it aimed for fundamental understanding of the object of study, but it was also positioned in "Pasteur's Quadrant," inasmuch as the research was motivated by the desire to solve practical problems. Since the early 1980s, the central role of the federal government in supporting academic research has been supplemented by increased funding from industry, and university-industry research linkages have attracted considerable comment. But as we pointed out earlier, these linkages were well established before World War II. Indeed, the share of university research expenditures financed by industry appears if anything to have declined during the early postwar period.[15] During 1953–58, industry supported 8 percent of annual academic R&D spending, on average, a share that declined to 2.7 percent by 1970, in part as a result of increased federal government funding of academic research. By 1980, industrial support for university research (excluding university-based FFRDCs) had rebounded to account for more than 4 percent of academic research spending, and this share increased further to approximately 7.4 percent by 1998 (National Science Board, 2002).

The structure of federal programs for support of academic R&D reinforced many of the internationally distinctive characteristics of the U.S. higher education system that were apparent before 1940. The large scale of postwar federal funding of academic research and the pluralistic, decentralized structure of federal R&D programs (even within a single, large R&D-supporting agency such as the Department of Defense) meant that numerous alternative paths of R&D were supported in such key technological areas as information technology, biomedical sciences, and materials science during the postwar period. The ability of federal R&D programs to support broad exploration of alternative applications of fundamentally uncertain technologies proved to be an important source of U.S. competitive advantage in such embryonic areas as computer hardware, semiconductors, and, eventually, the Internet (Mowery and Simcoe, 2002). Equally important, however, was the emphasis on peer review and interinstitutional competition in virtually all federal programs supporting academic R&D. The availability of funding from multiple federal sources, combined with the competitive processes allocating the bulk of this academic R&D support, powerfully reinforced the interinstitutional autonomy and competition for faculty, students, resources, and prestige that characterized the pre-1940 U.S. system of higher education. Moreover, the size of the federal academic R&D budget, as well as the reliance by most federal agencies on extramural research support rather than public laboratories, meant that U.S. universities' research enterprises dwarfed those of other industrial economies throughout the postwar period.

The "new structure" of U.S. academic R&D in the postwar period had important effects for industrial innovation and changed a number of its key characteristics. Although U.S. universities had played a significant role in industrial innovation in the pre-1940 U.S. economy, many of their important contributions were exploited by large, established industrial firms such as Standard Oil of New Jersey or Du Pont. During the postwar period, however, relatively new firms, many of which drew on universities for personnel or scientific and technological knowledge, played central roles in the commercial exploitation and growth of such "new industries" as computer hardware, semiconductors, computer software, and biotechnology. The economic role of these new firms in these postwar U.S. industries outstripped the importance of new firms in other industrial economies, such as Germany and Japan. Moreover, regions such as California's Silicon Valley or Massachusetts's Route 128 enjoyed significant advances in income and employment that were attributable in part to the presence of major research universities in these regions.

INDUSTRIAL INNOVATION AND UNIVERSITY RESEARCH: RECENT STUDIES OF THEIR INTERACTION

Thus far we have described the historical origins and development of the U.S. system of higher education, focusing on the ways in which its scale and structure created strong incentives for collaboration between university and industrial researchers well before the recent growth of university patenting and licensing. In this section, we summarize a number of recent studies of the contemporary relationship between university research and industrial innovation. To what extent do U.S. firms utilize the results of university research as the source of the technological innovations that they develop and commercialize, a view of industrial innovation that influenced the drafting of the Bayh-Dole Act? What importance do industrial managers assign to patenting and licensing as key channels for the flow of university research findings to industrial innovation? How, if at all, do managers' assessments of these issues vary among technologies and industries? The studies summarized in this section hed light on these key questions and provide a useful basis for examining university-industry collaboration and technology transfer.

All of the studies reviewed in this section relied on responses through interviews or surveys from senior industrial managers in industries ranging from pharmaceuticals to electrical equipment. The National Research Council's Government-University-Industry Research Roundtable (GUIRR) (1991) examined the contributions of university research to technological innovation, and Mansfield (1991) surveyed industry managers about the number of their

28   recent innovations that either could not have been developed, or could have
been developed only after significant delay, in the absence of recent academic
research. Two other studies relied on large-scale surveys of industrial R&D
managers. The "Yale survey" (results of which are summarized in Levin et al.,
1987) and the more recent "Carnegie-Mellon survey" (summarized in Cohen
et al., 2002) asked industrial research managers about the nature and scope of
the influence of university research on industrial R&D. The Carnegie-Mellon
survey also asked respondents to describe the most important channels
through which their firms gained access to the results of university research
for application in their industrial innovation strategies. The Yale survey focused mainly on large U.S. firms in the late 1970s and early 1980s, while the
Carnegie-Mellon survey focused on a broader range of large and smaller U.S.
firms in the early 1990s, thereby capturing insights from managers well after
the passage of the Bayh-Dole Act of 1980.

These studies also highlight the interindustry differences in the relationship between university and industrial innovation. Respondents in all four of
these studies characterize the biomedical sector, especially biotechnology and
pharmaceuticals, as unusual—university research advances affect industrial
innovation more significantly and directly in this field than is true of other sectors. Biotechnology firms' managers quoted in the GUIRR study stated that
they relied on university research as a source of inventions. Managers interviewed in the GUIRR study, however, differentiated between pharmaceuticals
based on biotechnology and other drugs, stating that university research rarely
was the source of new drugs not based on biotechnology, for which the key
work took place in industry. But university research affected the development
of these nonbiotechnology drugs as well—managers interviewed in the
GUIRR study highlighted a number of cases in which academic research had
illuminated the specific biochemical reactions that pharmaceutical firms
needed to find in searching for new drugs. In other cases, university research
advances permitted companies to make a more efficient assessment of possible
uses for drugs they were testing.

Mansfield (1991) found a similarly strong dependence on academic research in his survey of pharmaceutical industry managers, who stated that
more than a quarter of the new drugs commercialized by the companies could
not have been developed, or would have been developed only with substantial
delay, without academic research. These managers further asserted that the
development of an additional 20 percent of the drugs introduced by their firms
was substantially aided by academic research.

The nature of the relationship between university and industrial research and innovation in the biomedical sector contrasted with that in other industries in both the GUIRR and Mansfield studies. Interviewees from electronics firms reported in the GUIRR study that universities occasionally made relevant "inventions" but opined that most such inventions came from nonacademic research. University research did contribute to technological advances, but its contributions were largely in the form of knowledge of the fundamental physics and chemistry underlying manufacturing processes and product innovation, an area in which training of scientists and engineers figured prominently, and experimental techniques. Mansfield found that the reported percentage of new products that were "heavily dependent" on academic research for their introduction was significantly lower in areas other than pharmaceuticals. The executives from the information-processing equipment and instruments industries reported that 10–15 percent of their innovations depended on academic research (in the sense defined above in our discussion of Mansfield's work). Respondents from the metals industry estimated that slightly more than 10 percent of new products and processes would not have been developed in the absence of recent academic research. Even more striking is Mansfield's finding that in three industries—electrical equipment, chemical products, and metal products—at most 6 percent of new products depended on recent academic research.

The Yale and Carnegie-Mellon surveys of industry R&D executives corroborate the findings of these other studies concerning the differences in the relationship between university and industrial research in the biomedical and other industry sectors. The Yale survey queried R&D managers in industry about the sources of knowledge that affected innovation in their industries. Only fifteen of the fifty industries with three or more respondents in the Yale study rated university research as "important" or "very important" to technical advance in their line of business (Table 2.3). Once again, pharmaceuticals (which had only begun to recognize the significance of biotechnology at the time the survey was administered in the late 1970s) figures prominently on this list, but R&D managers in engineering and scientific instruments, semiconductors, and synthetic rubber also reported that university research was "important" or "very important" to their innovative activities. Interestingly, many of the other industries reporting that university research was important to their innovative activities are related to agriculture and forestry, prominent beneficiaries of federally funded university research for much of the twentieth century.

Another set of questions in the Yale survey asked R&D managers to assess the importance of specific fields of university science in their industries'

TABLE 2.3

Industries Rating University Research as
"Important" or "Very Important"

Fluid milk
Dairy products except milk
Canned specialities
Logging and sawmills
Semiconductors and related devices
Pulp, paper, and paperboard mills
Farm machinery and equipment
Grain mill products
Pesticides and agricultural chemicals
Processed fruits and vegetables
Engineering and scientific instruments
Millwork, veneer, and plywood
Synthetic rubber
Drugs
Animal feed

SOURCE: Previously unpublished data from the Yale Survey
on Appropriability and Technological Opportunity. For a description of the survey, see Levin et al. (1987).

innovative activities (Table 2.4). Virtually all of the fields of university research
that were rated as "important" or "very important" for their innovative activities by survey respondents are related to engineering or applied sciences. As
we noted previously, these fields of U.S. university research frequently developed in close collaboration with industry.

With the exception of chemistry, very few basic sciences appear on the list
of university research fields deemed by industry respondents in the Yale survey to be highly relevant to their innovative activities. But the absence of fields
such as physics and mathematics in Table 2.4 should not be interpreted as indicating that academic research in these fields does not contribute directly to
technical advance in industry. Instead, these results reflect the fact that fundamental advances in physics, mathematics, and related sciences penetrate
industry gradually. Their effects on industrial innovation are realized only after the passage of considerable time, a characterization very similar to that of
the GUIRR interviewees in the electronics industries. Indeed, in many cases
the effects of advances in these areas of science on industry are realized
through the incorporation of such advances into the applied sciences, such as
chemical engineering, electrical engineering, and material sciences.

The findings of the Carnegie-Mellon survey (Cohen et al., 2002) concerning interindustry differences in the importance of university research are similar to those of the Yale survey.[16] Although most industries do not assign great
importance to university research as a contributor to their innovation activi-

ties, pharmaceuticals stands out among the industries that view university research results as important, as do some of the electronics industries. The findings of the Carnegie-Mellon survey regarding the fields of university research
that industry considered important for innovation also were similar to those of
the Yale survey.

The Carnegie-Mellon survey included a number of additional questions
concerning the ways in which university research influenced the industrial
R&D agenda and the channels through which industry gained access to such
research results. On the first point, the responses summarized in Table 2.5 indicate that in most industries, university research results play little if any role
in triggering new industrial R&D projects; instead, the stimuli originate with
customers or from manufacturing operations. Here as elsewhere, pharmaceuticals is an exception — university research results trigger industrial R&D projects in a significant number of cases. But industry R&D managers reported
that university research results most often aided problem solving in the course
of a R&D project, rather than affecting the decision to initiate such projects.

The Carnegie-Mellon survey also queried R&D managers about their
use of different types of research from universities and government research

TABLE 2.4

The Relevance of University Science to Industrial Technology

Field	No. of industries with "relevance" scores of		Selected industries for which the reported "relevance" of university research was large (≥ 6)
	≥5	≥6	
Biology	12	3	Animal feed, drugs, processed fruits/vegetables
Chemistry	19	3	Animal feed, meat products, drugs
Geology	0	0	None
Mathematics	5	1	Optical instruments
Physics	4	2	Optical instruments, electronics
Agricultural science	17	7	Pesticides, animal feed, fertilizers, food products
Applied math/ operations research	16	2	Meat products, logging/sawmills
Computer science	34	10	Optical instruments, logging/sawmills, paper machinery
Materials science	29	8	Synthetic rubber, nonferrous metals
Medical science	7	3	Surgical/medical instruments, drugs, coffee
Metallurgy	21	6	Nonferrous metals, fabricated metal products
Chemical engineering	19	6	Canned foods, fertilizers, malt beverages
Electrical engineering	22	2	Semiconductors, scientific instruments
Mechanical engineering	28	9	Hand tools, specialized industrial machinery

SOURCE: Previously unpublished data from the Yale Survey on Appropriability and Technological
Opportunity in Industry. For a description of the survey, see Levin et al. (1987).

laboratories in their internal innovation activities, and these findings are strikingly similar to the other data discussed above on the types of knowledge outputs rated by managers as most important for industrial innovation. Respondents to the Carnegie-Mellon survey reported that general research findings from "public research" performed in government labs or universities were used more frequently (on average, in 29.3 percent of industrial R&D projects in respondents' firms) than prototypes emerging from these external sources of research (used in an average of 8.3 percent of industrial R&D projects). Interestingly, research techniques and instruments from these external research sources were rated as more important in their contributions to industrial R&D, used in an average of 22.2 percent of projects, than were prototypes. Respondents from the pharmaceutical industry reported that more than 40 percent of their R&D projects used research findings from universities and government laboratories, and more than 35 percent used techniques and instruments developed at these sites. But pharmaceutical industry respondents reported that only 12.3 percent of their industry projects relied on prototypes developed in university or government research facilities.

A similar portrait of the relative importance of different outputs of university and public-laboratory research emerges from the responses to questions about the importance to industrial R&D of various information channels (Table 2.6). Although pharmaceuticals once again is unusual in its assignment of considerable importance to patents and license agreements involving universities and public laboratories, respondents from this industry still rated research publications and conferences as more important sources of informa-

TABLE 2.5

*Rankings of Importance of External Information Sources in
Suggesting New R&D Projects and in Contributing to the
Completion of R&D Projects*

Information source	% of respondents indicating that source suggested new R&D project	% of respondents indicating that source contributed to project completion
Consultants	22.8%	34.2%
Joint or cooperative ventures	49.6	47.2
Competitors	40.5	11.7
Independent suppliers	45.6	60.6
Internal manufacturing operations	73.7	78.2
Customers	90.4	59.1
Universities/government labs	31.6	36.3

SOURCE: Cohen, Nelson, and Walsh (2002).

TABLE 2.6

Importance to Industrial R&D of Sources
of Information on Public R&D
(including university research)

Information source	% of respondents rating a source as "moderately" or "very" important for industrial R&D
Publications & reports	41.2%
Informal interaction	35.6
Meetings & conferences	35.1
Consulting	31.8
Contract research	20.9
Recent hires	19.6
Cooperative R&D projects	17.9
Patents	17.5
Licenses	9.5
Personnel exchange	5.8

SOURCE: Cohen, Nelson, and Walsh (2002).

tion. For most industries, patents and licenses involving inventions from university or public laboratories were reported to be of very little importance, compared with publications, conferences, informal interaction with university researchers, and consulting.

CONCLUSION

The U.S. "system" of higher education is internationally unique among the Organization for Economic Cooperation and Development (OECD) economies in its lack of strong central governmental controls of policy, administration, or resources; its large scale; its dependence on local sources of political and financial support; and its strong interinstitutional competition for resources, faculty, and prestige. These characteristics have distinguished U.S. higher education from the higher education systems of most other industrial economies through much of the twentieth and into the twenty-first centuries. More important for the concerns of this volume, these structural characteristics of U.S. higher education created strong incentives for faculty and university administrators to develop links with industrial research. Over the course of the past century, these close research links between U.S. universities and industry have produced important industrial innovations in fields ranging from pharmaceuticals to mining, as well as in agriculture. But these links also have influenced the development, indeed the creation, of new areas of engineering

34   and scientific research within U.S. universities. Knowledge, technology, and personnel have moved from universities to industry, and vice versa, throughout the history of this interaction between academic and industrial research.

Collaboration between university and industrial researchers in the United States meant that many U.S. universities and university faculty were actively patenting inventions and licensing these patents to industry well before the 1980s. But the flows of knowledge and technology transfer from U.S. universities to industrial innovation moved through many other channels in addition to those of patents and licensing. Indeed, as we have pointed out in this chapter, experienced managers of industrial research regard patents and licenses as important sources of industrial innovation in only a few industries. Instead, other types of interaction, ranging from publication of papers to the employment within industry of university-trained scientists and engineers with experience at the frontiers of research, are of greater importance for innovation in many technology-intensive and other industries.

Not only do channels other than patenting and licensing figure more prominently as sources of knowledge for industrial innovation in these industries, the evidence from expert surveys and other sources also highlights the substantial differences among industries and fields of research and innovation in the importance of different channels. Pharmaceuticals and the biomedical sector generally display a relationship between academic research and industrial innovation that most nearly approximates the "linear model" of innovation that influenced Vannevar Bush and numerous other leaders of U.S. science policy during the early postwar period. Not only do advances in fundamental scientific understanding influence the direction of industrial innovation, but in many cases the task of innovation involves the development and commercialization by industry of the fundamental advances achieved in academia. But the electronics, materials, and chemicals industries all exhibit very different patterns of interaction between university research and industrial innovation, a topic that we examine at some length in Chapters 6–8.

3

University Patent Policies and University Patenting Before the Bayh-Dole Act

This chapter examines the evolution of U.S. university patent policies and university patenting during the pre-Bayh-Dole era, spanning 1925–80. Although many of the issues in recent debates about the costs and benefits of university patenting had been articulated by proponents and opponents of university patenting as early as the 1930s, several arguments in favor of university patenting that figured prominently in these early debates were absent from the debates over the Bayh-Dole Act in the 1970s and subsequently. Interestingly, many proponents of university patenting argued in the debates of the 1930s that universities should avoid a direct role in managing patents and licenses, an argument that was rarely heard in the debates of the 1970s. The growth of university patenting and licensing throughout the 1925–80 period also exhibits many of the characteristics of the diffusion of a new organizational phenomenon, including emulation by universities of one another's approaches to patenting and licensing and considerable responsiveness to the demonstration by some universities of financial gains from licensing of faculty inventions.

Our examination of U.S. university patenting during the 1925–80 period focuses on the level and technological composition of university patenting and the characteristics of the universities active in patenting. Although some universities had begun to patent faculty inventions as early as the 1920s, few institutions had developed formal patent policies prior to the late 1940s, and many of these policies embodied considerable ambivalence toward patenting. Relatively few universities managed their patent portfolios themselves during the 1925–70 period, but this situation began to change during the 1970s. In particular, the 1970s are characterized by considerable growth in patenting by private U.S. universities. Our data also highlight steady growth in biomedical

36   patents as a share of overall university patenting during the postwar period. As
      we show in Chapters 6 and 7, the Bayh-Dole Act accelerated the growth of uni-
      versity patenting and resulted in the entry into patenting and licensing by
      many universities during the 1980s. But the "transformation" wrought by the
      1980 Act followed trends that were well established by the late 1970s.

A BRIEF HISTORY OF U.S. UNIVERSITY PATENT POLICIES

The Pre–World War II Debate

Just as the post-1970 surge in U.S. university patenting coincided with increased research collaboration between universities and industry (Henderson,
Jaffe, and Trajtenberg, 1998a), so did the first wave of university involvement
in patenting, which began after World War I. The expanding links between
university and industrial research during the 1920s and 1930s that we discussed
in Chapter 2 triggered a debate among U.S. research university administrators
over patent policy (McKusick, 1948; Palmer, 1934).[1]

In 1933, the American Association for the Advancement of Science (AAAS)
Committee of Patents, Copyrights, and Trademarks surveyed the different positions on the "patent problem," as it was then known, that faced university scientists. Among the questions addressed by the committee's report (AAAS,
1934) were: "Should [scientists] proceed to obtain patents? What are the advantages in doing this? What are the disadvantages?" (p. 7).[2]

One of the issues the committee considered was whether patenting was
necessary for "technology transfer." Although a common criticism of academic patenting was "that publication or dedication to the public is sufficient
to give the public the results of work of scientists" (AAAS, 1934, p. 9), the report concluded that this position was naive, for several reasons. Anticipating
an argument made during the 1970s in support of the Bayh-Dole Act, the committee opined that "discoveries or inventions which are merely published and
thus thrown open equally to all, unless of great importance to the industry, are
seldom adopted" (p. 9) and that "ordinarily no manufacturer or capitalist
would be willing to-day to risk his money, and expend time and energy in developing on a commercial scale a new product or process without being assured that his investment in developing the invention would be protected in
some measure" (p. 10).[3]

The committee argued that a scientist could not expect that publication of
the technical details of his invention would yield social benefits, because of
the presence of "patent pirates" who would "wrongfully appropriate his work"
and "deny the public what he thought he gave it," either by charging monop-

oly prices or withholding the invention from use (AAAS, 1934, p. 10). Were the inventor or his university, rather than a "pirate," to obtain a patent on the invention, this risk would be reduced.[4]

A related argument stated that patents on university inventions were necessary for "quality control" reasons. Patenting of university research advances would prevent the unsuccessful or even harmful exploitation of university research advances by unqualified individuals or firms. Patenting of such advances by the university, according to this argument, prevented incompetent exploitation of academic research that might discredit the research results and the university.[5]

Proponents of university patenting thus concluded that doing so enhanced the public good. University patents advanced social welfare by inducing private parties to develop and commercialize university research results, by preventing "patent pirates" from patenting the research and charging monopoly prices, and by allowing institutions to ensure that only reputable parties developed the research, protecting the reputations of the invention and the university itself.

As we note in Chapter 5, the first of these three arguments ("patents induce development") figured prominently in debates about university patent policy in the 1960s and 1970s (Eisenberg, 1996), which often asserted that commercialization of a university invention might require that any patented research results be licensed on an exclusive or semiexclusive basis. Prevention of "patent piracy" and protection of universities' reputations, however, require only that an institution obtain a patent and license it widely at low or no royalties.

The committee's report also addressed the potentially negative effect of patents on the progress of research in fields where advances are cumulative, that is, the possibility "[t]hat patents will place unfortunate strictures on other men who subsequently do fundamentally important work in the same field" (AAAS, 1934, p. 12). The committee acknowledged such dangers, but argued that universities could avoid them "by permitting the use of patents on liberal terms . . . [which] is particularly necessary in the case of broad or basic inventions" (p. 12).

A third class of issues in the committee's report dealt with the tension between university patenting and the "open science" norms and institutions of academe (Merton, 1973). Objections to patenting based on this view included the assertion "that it is unethical for scientists or professors to patent the results of their work" (AAAS, 1934, p. 8; the committee's report indicated that "this objection is probably the vaguest and most frequent one raised"). Although the committee considered the risk that patenting by university scientists would

38   hinder communalism and bias academic inquiry away from basic research, a
concern echoed in more recent debates over university patenting (Dasgupta
and David, 1994), its report dismissed these fears.[6]

The debates over university patent policies in the 1930s treated medical patents as a special case. Opposition to medical patents was widespread, based on
the argument that patents restricted the use of new discoveries and therefore
had no place in the medical community (Weiner, 1986).[7] Opponents of medical patents also expressed concern over perceptions of university profiteering
at public expense in the field of public health (McKusick, 1948). The AAAS
committee acknowledged the "special" nature of patents in the field of public
health (with little elaboration) but suggested that the benefits of patenting discussed above, particularly those associated with using patents as a "quality
control" mechanism, were sufficient to warrant patenting of such discoveries.

Although the AAAS report favored university patenting of faculty inventions, the committee did not endorse direct involvement by universities in patent management, arguing instead that "this can preferably be done by independently organized foundations, holding companies or other suitable
experienced organizations" (AAAS, 1934, p. 14). This position reflected the
reluctance of many U.S. universities during the 1925–70 period to directly
manage patenting and licensing, a reluctance that faded somewhat during
the 1970s.

This review of the early debates about university patenting underscores
the widespread awareness of and interest in patenting by U.S. university scientists and administrators well before the 1970s and 1980s. The primary moti-
vation for patenting was the protection of the public interest and the preservation of academic institutions' reputations. The prospect of licensing income
influenced the entry by several universities into patenting and licensing during the 1930s and subsequently; but through much of the 1925–80 period,
many academic scientists and administrators preferred to avoid direct involvement in the management of these patents. These tensions were reflected
in the patent policies adopted by leading pre-1940 institutional patenters and
licensors.

Pre–World War II University Patent Policies: An Overview

Since one of the forces that sparked the debate over university patenting was
the growth of research collaboration between U.S. universities and industry, it
is not surprising that the first group of universities to become involved with
patents were land-grant institutions, which, as we noted in Chapter 2, conducted a good deal of applied research of interest to industry and agriculture.

A number of these public universities sought patents for faculty inventions in
the expectation that state taxpayers and the local economy would benefit from
their research. But land-grant institutions frequently avoided a management
role in patenting and licensing (Committee on Uniform Patent Policies in
Land Grant and Engineering Experiment Stations, 1922). Instead, several
land-grant and other universities "outsourced" their patent management to affiliated but legally separate foundations or to a third-party technology transfer
agent, the Research Corporation (see Chapter 4 for more discussion of the Research Corporation).

The first university-affiliated research foundation was the Wisconsin
Alumni Research Foundation (WARF). In 1924, Dr. Harry Steenbock of the
University of Wisconsin developed a method for increasing the vitamin D
content of food and drugs via the process of irradiation. Despite criticism by
many in the medical community and his colleagues at the university, Steenbock decided to patent his findings, based partly on his desire to protect the
public from unscrupulous or incompetent firms and from monopolization of
the industry by a private patentee (Apple, 1996).[8] Steenbock offered to assign
his patent to the University of Wisconsin, but the university thought that the
creation of a specialized office to handle patents was not worth the necessary
investment (Apple, 1996). Instead, Steenbock convinced several alumni to create the WARF, an entity affiliated with but legally separate from the University
of Wisconsin that would accept assignment of patents from university faculty,
license these patents, and return part of the proceeds to the inventor and the
university. According to Apple (1996, p. 42), "[w]ith this structure, business
matters would not concern or distract the university from its educational mandate; yet academe could reap the rewards from a well-managed patent whose
royalties would pay for other scientific work."

In an action that illustrates the tension between pecuniary and other motives (such as those articulated by Steenbock) in university licensing policy,
WARF licensed the Steenbock patents to Quaker Oats on an exclusive basis
for the production of vitamin-enriched cereal products. The foundation also
negotiated a limited number of licenses with pharmaceutical firms in other
fields of use covering the development of vitamin D supplements. These licensing agreements were criticized by some observers, who argued that they
raised the cost of enriched food products that were beneficial to the public
health. Such criticism received additional impetus from the considerable income that the Steenbock patents earned for the University of Wisconsin
(Weiner, 1986).[9]

WARF's success and substantial licensing income influenced the development of patent policies at other U.S. universities during the 1930s, when many

institutions revised and formalized their patent policies in response to several forces. First, the Depression's devastating effects on university finances forced many institutions to seek new sources of income, and the widely acknowledged profitability of WARF offered an attractive model for emulation. Second, the post–World War I growth in industry-funded research at universities had led some universities to clarify or codify policies affecting ownership of faculty inventions. Land-grant universities were the most active in this area, and Purdue University, the University of Minnesota, and Cornell University established affiliated but legally separate research foundations that were similar to WARF during the late 1920s and early 1930s. In some cases, these research foundations also sought to increase university research funding from industry: McKusick (1948, p. 2) noted that "patent administration was only incidental to [their] primary purpose." Although this group of schools typically did not assert rights to all university inventions, faculty with patentable inventions frequently asked their university's research foundation to hold and administer the inventions. Still other universities referred their faculty to third-party patent management agents, including the Research Corporation. During the 1930s and 1940s, several universities, including MIT, Princeton, and Columbia, signed formal Invention Administration Agreements (IAAs) with the corporation.

Table 3.1 summarizes the 1940 patent policies of the sixteen institutions classified by Geiger (1986) as the leading U.S. research universities before World War II: Illinois, Michigan, Minnesota, Wisconsin, California, Columbia, Harvard, Pennsylvania, MIT, Cornell, Johns Hopkins, Princeton, Yale, Stanford, Chicago, and the California Institute of Technology. As of 1934, only two of these institutions had adopted formal patent policies. By the end of the 1930s, however, twelve had done so, an indication of increased institutional interest in patent management.[10]

Several elements of these policies deserve mention. First, despite increased interest in patenting among the leading U.S. research universities and a few other institutions, most U.S. universities still lacked patent policies before World War II (Palmer, 1957). Several of the universities that had adopted patent policies, including Harvard, Penn, Chicago, and Johns Hopkins, discouraged patenting or prohibited university faculty from patenting, especially in the field of medicine. Nonetheless, with the exception of the University of Chicago, each of these "antipatent" institutions acknowledged that, under special circumstances, patents might be necessary, even in medicine, for "quality control" purposes of the sort discussed earlier. A number of the institutions that allowed faculty patenting used research foundations or the Research Corporation for patent management (Table 3.1), reflecting their

TABLE 3.1

University Patent Policies and Procedures, 1940

Institution	Formal systemwide patent policy	University asserts rights to nonsponsored research	Restrictions on medical patents	Patent management
Illinois	Yes	Yes	No	
Michigan	No	No	No	
Minnesota	No	No	No	University of Minnesota Research Foundation
Wisconsin	Yes	No	No	Wisconsin Alumni Research Foundation
California	Yes	No	No	
Columbia	Yes	No	No	University Patents Inc; Research Corporation
Harvard	Yes	No	Yes	
Penn	Yes	No	Yes	
MIT	Yes	Yes	No	Research Corporation
Cornell	No	Yes	No	Cornell Research Foundation, Inc.
Johns Hopkins	Yes	No	Yes	
Princeton	Yes	No	No	Research Corporation
Yale	Yes	No	No	
Stanford	Yes	Yes	No	
Chicago	Yes	No	Yes	
California Institute of Technology	No	No	No	

SOURCES: Spencer (1939); Potter (1940).

aversion to in-house patent management. The onset and aftermath of World War II changed this landscape, as we discuss in the next section.

The Impact of World War II

As we noted in Chapter 2, World War II and the Cold War that followed transformed the structure of the U.S. national innovation system. Nowhere was this transformation more dramatic than in U.S. universities. Formerly funded largely by state governments, the U.S. Department of Agriculture, and industry, academic research experienced a surge of federal funding. As the growth in university-industry research links had done during the 1920s and 1930s, increased federal funding of university research strengthened two motives for university involvement in patenting. First, the expanded scale of the academic research enterprise increased the probability that universities would produce patentable inventions. Second, many federal research sponsors required the development of a formal patent policy.

42   By the late 1940s, virtually all major U.S. universities had developed patent policies, a considerable increase from the situation in the late 1930s
(McKusick, 1948). Summarizing his survey of U.S. universities in the late
1950s, Palmer (1962) found that eighty-five institutions had adopted or revised
patent policies during the 1940–55 period; more than half of these new or
revised policies were announced during 1946–55.[11] Typically, patents from
government-funded work were governed by the policies of the sponsoring
agency (see below); privately sponsored research was managed on a case-by-
case basis, although research sponsors often received preferential treatment.
Significant differences nonetheless remained among U.S. universities in their
assertion of rights to faculty inventions and their willingness to pursue patent
licenses.

As in the prewar period, many universities during the 1950s and 1960s outsourced patent management (McKusick, 1948). Data on Research Corporation IAAs reveal the dimensions of this trend: as of 1940, only three of the nation's eighty-nine "Research Universities" (as classified by the Carnegie
Commission on Higher Education's 1973 taxonomy; see below for details) had
signed IAAs with the Research Corporation. By 1950, this number had increased to twenty (Table 3.2), and by the mid-1960s nearly two-thirds of the
Carnegie Research Universities were Research Corporation clients.

Well into the 1960s, U.S. university patent policies and procedures reflected the ambivalence toward patents that was revealed in the debates of the
1930s. Many institutions continued to avoid direct involvement in patent administration, and others maintained a hands-off attitude toward patents altogether. Columbia's policy left patenting to the inventor and patent administration to the Research Corporation, stating that "it is not deemed within the
sphere of the University's scholarly objectives" to hold patents, and Harvard,

TABLE 3.2

Carnegie Research Universities with Research Corporation IAAs

Type of University	Number with IAAs with the Research Corporation *Percentage of category with IAAs with the Research Corporation*						
	1950	1955	1960	1965	1970	1975	1980
RU1 and RU2	20	39	51	59	62	68	68
(N = 89)	22%	44%	57%	66%	70%	76%	76%
Public	11	22	33	40	40	43	43
(N = 54)	20%	41%	61%	74%	74%	80%	80%
Private	9	17	18	19	22	25	25
(N = 35)	26%	49%	51%	54%	63%	71%	71%

Chicago, Yale, and Johns Hopkins adopted similar positions. All of these universities, as well as Ohio State and Pennsylvania, discouraged or prohibited medical patents. Other universities allowed patents on biomedical inventions only if it was clear that patenting would be in the public interest.[12] This institutional ambivalence toward patenting began to change during the 1960s, although the prohibitions on medical patenting at Columbia, Harvard, Johns Hopkins, and Chicago were not dropped until the 1970s. The pace of change accelerated during the 1970s in response to federal initiatives in R&D funding and patent policy.

The Growth of University Involvement in Patent Management, 1960–80

The Rise of Federal Support for Academic Research

Although federal funding of academic research grew during the first postwar decade, the rate of growth in such support accelerated in the late 1950s, and the composition of this support shifted in favor of basic research. U.S. universities' share of total U.S. basic research performance (excluding university-operated Federally Funded Research and Development Centers [FFRDCs]) nearly doubled from 27 percent in 1953 to 50 percent in 1968, while federal funds for basic research in U.S. universities increased more than five-fold during the 1958–68 period (National Science Board, 2002). The greatest increases in funding in the late 1950s and 1960s occurred in the biomedical sciences, funded largely by the National Institutes of Health (NIH) within the Department of Health, Education, and Welfare (HEW). By 1971, NIH supported nearly 37 percent of academic R&D, a share that grew to more than 46 percent by 1981 (Table 2.2). These increases in federal research funding, especially in biomedical research, transformed the content of academic research and elevated the salience of patent management issues at many universities.

Increased federal research funding also broadened the number and characteristics of U.S. research universities. The interinstitutional concentration of federal support for university research was high during the 1940s and early 1950s but declined during the 1950–80 period. The share of federal R&D funds accounted for by the ten leading academic recipients of these funds shrank from 43 percent in 1952 to 37 percent in 1958 and declined further still during the 1960s and 1970s (Table 3.3). In the life sciences, where funding was less institutionally concentrated than overall federal academic research funding (Geiger, 1993), the dispersion of funding also grew during the 1960s and

44

TABLE 3.3

Concentration of Federal R&D Funds in Universities
Receiving the Largest Federal Obligations, 1963–75

Year	Top 10	Top 20	Top 50	Top 100
1963	32.8%	49.5%	71.9%	89.5%
1964	30.8	47.1	71.6	88.9
1965	30.0	45.8	70.5	88.8
1966	29.6	45.4	69.9	88.7
1967	29.1	44.9	69.6	88.1
1968	27.7	43.1	67.4	86.7
1969	27.4	43.2	67.3	86.1
1970	27.8	43.3	67.6	86.1
1971	27.1	42.7	67.2	85.8
1972	27.4	42.8	67.0	85.3
1973	27.1	42.4	67.1	85.1
1974	27.3	42.8	67.2	85.7
1975	25.8	41.4	66.2	85.0

SOURCE: Smith and Karlevsky 1975.

1970s. Reduced concentration in federal support for academic research owed much to the redistributive instincts of Congress and the actions of research agency administrators who sought to accommodate these instincts (Graham and Diamond, 1997).

Changes in Policy, Appropriability, and Opportunity
During the 1960s and 1970s

U.S. universities' patent policies and practices changed significantly during the 1970s. First, the Research Corporation, which by 1970 was administering inventions for more than 200 institutions, began to encourage and assist its client universities in developing capabilities to manage the early stages of the technology transfer process, particularly invention screening and evaluation.[13] A second development resulting from the growth in federal support for biomedical research was the emergence during the 1970s of molecular biology as a field characterized by numerous advances in basic science that promised commercial applications of considerable interest to industry. The growth of biomedical research increased universities' interest in capturing revenues from licensing of biomedical patents in an era of slower growth in overall federal research funding and accelerating growth in research costs. A growing number of U.S. universities began to seek patents for faculty inventions and (their former ambivalence notwithstanding) began to manage their patenting and licensing activities themselves (Weiner, 1986).

Change also occurred during this period in federal patent policies. Before
the 1960s, federal agencies lacked any policy beyond case-by-case negotiations
for dealing with requests from universities for title to inventions resulting from
federally funded research. In the mid-1960s, the Department of Defense
(DOD) began to grant title to inventions resulting from DOD-financed research to universities with "approved" patent policies, that is, policies that
required faculty to report inventions resulting from sponsored research and
allowed universities to obtain patents on these inventions. As we point out in
Chapter 5, two other federal sources of academic research funding, HEW and
the National Science Foundation (NSF), began to negotiate Institutional Patent Agreements (IPAs) with universities in 1968 and 1973, respectively. IPAs
eliminated the need for case-by-case reviews of the disposition of individual
academic inventions resulting from federally funded research and facilitated
licensing of such inventions on an exclusive or nonexclusive basis.

A fourth impetus for increased university involvement in patenting and
licensing resulted from the early successes of Stanford University's Office of
Technology Licensing (OTL). Niels Reimers, the associate director of Stanford University's Sponsored Projects Office and the founding director of
Stanford's OTL, noted that shortly after he was hired by the university in
1968: "I looked up the income we had from Research Corporation from '54
to '67, and it was something like $4,500. I thought we could do a lot better
licensing directly, so I proposed a technology licensing program" (Reimers,
1998).

Reimers's technology licensing program, which had begun in 1968 as an experiment, focused more on marketing and less on the administrative and legal
details of patent management. Reimers staffed his licensing program with individuals skilled in technology evaluation and marketing, rather than the attorneys who dominated the staffs of most U.S. university licensing programs in
the 1960s. The pilot program increased university licensing income to $55,000
in its first year (more than twelve times what it had earned via its contract with
Research Corporation in the previous thirteen years), the experiment was
judged a success, and Stanford created its OTL in 1970.

All of these developments sparked considerable interest among U.S. universities in expanding or establishing university technology licensing offices.
The dimensions of this increased university involvement in patent management and technology transfer during the 1970s are apparent in Figure 3.1,
which shows "entry" into technology transfer activities by year, based on data
from the Association of University Technology Managers (AUTM, 1998).[14] As
the figure shows, the number of universities establishing technology transfer

46   offices and/or hiring technology transfer officers began to grow in the late 1960s, well before the passage of the Bayh-Dole Act. Although the Act was followed by a wave of entry by universities into management of patenting and licensing, growth in these activities was well established by the late 1970s.

UNIVERSITY PATENTS, 1925–80

A number of scholars have documented the role of the Bayh-Dole Act in the growth of patenting and licensing by universities since 1980 (Henderson, Jaffe, and Trajtenberg, 1998a,b). But Bayh-Dole is properly viewed as initiating the latest, rather than the first, phase in the history of U.S. university patenting. And this latest phase is characterized by a higher level of direct involvement by universities in management of their patenting and licensing activities, in contrast to the reluctance of many U.S. universities to become directly involved in patenting prior to the 1970s. Public universities were more active in patenting than private institutions during much of the pre-Bayh-Dole era, reflecting the strong incentives that they faced to reap the benefits of university research for local taxpayers and the importance of applied research at many of these institutions. By the 1970s, however, both public and private universities had become directly involved in patenting.

In this section, we examine the growth of U.S. university patenting during 1925–80. We provide an overview of the characteristics of active university patenters and changes in the technological fields of university patents during

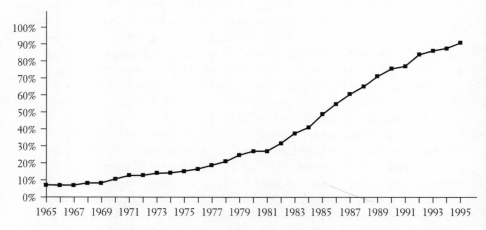

FIGURE 3.1   Proportion of Carnegie RU1s with > 0.5 FTE technology transfer personnel, 1965–95

this period. We also consider some reasons for the increased direct involvement of universities in patent management that became apparent in the 1970s.

Basic Trends

Figure 3.2 plots the number of patents assigned to American universities from 1925 to 1980. Our data cover university patents for every fifth year during 1925–45 and annual counts for 1948–80.[15] During the 1925–80 period, U.S. universities' share of all domestically assigned U.S. utility patents grew from zero to slightly less than 1 percent. After growing during the 1940s and 1950s, the number of university patents remained roughly constant until the 1970s, when university patenting increased significantly. The total number of university patents issued during the 1970s alone is 1.5 times the total number of university patents issued in the previous two decades.[16] Although the surge in U.S. university patenting after the passage of the Bayh-Dole Act in 1980 has been widely noted, Figure 3.2 suggests that university patenting began to grow as a share of U.S. patenting during the decade prior to Bayh-Dole.

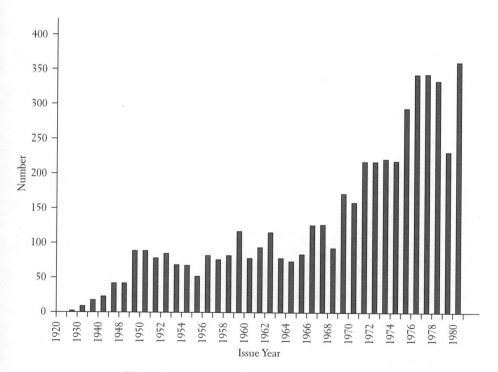

FIGURE 3.2   University patents, 1925–80

48   Further evidence that the growth in university patenting predates Bayh-Dole is seen in Figure 3.3, which shows the ratio of total U.S. university patenting to total prior-year academic R&D expenditures for application years 1963–93.[17] Aggregate university "patent propensity" does increase after 1981 (as pointed out by Henderson, Jaffe, and Trajtenberg, 1998a,b), but the trend rate of growth is stable during and after the 1970s; there is no evidence of a sharp increase in the rate of growth in the patent propensity of universities after Bayh-Dole.

The heterogeneity among U.S. universities' patent policies that we noted earlier is reflected in considerable differences in the size and characteristics of the patent portfolios that each university acquired during the 1925–45 period. Patents issued to the nation's leading pre-1940 research universities (the "Geiger 16") accounted for just over half of the academic patents (excluding Research Corporation patents) issued during the 1925–45 period (Table 3.4).

Ivy League institutions such as Harvard and Yale are missing from the list of "Geiger 16" universities in Table 3.4 that obtained patents during 1925–45, reflecting their aversion to direct institutional involvement with patents that was discussed earlier. Individual faculty from these universities, however, used the Research Corporation for patent administration beginning in the late 1920s.[18] Since MIT signed an IAA with the Research Corporation in 1937 (see Chapter 4), the data in Table 3.4 omit considerable patent activity at MIT after this year.[19] The table shows that several other private universities active in both engineering and the applied sciences before World War II, such as the

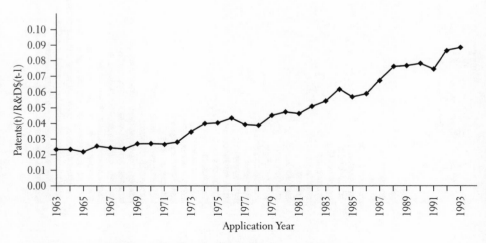

FIGURE 3.3   University patents per R&D dollar, 1963–93

TABLE 3.4

Patenting by U.S. Universities, 1925–45

Geiger 16	Total patents	Others	Total patents
California Institute of Technology	10	Purdue University	13
University of Illinois	7	Washington State University	7
University of Minnesota	7	Iowa State University	6
Stanford University	5	Illinois Institute of Technology	4
University of Michigan	4	Carnegie Mellon University	3
University of Pennsylvania	4	Ohio State University	2
University of Wisconsin	4	University of Kansas	2
University of California	3	Fordham University	1
Cornell University	2	Louisiana State University	1
MIT	2	Saint Louis University	1
		Tennessee State University	1
		University of Cincinnati	1
		University of Iowa	1
		University of New Hampshire	1
		Other	2
Total	48	Total	46

NOTE: Data collected at five-year intervals.

California Institute of Technology and Stanford University, accounted for a substantial number of patents during the 1925–45 period.[20]

Public universities were more heavily represented in patenting than private universities during the 1925–45 period, both within the top research universities and more generally (Table 3.4). As we noted earlier, a number of public universities had established affiliated but legally separate research foundations that were similar to WARF in the late 1920s and early 1930s. Patents assigned to these university-affiliated foundations show up as "university patents" in Table 3.4, although the parent university was not directly involved in management of patenting and licensing.

This dominance of overall academic patenting by state universities persisted through much of the postwar era. But private universities increased their share of academic patenting from 14 percent in 1960 to 39 percent in 1970 and 45 percent in 1980.[21] This growth in the share of private-university patents is particularly noteworthy, inasmuch as it occurred during a period of rapid growth in overall U.S. university patenting. The era of increased public funding for academic research thus was associated with an expanded role for private universities in managing the patents received by their faculty on publicly and privately funded research.

Dispersion and Entry in University
Patenting During the 1970s

The 1970s represented the most dramatic period of change in U.S. university patenting during the 1945–80 period, and arguably during the entire 1925–80 period. Overall university patenting grew significantly and became less concentrated; more and more universities chose to manage their patents themselves; and biomedical inventions increased in importance within university patenting and licensing. Here, we analyze the sources of expanded university patenting, focusing on the increased dispersion of patenting among universities and the sources of entry into patenting by universities with limited experience in these activities.

The dynamics of federal support affected growth in the number of university patents and change in the characteristics of universities that were active patenters. Increased federal funding of academic R&D was a necessary condition for the growth of university patenting depicted in Figure 3.2. But increases in the interinstitutional dispersion of federal research funds during the 1960s and 1970s also appear to have affected the concentration of academic patenting among U.S. universities.

In order to explore the existence and extent of such dispersion in patenting, we examined the distribution of university patents among the institutional categories established by the Carnegie Commission on Higher Education in 1973. The Carnegie Commission classified the nation's 173 doctorate-granting institutions as "Research Universities" or "Doctoral Universities." Institutions that awarded at least fifty doctorates in 1969–70 and were among the fifty leading recipients of federal financial support in at least two of the three years 1968–69, 1969–70, and 1970–71 were placed in the "Research University 1" (RU1) category. An institution that awarded at least fifty doctorates in 1969–70 and ranked between fifty and one hundred in federal financial support in two of the three years was categorized as a "Research University 2" (RU2). The commission's Doctoral Universities category includes all other institutions that granted more than ten doctorates in the 1969–70 period.[22]

Figure 3.4 shows postwar patenting by Research Universities, Doctoral Universities, and Other Institutions (including those not classified by the Carnegie Commission). The Research Universities account for the majority of university patents throughout the 1948–80 period. But the share of patents accounted for by RU2s increased from 5 percent to 12 percent during this period, and the concentration of patents within the overall Research Universities category decreased considerably, especially after 1970. Increases in the level and interinstitutional dispersion in university patenting thus appear to track the growth and dispersion of federal funding of U.S. academic research.

Growth in university patenting during the 1970s reflected expanded patenting by Carnegie Research Universities (RU1s and RU2s) with little or no previous experience in patenting. We defined Carnegie Research Universities
with ten or more patents in the 1950–69 period as "incumbents" and those
with fewer than ten patents in the 1950–69 period as "entrants."[23] Of the
seventy-seven Carnegie Research Universities that obtained patents during
the 1970s, fifty-three were entrants according to our definition. Figure 3.5
shows that growth in university patenting during the 1970s is due in large part
to increased patenting by entrants.

These entrants came disproportionately from the ranks of the second tier of
the Carnegie Research University category, the RU2 institutions, which are
more heavily represented among entrant institutions than among incumbents.
This increased patenting by relatively inexperienced academic patenters may
reflect increased dispersion of federal research funding (especially biomedical
research funding) among institutions. Overall and within the two classes of
universities, entrants' patents include a higher share of biomedical patents
than do those of incumbents.

A second factor that affected growth in patenting by universities during the
1970s was the negotiation of IPAs with federal research funding agencies by

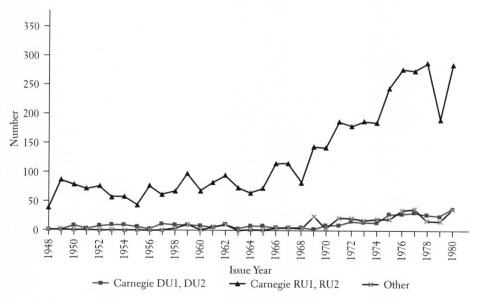

FIGURE 3.4   University patents by university category, 1948–80

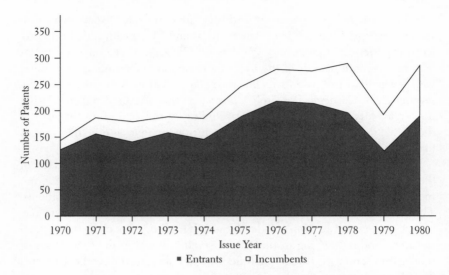

FIGURE 3.5   Patenting in 1970s by entrants and incumbents (Carnegie RU1s and RU2s)

academic institutions. As we noted earlier, IPAs lowered the costs of patenting university inventions that resulted from federally funded research, albeit less significantly than the subsequent Bayh-Dole Act. Slightly more than half (52 percent) of the seventy-seven Carnegie Research Universities receiving patents during the 1970s had IPAs with either the NSF or HEW.[24] IPAs were somewhat more common for incumbent institutions (68 percent had IPAs) than entrants (46 percent) and much more common for RU1s (64 percent had IPAs) than RU2s (31 percent). Figure 3.6 shows that institutions with IPAs dominated the growth of university patenting during the 1970s. Nonetheless, although IPAs may have encouraged entry by lowering the costs of patenting and licensing, fewer than half of entrant institutions had IPAs; patenting during the 1970s grew for both entrants with IPAs and entrants without IPAs. The diffusion of IPAs alone thus does not explain entry by universities into patenting.

These data on the changing sources of university patenting during the 1970s highlight three aspects in which this decade departed from historical trends and prefigured the 1980s and 1990s. First, during the 1970s private universities expanded their patenting and licensing of faculty inventions. A second and closely related shift was the growth in the role of public and private universities in directly managing these activities. Finally, the 1970s were characterized by increased entry into patenting and licensing by universities with little experience in these activities, a cohort of entrants drawn primarily from RU2 institutions that specialized in biomedical patenting to a greater degree than incumbents. All of these trends in university patenting were influenced by increased interinstitutional dispersion of federal research funding, the growth of IPAs, and the success of entrants such as Stanford University. Determining the relative importance of these various factors in affecting the three key trends discussed above remains an important task for future research. Interestingly, only one of these factors (the IPAs) represented a change in federal policy toward the patenting of publicly funded research. It is likely that a similarly diverse range of factors, and not the Bayh-Dole Act alone, underpinned the continued growth of U.S. university patenting after 1980.

University Patents by Technological Field

A final issue of interest in academic patenting is the distribution among technology fields of university patents during 1925–80. Figure 3.7 displays this information for university patents during 1925–45, and Figure 3.8 displays similar data for the 1948–80 period (both figures exclude Research Corporation patents). The data in Figure 3.7 highlight the importance of "chemical" patents during the pre-1940 period. The prominent role of these patents reflects

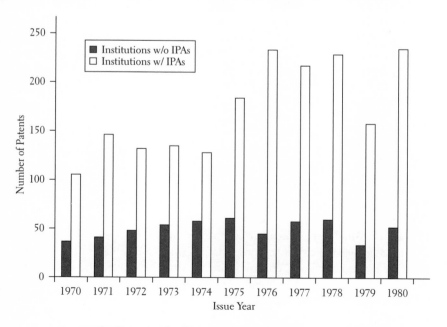

FIGURE 3.6   Patenting by Carnegie Research Universities by IPA status

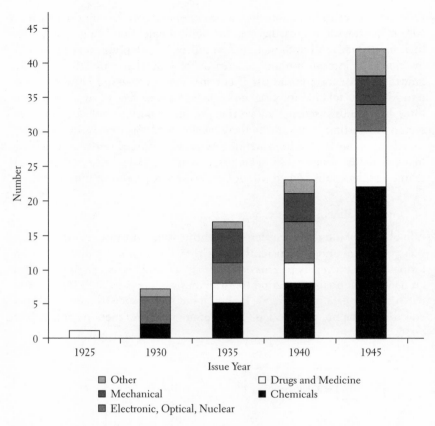

FIGURE 3.7   Distribution among technology classes of university patents, 1925–45

interwar academic research in fields including agricultural chemistry, industrial chemistry, and chemical engineering, as well as the strong university-industry linkages in those fields of research (Rosenberg and Nelson, 1994). Nearly 60 percent (22/37) of the chemical patents issued to universities during this period covered organic compounds. Some of the "organic compounds" that are classified as chemicals in Figure 3.7 are vitamins and could also be classified as biomedical inventions.[25] During the interwar period, U.S. universities made significant contributions to vitamin research and synthesis (Apple, 1996), and the most lucrative academic patent licenses in this period involved vitamin-related inventions. These included the Williams-Waterman method for synthesizing vitamin B_1 (developed at the University of California,

Berkeley and administered by the Research Corporation), Milas's vitamin A and B formulations (developed at MIT and administered by the Research Corporation), and Steenbock's method for producing vitamin D (administered by WARF).

Although data on the distribution of licensing revenues among university patents are limited, biomedical inventions (including vitamins) appear to have accounted for the majority of licensing revenue from university patents issued before Bayh-Dole. Blumenthal, Epstein, and Maxwell (1986) suggest

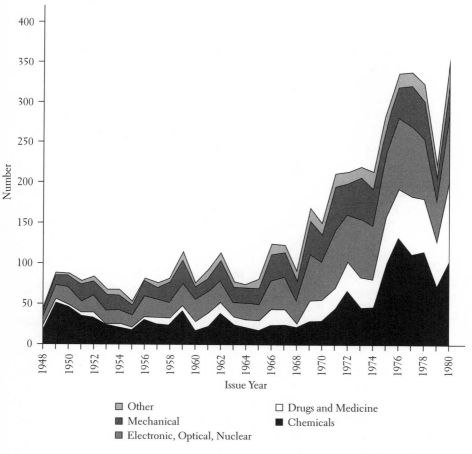

FIGURE 3.8 Distribution among technology classes of university patents, 1948–80

56   that throughout its history, WARF earned most of its revenues from a handful
of biomedical inventions, and Chapter 4 shows that this was also true for the
Research Corporation from the 1940s to the 1970s. In spite of the reluctance
of many universities to seek such patents prior to the 1970s, medical patents
have been important revenue sources for academic licensors throughout the
twentieth century.

Increased federal financial support for biomedical research during the
postwar era is reflected in the growing share of biomedical patents within
our university patent data during and after the 1970s. Much of the growth in
university patenting during the 1970s occurred in the biomedical area (Figure 3.8). Nonbiomedical university patents increased by 90 percent from the
1968–70 period to the 1978–80 period, but biomedical university patents increased by 295 percent. This rapid growth in biomedical patents also reflected
the expansion of the IPA program associated with the major biomedical funding agency (HEW) during the 1970s. The increased share of the biomedical
disciplines within overall federal academic R&D funding, the dramatic advances in biomedical science that occurred during the 1960s and 1970s, and
the strong industrial interest in the results of this biomedical research all affected the growth of university patenting during this period.

CONCLUSION

Patenting and licensing by universities of faculty inventions have a long history in the United States. For much of the 1925–80 period, the appropriateness
of this activity as one of the many missions of U.S. universities was itself a subject of debate, the terms of which anticipated many of the arguments articulated during and after the framing and passage of the Bayh-Dole Act of 1980.
As we point out in our discussion of the origins of the Bayh-Dole Act in Chapter 5, the terms of the debate over university technology licensing shifted
somewhat between the 1930s and the 1970s from an emphasis on the regional
economic benefits associated with the licensing by land-grant universities of
faculty inventions to a focus on the benefits to the national economy associated with the more rapid and successful technology transfer that (according to
supporters of the Bayh-Dole Act) could be attained by patenting and licensing
faculty inventions. This shift in the terms and geographic delimitation of the
economic benefits highlighted in debates over university technology licensing
reflected, of course, the shift in the scale and sources of financial support for
university-based research.

Concern among many university administrators about their exposure to political criticism appears to have limited the willingness of at least some U.S.

universities to assume a direct role in the management of patenting and licensing for much of the 1925–70 period. But the 1970s witnessed an upsurge in entry by universities, particularly private universities, into direct management of patenting and licensing activities. The growth in university patenting during the 1970s reflected shifts in the underlying content of academic research, the effects of the longer-term tendency for federal funding of academic research to become more concentrated in biomedical research and simultaneously less concentrated among institutions, and a shift (before Bayh-Dole) in federal policy toward university patenting and licensing. Nonetheless, prior to 1980, federal policy remained ambivalent toward university licensing, evidenced in the debates over the appropriateness of exclusive licensing under IPAs that we discuss in Chapter 5.

The historical evolution of university patenting behavior in the United States reflects the unanticipated interaction of an array of federal and state policies, rather than intellectual property regimes alone. Indeed, many of the features of university patenting commonly associated with the post-Bayh-Dole period have deep roots in the pre-1980 period. And as we emphasized in Chapter 2, this lengthy involvement in patenting has been influenced by the unusual structure of the U.S. university system. The decentralized system for funding of universities created strong incentives for public universities to pursue research of interest to local firms and to patent their inventions for the benefit of state taxpayers. But the broader environment of interinstitutional competition, administrative autonomy, and the constant search for resources created strong incentives for both public and private universities to develop strong links with industrial research. The changing structure of these incentives, especially change in the sources and structure of funding for university research, has been the most powerful influence on the long history of U.S. university patenting and licensing, before and after the Bayh-Dole Act.

4

THE RESEARCH CORPORATION AND UNIVERSITY
TECHNOLOGY LICENSING, 1912–80

We argued in Chapter 3 that U.S. universities' reluctance to become directly involved in patenting and licensing during much of the 1925–80 period led many of them to contract with the Research Corporation to manage these activities. This chapter discusses the history of the Research Corporation in detail. The corporation played a central role in university patenting and licensing before 1980, and its history anticipates many of the issues currently confronting contemporary university technology transfer offices. These include the high costs of patent management, the severe uncertainty over the infrequent and unpredictable "arrival rate" of the "home run" patents that account for the majority of licensing revenues, the need for close interaction with faculty inventors, and the difficulties in balancing licensing revenues with other objectives of university patent and licensing programs.

Immediately below, we discuss the origins of the Research Corporation in the patenting activities of Frederick Cottrell of the University of California. The next section describes the corporation's evolution by 1945 into a manager of patenting and licensing of university inventions for many of the leading research universities in the United States. The section that follows examines the zenith during the 1950s and 1960s of the Research Corporation's importance as a technological intermediary operating on behalf of academic inventors, with the foundation and growth of the corporation's Patent Management Division. But even during its period of greatest activity and influence, the Research Corporation experienced low profitability and high costs, and the final section examines its decline during the 1970s and 1980s.

The Research Corporation originated from the research of Frederick Gardner Cottrell of the University of California at Berkeley during the early twentieth century. Consistent with Chapter 2's portrayal of the practical motives for much U.S. university research, Cottrell's research was motivated in part by his interest in problems of industrial technology and practice (Cameron, 1993). Beginning in 1905, Cottrell conducted research on industrial air pollution control, responding to a growing nuisance in his native San Francisco. Building on the work of the British scientist Sir Oliver Lodge, Cottrell invented the electrostatic precipitator, a device that removed dust and fumes from smokestacks by electrically charging them and collecting them on an oppositely charged plate.

Cottrell received the first of six patents on the electrostatic precipitator in 1907. Although he was not interested in amassing a personal fortune from his inventions, Cottrell opposed placing his intellectual property in the public domain, arguing that

> a certain minimum amount of protection is usually felt necessary by any manufacturing concern before it will invest in machinery or other equipment, to say nothing of the advertising necessary to put a new invention on the market. Thus a number of meritorious patents given to the public absolutely freely by their inventors have never come upon the market chiefly because "what is everybody's business is nobody's business." (Cottrell, 1912, p. 865)

In other words, Cottrell believed that clearly defined intellectual property rights were needed to provide firms with the incentives to undertake the costly research, development, and marketing activities necessary to bring an embryonic invention such as the precipitator to commercialization. In this argument, Cottrell anticipated subsequent work by scholars such as Kitch (1977) and the arguments set forth by the supporters of the Bayh-Dole Act (see Chapter 5).

Cottrell intended to license his patents and use the proceeds to support scientific research. Implementation of this plan, however, required an organization to manage the licenses. Cottrell first considered using the University of California as a licensing manager but rejected this possibility because of his belief that the involvement of university administrators in licensing management could have detrimental consequences for the culture of scientific research at the university, anticipating some of the concerns discussed in the report of the American Association for the Advancement of Science (AAAS) Committee on Patents, described in Chapter 3:[1]

60 A danger was involved, especially should the experiment prove highly profitable to the university and lead to a general emulation of the plan. University trustees are continually seeking for funds and in direct proportion to the success of our experiment its repetition might be expected elsewhere . . . the danger this suggested was the possibility of growing commercialism and competition between institutions and an accompanying tendency for secrecy in scientific work. (Cottrell, 1932, p. 222)

Cottrell approached the Smithsonian Institution, where his plan was embraced by Secretary Charles Walcott but rejected by the Institution's regents, reflecting their desire to avoid any involvement in patent administration. Instead, a corporation, in which Walcott played an advisory role, was formed to oversee patenting and licensing. The Research Corporation was founded in 1912 with the assistance of none other than William Howard Taft, then a Smithsonian regent, in drafting its charter.

Although he originally intended to assign the corporation's licensing royalties to the Smithsonian for the "increase and diffusion of knowledge," Cottrell subsequently decided to use the organization's earnings to support scientific research at institutions other than the Smithsonian. The corporation also managed the licensing and development of the electrostatic precipitator patents, and Cottrell argued that the corporation should assume responsibility for managing the licensure of donated patents in other technological areas:

The ever growing number of men in academic positions who evolve useful and patentable inventions from time to time in connection with their regular work and without looking personally for any financial reward would gladly see these further developed for the public good, but are disinclined either to undertake such developments themselves or to place the control in the hands of any private interests. (Cottrell, 1912, p. 865)[2]

In Cottrell's view, the purpose of the Research Corporation "was not merely to produce revenue for scientific research, but to act as a sort of laboratory of patent economics and to conduct experiments in patent administration" (as cited in McKusick, 1948, p. 208). From its inception, he envisioned the Research Corporation as an entity that would develop and disseminate techniques for managing the intellectual property of research universities and similar organizations.

During its first twenty-five years, the Research Corporation focused on three activities: (1) designing, manufacturing, and installing electrostatic precipitation and other equipment arising from patents that it owned, administered, or purchased; (2) managing patentable inventions from educational or research institutions that were donated to the corporation; and (3) providing grants for scientific researchers. The first of these three tasks, however, accounted for the bulk of the corporation's activities during this period.

THE EVOLUTION OF THE RESEARCH CORPORATION, 1912–45   61

Early Activities: 1912–36

Frederick Cottrell played no official role in the Research Corporation once it was founded, although he exerted considerable influence on its early decisions and took part in a number of the corporation's activities until his death in 1948.[3] The corporation's directors and managers quickly learned that administration of the Cottrell patents was more difficult than they had anticipated. Merely licensing the precipitation patents to firms resulted in minimal technology adoption and modest royalty income, since application of the precipitator technology required customization to meet the technical needs of different industries. Few engineers outside the corporation had the skills necessary to adapt the electrostatic precipitator to these varied applications. As a result, the Research Corporation extended its activities beyond those of a "pure" technology intermediary and entered the precipitator installation and design business. Research Corporation staff (which by 1917 included forty-five engineers) performed research and development to adapt precipitator technologies to licensees' plants.

Despite these unanticipated investments, the electrostatic precipitation business became profitable by 1915, and the Research Corporation began to award research grants in 1924. During the next several decades, the Research Corporation dominated the electrostatic precipitator market (White, 1963). Since the corporation's "endowment" of Cottrell's patents proved insufficient to support its licensing activities, the organization acquired additional patents from other inventors and pursued R&D in this technology field.

As a by-product of its work in the precipitation industry, the Research Corporation developed considerable expertise in patent management and litigation. As early as 1913, it began to pursue infringers of the Cottrell patents. By 1918, the Research Corporation was "making the securing of business secondary to the protection of patent rights" in the precipitation field, devoting more effort to the management of its patent portfolio than to the installation of precipitators.[4] Their experience with the precipitation patents expanded the skills of Research Corporation staff in seeking out potential licensees, negotiating license agreements, and overseeing the development and marketing of inventions.[5] The corporation also developed numerous contacts with patent attorneys throughout the country and with scientists at several university laboratories, the site of much of the development work on the electrostatic precipitators.

The successes of the Research Corporation in managing its precipitation patent portfolio drew the attention of a number of university scientists and

62   independent inventors who sought assistance with the patenting and licensing of their inventions in fields other than precipitators. Following Cottrell's example, several of these scientist-inventors wished to assign their licensing royalties to the Research Corporation to support its philanthropic activities. The expanding research collaboration between U.S. universities and industry and the related growth of science-based industry increased the volume of commercially valuable academic research in the 1920s and 1930s, resulting in more and more requests from academic inventors to the Research Corporation for assistance in the management of patenting and licensing.

Beginning in the late 1920s, the Research Corporation began to accept donations of patents outside of the precipitation field and received a number of patents in a diverse array of technical fields.[6] Among the most important of these inventions was the Williams-Waterman process for synthesis of vitamin B_1. Developed in Robert R. Williams's laboratory at the University of California in 1932, the Williams-Waterman process was important in the fight against malnutrition and was immediately recognized to have significant income potential. Williams and Robert E. Waterman filed for a patent on their new process with the aid of the Research Corporation, which also assisted the inventors in the successful prosecution of an interference hearing. The patent issued in 1935 and was assigned to the Research Corporation.

The Williams-Waterman invention was an important development in the history of the Research Corporation for several reasons. One of the first in a series of public health–related inventions that accounted for a growing share of the Research Corporation's licensing revenues during the next two decades, the patent was the first "home run" in a field other than electrostatic precipitation. Income from this and other biomedical patents proved indispensable to the corporation's growth. The corporation's involvement in the Williams-Waterman interference hearing also expanded its activities in nonprecipitation technologies from administering patents to helping secure them. Like contemporary university technology licensing offices, the corporation recognized that it had to assume responsibility for a number of activities in addition to the administration of patents and licenses.

The Research Corporation's reputation in academic patent management also benefited from its successful management of the precipitation patents, as well as the marketing efforts of Cottrell, who frequently visited leading colleges and universities to advise administration and faculty on matters of patenting and to promote the Research Corporation's services. In addition, the Research Corporation's research grants to university researchers had produced a number of potentially patentable inventions by the 1930s. Although they

were not obliged to do so, many of these inventors turned to the Research Corporation for patent assistance.

Another development that aided the Research Corporation's growth was the increased interest of U.S. universities during the 1930s in the financial returns from patenting and licensing of faculty inventions. But as we pointed out in Chapter 3, many U.S. universities in the 1930s avoided direct management of patent prosecution and licensing, in contrast to their embrace of this role during the 1970s and 1980s. This reluctance was partly due to the political controversy that had erupted over the University of Wisconsin's patenting and licensing activities (although these were managed by the Wisconsin Alumni Research Foundation), as well as the fact that the scale of the research enterprise at most universities during this period was too small to justify direct involvement in patent administration. As the Research Corporation noted, "University staffs were not equipped to handle such problems — the number [of patents] arising in any one year at a single institution would be too small to justify having expert patent personnel" (Research Corporation, 1972, p. 15). Faculty inventors therefore were encouraged by administrators, colleagues, and the broader scientific and technological community to work through the Research Corporation (Palmer, 1948).[7]

Nevertheless, despite expanded discussions with U.S. universities and inventors over management of their patents, management of nonprecipitation patents accounted for a relatively small part of the Research Corporation's activities during the 1930s. Although it handled inventions for individual faculty members and universities on a case-by-case basis, the corporation had no formal agreements with universities. This situation began to change, however, with the negotiation of the Research Corporation's first Invention Administration Agreement (IAA) with MIT in 1937.

The MIT Invention Administration Agreement

As key precipitation patents expired and the market for electrostatic precipitators declined during the Depression, the Research Corporation sought to develop new revenue sources.[8] In addition to its work with precipitator patents, the corporation's management of its portfolio of nonprecipitation patents had contributed to the development of unique competencies that could be exploited for the mutual benefit of the Research Corporation and academic institutions, while sustaining Cottrell's original vision for the corporation as a source of funding for scientific research. In addition, as the Research Corporation argued in a 1972 document, centralized management of patenting and licensing on behalf of universities by a specialist could be less costly for each

64   institution than independent management of their faculty patents: "if there were an inter-university clearing house for handling patents, experts could be engaged, contacts with industry could be maintained, legal costs could be spread, and many other advantages gained for the whole group" (Research Corporation, 1972, p. 15).

The Research Corporation's search for new income sources, along with the increased interest of U.S. universities in licensing income, led it to expand its activities in patent management by negotiating agreements with U.S. universities. The Research Corporation's 1937 IAA with MIT laid the groundwork for the corporation's emergence as a national technology licensing intermediary for U.S. universities.[9]

Prior to the arrival of Karl Compton as its president in 1930, MIT did not have a well-defined institutional patent policy. Instead, the Institute either ceded rights to the individual inventor or deferred to the requirements of research sponsors. Shortly after becoming president of MIT, Compton organized an internal study of all aspects of its industrial relations, including its patent policy. After some debate, the Institute's Committee on Patent Policy (chaired by Vannevar Bush) decided that MIT would assert rights to any faculty inventions resulting from research financed by the Institute. The committee recommended that procedures be developed "to relieve the Institute of all responsibility in connection with the exploitation of inventions while providing for a reasonable proportionate return to the Institute in all cases in which profit shall ensue."[10] Accordingly, MIT sought outside parties to administer its patents and aid in the patent application process.

The eventual choice of the Research Corporation as MIT's patent manager reflected a number of ties linking corporation managers with MIT staff and administration. Howard Poillon, the Research Corporation's president since 1928, was a close friend of Karl Compton's and lobbied him for the right to market MIT's inventions. The Research Corporation also administered patents that covered the inventions of several MIT faculty members, such as Robert Van de Graaf's electrostatic generator and Nicholas Milas's vitamin formulas, both of which were based on research funded by the corporation.

An IAA between MIT and the Research Corporation was signed in 1937. The agreement called for the corporation to establish a Boston office to manage the review and evaluation of MIT inventions. Under the terms of the IAA, MIT disclosed potentially patentable inventions to the Research Corporation, which evaluated them and accepted for administration those deemed to have commercial promise. The corporation agreed "to use its best efforts to secure patents on inventions so assigned to it and to bring these inventions into use and derive a reasonable income therefrom" and further to "use its best efforts

to protect these said inventions from misuse and to take such steps against infringers as [it] may deem for the best interest of the parties hereto, but with the
general policy of avoiding litigation wherever practicable." All services were
provided at the expense of the Research Corporation, although the corporation assumed no financial responsibility for any additional development costs
for MIT inventions. Any licensing income net of expenses was to be divided
between MIT and the corporation on a 60-40 basis. The Research Corporation used its portion of the earnings to support its operating expenses and philanthropic activities.

The outbreak of World War II cut off the flow of inventions from MIT and
other universities, and the Research Corporation virtually ceased its patent administration efforts.[11] Shortly after the return of peace, the corporation re-
assessed its patent management activities, most of which had involved MIT inventions, noting that they had produced net losses during the 1937–47 period
(1947 *Annual Report*, p. 1).[12] Although none of the forty MIT inventions and
none of the handful of inventions it was administering for other universities
had yet produced significant returns, the corporation opined that four MIT inventions had "bright futures" and asserted that "after ten years of trial of the
economic soundness of the type of educational institution patent management agreement initiated in 1937, the soundness of the idea, in spite of the dor-
mant war years, seems to be confirmed" (1947 *Annual Report*, p. 1).

Nevertheless, this internal review argued that the scale of the Research
Corporation's patent-management operations was too small to be economical,
noting that

> the handling of inventions for educational institutions can be successful only if the
> service can be rendered to a considerable number of such institutions so that a large
> number of potentially valuable inventions can be administered . . . unless a sizable
> number of such inventions is available for administration the numerical odds of un-
> successful developments to successful ones would render the management under
> such circumstances too great a risk. (1947 *Annual Report*, p. 3)

By the time the 1947 *Annual Report* was published, the corporation had begun
a program to attract more university clients to its intellectual property management services.

THE PATENT MANAGEMENT DIVISION

The MIT agreement sparked interest in patent licensing by other universities.
Although the Boston office had originally been established to handle MIT's inventions, it also began to handle patent matters for other universities. In 1946,
the Research Corporation established the Patent Management Division to

66   handle all nonprecipitation patents, consolidating the work previously done in the Boston and New York offices. Following the policies established in the MIT agreement and in contrast to the corporation's activities in precipitator technologies, the Patent Management Division had the following responsibilities:

1. Negotiation of agreements with educational and scientific institutions for the administration and development of their patents;
2. Evaluation of inventions submitted under these agreements, as well as those submitted by individual inventors;
3. Submission of patent applications for promising inventions; and
4. Licensing patents to industry.

The Patent Management Division assumed no responsibility for the development of university inventions but worked with universities to improve their expertise in patenting and licensing of faculty inventions. The division sought to expand university patenting, thereby increasing the volume of business for the Research Corporation, and its efforts contributed to growth in the number of universities initiating formal technology transfer activities during the 1960s and 1970s (see below for further discussion).[13]

The combined effects of the formation of the Patent Management Division and the MIT agreement were significant. The expansion of military and biomedical research conducted in U.S. universities during and after the war had increased the pool of potentially patentable academic inventions, and federal funding agencies compelled universities to develop formal patent policies during the early postwar period. The Research Corporation negotiated IAAs,

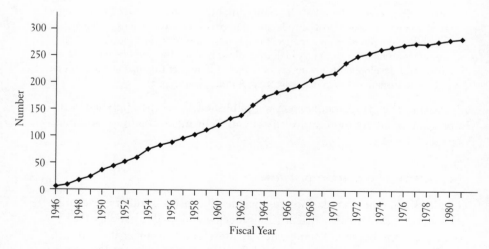

FIGURE 4.1   Research Corporation Invention Administration Agreements, 1946–81

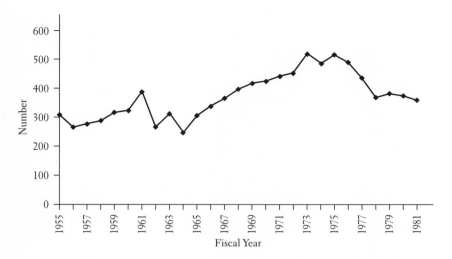

FIGURE 4.2 Invention disclosures to the Research Corporation, 1955–81

modeled on the MIT agreement, with several hundred other U.S. universities during the 1940s and 1950s (Figure 4.1). Under the terms of these agreements, university faculty submitted invention disclosures to the Patent Management Division, which bore all costs of invention evaluation, patent prosecution, and licensing. Any royalty income was divided among the academic institution, the inventor, and the Research Corporation. The Research Corporation's share of the royalties, after deduction of operating expenses, funded its research grants.

Growth in the number of university clients was paralleled by expansion in the annual number of inventions disclosed to the Research Corporation (Figure 4.2). The average annual flow of disclosures, which never fell below 200 during this period, represented a sharp increase from the average of roughly 50 disclosures per year received by the corporation (primarily from MIT) at the time the Patent Management Division was established. But this increased flow of disclosures did not produce a comparable increase in patents (Figure 4.3) or gross royalties (Figure 4.4), an issue that we discuss in greater detail below.

As was noted earlier, the Research Corporation's Patent Management Division had hoped that its expanded activities in managing university inventions would increase the corporation's licensing income while reducing its reliance on a small number of donated inventions for the bulk of its income. Nonetheless, the corporation's 1951 *Annual Report* noted that institutional inventions still accounted for a small share of licensing royalties:

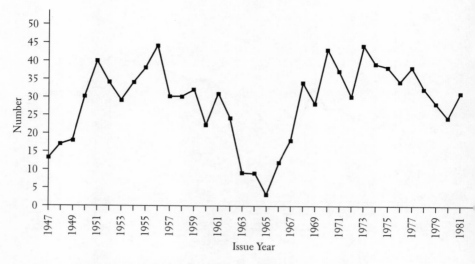

FIGURE 4.3   Patents issued to the Research Corporation, 1947–81

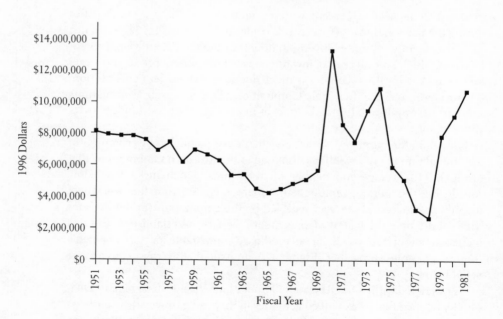

FIGURE 4.4   Research Corporation gross royalties, 1951–81

[Most revenues] have been derived from agreements covering specific projects; and not from the over-all patent management contracts . . . the blanket agreements still have not "paid off." The corporation's experience shows that this is not to be expected except over a period of many years, and even then only in a few instances. It is important only that there be a sufficient number of these "few instances" and to that end, it is important that more institutional agreements be secured. (1951 *Annual Report*, p. 42)

This problem was a persistent one for the Research Corporation. In 1947, it had noted that "none of our other [other than MIT] general agreements with educational institutions to date show any promise of financial return, but we continue optimistic of future developments, particularly as the number and scope of such agreements continues to increase" (1947 *Annual Report*, p. 2). Although its portfolio of institutional agreements, patents, and licenses grew during the 1950s, growth in net revenues proved elusive.

The Patent Management Division's Invention Portfolio

From the inception of the Patent Management Division, licensing royalties were dominated by income from a small number of inventions, most of which were in the biomedical field (Table 4.1). Throughout the 1945–85 period, the corporation's top five inventions accounted for the lion's share of gross revenues, a characteristic of the corporation's licensing portfolio that also is apparent in contemporary data on the royalty income of leading U.S. academic licensors (see Chapter 6).

By the mid-1950s, the Research Corporation's heavy reliance on biomedical inventions for income had begun to raise concerns among the corporation's management. The 1955 *Annual Report* noted that wide fluctuations in the prices of vitamins had affected the corporation's royalty income (see Table 4.1). Although the report forecast that other types of inventions would "soon" begin to contribute significantly to the royalty stream, these new revenue sources failed to materialize.

This problem was attributable in part to the fact that the Research Corporation's considerable expertise in prosecuting, managing, and licensing patents in the areas of precipitation technology and the life sciences did not translate into comparable strength in other technical fields. As a result, the corporation's activities in nonbiomedical fields were limited. Indeed, Fishman (1996) notes that one reason for MIT's 1946 decision to stop using the Research Corporation as the sole agent for administration of its patent portfolio was concern over the corporation's lack of expertise in fields other than the life sciences.[14]

Another striking characteristic of the biomedical "home runs" that accounted for the bulk of the Research Corporation's income through the early

TABLE 4.1
Research Corporation Gross Income from "Home Run" Inventions, 1945–85

Year	Gross income*	Gross income from top 5 earners	Share of gross income from top 5 earners	Share of income from biomedical inventions in prev. column	Top 5 grossing inventions (descending order)
1945	4,713,417	4,604,511	98%	100%	Eschatin Ergotrate Merthiolate Pantothenic acid Vitamin B1
1950	5,528,142	5,165,811	93%	90%	Panthothenic acid Vitamin B1 Ergotrate Electromagnetic horns* Merthiolate
1955	7,485,868	5,996,276	80%	100%	Cortisone Vitamin B1 Vitamin A Pantothenic acid Ergotrate
1960	6,516,215	5,389,883	83%	100%	Cortical hormones Vitamin A Pantothenic acid Nystatin Vitamin K
1965	4,155,908	3,684,411	89%	93%	Nystatin Cortical hormones Pantothenic acid Glass strength promoter* Reserpine
1970	13,070,160	12,433,948	95%	43%	Hybrid seed corn** Nystatin Cortical hormones Plant growth regulants* Reserpine
1975	5,823,032	4,755,064	82%	63%	Quinoxaline-di-n-oxides Plant growth regulants* Nystatin Maser* Antibacterial agent
1980	9,041,497	6,547,132	72%	96%	Platinum anti-tumor compounds Burn ointment Quinoxaline-di-n-oxides Radiopharmaceuticals for skeletal imaging Delayed release mushroom nutrients*
1985	13,869,300	12,776,616	92%	96%	Plantinum anti-tumor compounds Antibacterial agent Quinoxaline-di-n-oxides Delayed release mushroom nutrients* Radiopharmaceuticals for skeletal imaging

NOTES: Income numbers are in 1996 dollars. * Nonbiomedical invention. ** Includes back royalties paid as a result of infringement suit.

1970s was the prominence within this group of donated inventions. The most important invention in the first decade of the Patent Management Division (although it was donated to the corporation before the establishment of the division) was the method for synthesis of vitamin B_1 that we discussed earlier. The corporation's most lucrative invention after the expiration of the vitamin B_1 patents was nystatin, an antifungal antibiotic developed by Rachel Brown and Elizabeth Hazel of the New York State Department of Health that the inventors had donated to the corporation.[15] During the 1960s and early 1970s, nystatin, two other donated biomedical inventions (Edward Kendall's cortical hormones and Robert Woodward's reserpine), and one donated agricultural invention (the Jones-Mangelsdorf hybrid seed–growing process) were the corporation's most important sources of royalty income.

Although donated inventions had been important to the Research Corporation's revenues since the beginning of its patent management activities, the extent of the corporation's reliance on donated inventions had increased by the mid-1960s. This is apparent even if we restrict our attention to the donated inventions among the top five gross revenue earners, or the donated "home runs." Having accounted for 48 percent of total gross royalty revenues in 1955 and 50 percent in 1960, the donated inventions among the top five gross revenue earners accounted for 69 percent of gross royalties in 1965 and 91 percent in 1970.[16] Only after 1975, when the patents on the last of the donated "home runs" expired, did the entirety of the Research Corporation's income depend on inventions administered through institutional IAAs.

The Cancellation of the MIT Invention Administration Agreement

The Research Corporation's failure to attract economically valuable institutional inventions came into sharp focus following the 1963 cancellation of the IAA with MIT. The events that led to MIT's termination of its agreement with the Research Corporation merit discussion not only because of their importance for the subsequent history of the Research Corporation but also because they illustrate some of the difficulties of academic patent management.

The immediate catalyst for the series of events that led to the cancellation was the dispute between the Research Corporation and MIT over the corporation's management of the Forrester patent on magnetic core memories for computers (see Pugh, 1984).[17] In 1951, the Research Corporation filed a patent application on Jay Forrester's invention under the MIT IAA. A similar patent application was filed by Jan Rajchman at RCA in 1950, and an interference was declared in 1956. In the meantime, IBM had become interested in using the core memory technology in its mainframe computers and entered a cross-

72   licensing agreement with RCA in 1957. IBM also entered into negotiations with the Research Corporation to negotiate a license should Forrester win the case. But IBM and the corporation failed to agree on royalty rates, and the negotiations collapsed. IBM, which had a long history of donating funds and equipment to MIT, expressed concern to Institute administrators that the Research Corporation was taking a hard line in the negotiations. Indeed, Pugh (1984) reports that IBM may have threatened to withhold future funding to MIT if the Research Corporation did not compromise.

In 1960, the Board of Patent Interferences declared Rajchman victorious on ten significant claims and awarded several narrower claims to Forrester. The Research Corporation launched a civil action to attempt to recover the ten claims awarded to Rajchman and initiated a patent infringement suit against RCA and IBM.[18] By this time, the interests of MIT and the Research Corporation seem to have diverged. As Pugh (1984, p. 211) describes it:

> As the attorneys prepared for the court case, MIT decided that its interests were not properly represented by Research Corporation. Research Corporation wanted patent fees paid over time, based on use, so that a predictable revenue stream would permit orderly operation of its business. MIT preferred a single payment to help cover the costs of a building program. Even more importantly MIT was concerned about its long-term relationship with IBM and the rest of the computer industry.

In 1962, MIT terminated its IAA with the Research Corporation. Under the terms of the termination agreement, the Research Corporation received a $1.6 million cash settlement, and MIT retained all residual rights to the patents it had assigned to the Research Corporation.

The Forrester case was a pivotal development in the Research Corporation's history, since it led to the termination of the IAA that had been the foundation for the corporation's patent management activities. But this case also illustrates the potential conflicts between the incentives of patent management agents and those of their academic principals. Similar tensions between the goals of maximizing licensing income and maintaining or deepening relationships with industrial firms (relationships that ultimately may prove to yield substantially more research funding or income) are not uncommon within contemporary university technology licensing offices and faculties.[19]

The Growing Costs of Patent Management

Although the Research Corporation had expanded its operations in the early postwar period in order to reduce the unit costs of patent management, these cost savings proved to be elusive. As we noted above, the corporation's expertise in locating licensees and negotiating licensing agreements in one technology field appears to have had limited relevance to other technological

areas. Other costs of the corporation's operations, such as legal and "visitation"
expenses, also grew as its activities and client list expanded. Instead, dis-
economies of scale and scope increased the Research Corporation's operating
costs and reduced net revenues. This section examines several of these sources
of increasing costs, which highlight challenges faced by many contemporary
university technology licensing offices.

Expanded Visitation and Marketing Efforts

Following the cancellation of its agreement with MIT, the Research Corporation reorganized its patent management program. Although the corporation
maintained its support for a specialized Patent Management Division that
served multiple institutional clients, the 1963 *Annual Report* argued that the
corporation's efforts had been "too conservative." In 1963, the corporation expanded its efforts in patent management and marketing. These intensified
efforts included an increase in staff and greater reliance on technical consultants (and outside patent counsel) for evaluating and licensing inventions.
The increased reliance on consultants was most pronounced in the mechanical and electronics fields, where the corporation had developed little expertise and (as we discuss below) generated little royalty income.[20] Figures 4.5

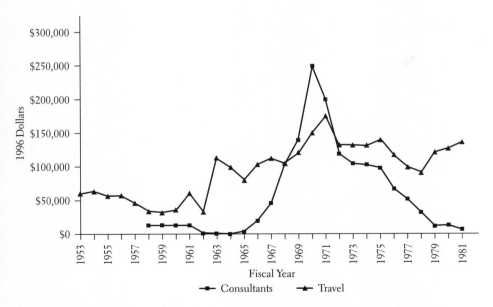

FIGURE 4.5   Research Corporation expenditures on consultants and travel, 1953–81

and 4.6 illustrate the rapid growth during 1964–74 in expenditures on consultants, travel, litigation, and staff.[21]

As part of the expansion of its marketing and patent management activities during the 1960s, the Research Corporation had initiated an ambitious visitation program to foster "a closer working relationship with institutional inventors and their administrators, more expeditious handling of invention disclosures submitted for evaluation, and improved understanding of the problems involved in bringing inventions from the laboratory to the marketplace" (1965 *Annual Report*, p. 2). The corporation made 81 visits to academic institutions in 1964, 116 in 1965, and 120 in 1966.[22] In 1966, the Research Corporation announced plans for annual visits to large universities and technical schools with which it had agreements and biennial visits to smaller schools (1966 *Annual Report*). These increased travel and visitation activities contributed to growth in the corporation's travel costs during the 1960s. Moreover, the higher number of invention disclosures produced by expanded visitation activities (see Figure 4.2) required the hiring of additional staff and consultants, further increasing costs.[23]

These increased costs of travel and related activities reflected the importance of face-to-face interactions between Research Corporation staff and uni-

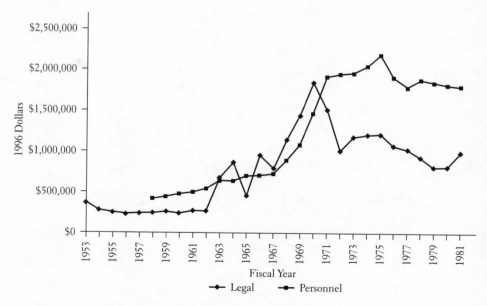

FIGURE 4.6   Research Corporation legal and personnel expenditures, 1953–81

THE RESEARCH CORPORATION AND LICENSING

versity administrators and inventors, a theme that runs through the corporation's history. MIT had insisted that the Research Corporation establish a Boston office as a condition of the 1937 Invention Management Agreement. Even
after the corporation's Boston office was closed in 1946, Research Corporation
staff continued monthly visits to MIT to evaluate and discuss Institute inventions through the late 1950s. For the Research Corporation (as for contemporary licensing offices), patenting and licensing transactions required significant investments of time in the development of close relationships with
inventors and their parent institutions, reflecting the substantial "relational"
component of such transactions. Evaluation of inventions, especially those in
their embryonic stages, requires inventor cooperation, guidance, and equipment. Inventors also are often more knowledgeable about markets for licenses
and may be willing to contribute consulting assistance to transfer important
know-how along with the patent license. Inventor assistance and cooperation
may be needed to write and prosecute patent applications.[24]

The importance of these relational aspects of technology licensing operations helps explain the role of geographic proximity in markets for technology.[25] Indeed, the need for frequent interaction between licensing professionals and university inventors has provided one impetus for the decentralization
of technology licensing offices in large, multicampus university systems such
as the University of California.

Training Universities in Patent Management

During the 1970s, the Research Corporation initiated an ambitious training
program to teach university administrators and faculty to evaluate the
patentability and licensing prospects for faculty inventions. The "outreach
program" included a newsletter, *Research and Invention*, which began publication in 1971; an instructional pamphlet for university inventors and administrators entitled "Evaluating and Patenting Faculty Inventions"; and sponsorship of conferences and seminars on university-industry technology transfer.
In addition, with funding from the National Science Foundation, the corporation began a "Patent Awareness Program" in 1973 that sought to "increase
the ability of faculty members and administrators alike to recognize inventions
developed at educational institutions" (Marcy, 1978, p. 156).

The expanded training program and associated efforts to shift more responsibility for invention evaluation and patent management to client universities represented a change from the Research Corporation's previous position that universities should not get involved in patenting.[26] The corporation
now argued that the early stages of invention screening and evaluation (that is,
persuading faculty members to disclose valuable inventions and collecting

76   properly written invention disclosures) were best done by the universities themselves. This shift in policy may have reflected the inability of the expanded visitation program to support the close interactions between inventor and patent agent needed to facilitate the early stages of the patenting and licensing process. But these policy changes also were a response to the Research Corporation's deteriorating financial situation.[27]

In addition to their costs, the extensive visitation and outreach activities associated with the more aggressive patent management activities had another unanticipated effect. As we noted in Chapter 3, by the 1970s the corporation's activities and other developments in federal policy and the content of university research had led a growing number of U.S. universities to assume a larger role in patent management. Paradoxically, the efforts of the Research Corporation to train a larger group of faculty and administrators in patenting and licensing eroded its competitive advantage in patent administration.

The Paucity of "Home Runs"

The Research Corporation's efforts during the postwar period to expand the number of universities with whom it worked, as well as its more intensive marketing activities of the 1950s and 1960s, do not appear to have offset the detrimental financial effects of higher operating costs, declining royalties, and the expiration of key donated patents on "home runs." In the face of the imminent expiration of the last of its lucrative donated patents in 1975, the corporation noted that

> while it is possible that other substantial income producing inventions will become available in the future, it will be a rare occurrence. Therefore, if the invention administration operation is to continue, total reliance must be put on finding and developing commercially viable shared inventions. One consequence of this situation is that a major effort will be required in the future to develop and enhance relationships with universities and faculty inventors. (1974 *Annual Report*, p. 3)

Unfortunately, this statement overlooked the fact that such efforts had been under way for more than a decade, with little effect. The "arrival rate" of highly profitable inventions proved to be unresponsive to the Research Corporation's efforts to increase it. This inability to obtain and license additional "home runs" in the face of growing needs for revenues foreshadows the challenges that technology licensing offices and administration at a number of prominent universities face as patents on key inventions from the early 1980s, many of which are associated with the rise of biotechnology, begin to expire.

Did the Research Corporation fail to capture more profitable institutional inventions because its client universities began to "cherry-pick" their faculty

inventions, choosing to license their most valuable inventions independently? 77
To examine this possibility, we collected data from the annual reports of the
U.S. Patent and Trademark Office on independent patenting by the corporation's clients in each of six years (1950, 1955, 1960, 1965, 1970, and 1975) during
the 1950–75 period.[28] These data suggest that there was little cherry-picking in
the first two decades of the period, although this began to change during the
late 1960s and 1970s. Specifically, fewer than 10 percent of institutional clients
received patents (patents assigned to themselves rather than to the Research
Corporation) before 1970. Fully 95 percent of these "independent" patents
were in fields outside of the life sciences, and the apparent decision of its institutional clients to bypass the Research Corporation may have reflected the
corporation's lack of experience in fields outside of biomedical technology.[29]
But cherry-picking appears to have expanded during the 1970s. The number
of patents assigned to Research Corporation clients nearly doubled between
1970 and 1975, and much of this growth resulted from increased independent
patenting by Research Corporation institutional clients in the life sciences.
The corporation's 1975 *Annual Report* noted that many universities were beginning to withhold valuable inventions.[30]

The Limits of Scale Economies

The failure to attract highly profitable inventions from its client universities
suggests that the benefits for the Research Corporation resulting from diversification among technologies and institutional clients were limited. Despite increased expenditures on consultants and specialized staff, the corporation patented few lucrative inventions. This failure was surprising in view of
the fact that during the 1950s and 1960s, the Research Corporation had access
to the patentable inventions of many of the nation's most prominent research
universities.

The effects of slower revenue growth were exacerbated by continued
growth in the corporation's total operating costs during the 1960s (Figure 4.7).
Beginning in the mid-1970s, the visitation program and the more aggressive
patent management program were curtailed, and the rate of growth of expenditures on consultants, legal services, personnel, and travel declined (revealed
in the downward trend after 1975 in consulting, legal, and personnel expenses
in Figures 4.5 and 4.6).

Another source of scale economies that the Research Corporation had
hoped to exploit, dating back to Cottrell's original vision, was the spreading
of "fixed" costs over a large number of institutions and inventions. Nonetheless, its growing client roster failed to prevent the corporation's total costs per

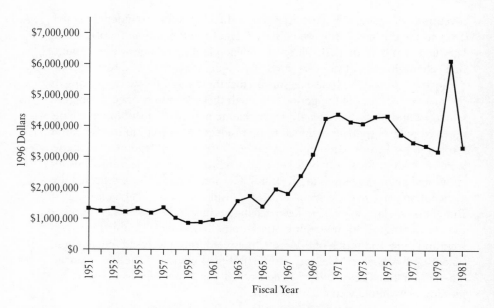

FIGURE 4.7   Research Corporation total operating costs, 1951–81

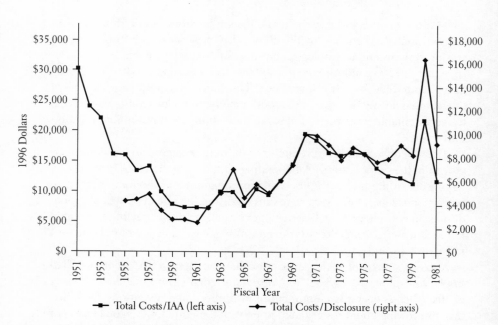

FIGURE 4.8   Total costs per Invention Administration Agreement and disclosure, 1951–81

invention agreement and per disclosure from increasing, rather than decreasing, in the late 1960s (Figure 4.8).

By the mid-1970s, the Research Corporation's net royalty income had declined sharply (Figure 4.9), and a "Committee on Goals and Objectives of the Corporation" was convened to conduct a strategic review. The committee's report concluded in 1979 that "if in the years 1980–1983 forecasts of enhanced income do not begin to be realized, significant changes in programs will be necessary" (Research Corporation, 1979, p. 5). In the event, these "significant changes" included closing the Patent Management Division.[31]

FEDERAL POLICY CHANGES, LOSS OF MARKET SHARE, AND THE DECLINE OF THE RESEARCH CORPORATION

The Research Corporation played an important role in assisting U.S. universities in responding to the changes in federal policy toward university patenting during the 1960s and 1970s that were described in Chapter 3. For example, the Research Corporation helped universities to bring their policies and procedures into conformity with new guidelines for patenting developed by the Defense Department, the National Science Foundation, and the Department of Health, Education, and Welfare during the 1970s, in hopes that doing so

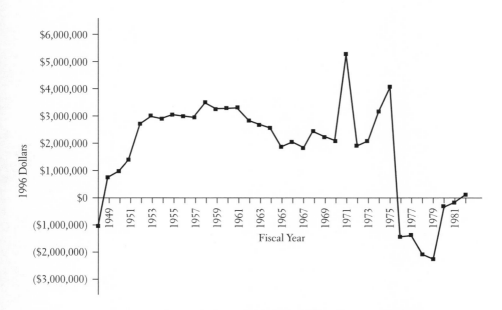

FIGURE 4.9   Research Corporation net royalty income, 1948–82

80   would ultimately increase the demand for its services.[32] But the corporation's assistance to U.S. universities in responding to these changes in federal policy may have hastened its eclipse, as U.S. universities expanded their independent management of patenting and licensing activities.

In responding to requests for assistance from U.S. universities, the Research Corporation supported the growth of independent technology transfer operations at a number of institutions. By teaching university administrators about the processes of invention evaluation and administration, the Research Corporation helped academic institutions develop the capabilities needed to manage patenting and licensing.[33] The corporation's 1974 *Annual Report* noted that almost every major U.S. university was considering the establishment of an internal technology transfer office, and the 1975 *Annual Report* stated that a growing number of client universities no longer asked the corporation to evaluate particularly valuable inventions, choosing instead to manage them internally.[34] The potential for significant royalty income in these fields thus appears to have contributed to growth in cherry-picking by universities after the early 1970s, ironically reducing the Research Corporation's ac-

FIGURE 4.10   Research Corporation share of U.S. university patents, 1969–87

cess to university inventions at the same time that the pool of commercially valuable academic inventions was expanding.

The passage of the Bayh-Dole Act, which the Research Corporation supported, was another important factor in the corporation's decline. Growth in independent university technology licensing operations, which accelerated after the passage of Bayh-Dole, reduced the Research Corporation's share of the market for academic patents. As the number of universities that entered into patenting and licensing activities increased (see Chapter 3), the Research Corporation's share of all university patents decreased dramatically, as seen in Figure 4.10.

In a recent review of its patent management activities, the Research Corporation noted that "the Bayh-Dole Bill, which the foundation strongly supported and testified in favor of, curtailed this pioneering initiative as the nation's colleges and universities developed their own technology transfer offices and staffs of legal and technical experts" (1997 *Annual Report*, p. 16). Our analysis above supports this view but suggests that the internal operating and financial difficulties that ultimately caused the Research Corporation to curtail its patent management activities predated the passage of Bayh-Dole.

The Research Corporation After 1980

The Research Corporation remained active during the 1980s in the face of Bayh-Dole and the growth of independent university-based technology transfer operations, but its importance declined. The ability of the corporation to compete in this arena was further hindered by its status as a charitable foundation. In the early 1980s, the Internal Revenue Service ruled that the Research Corporation's technology transfer activities were an "unrelated trade or business." As a result, the corporation was prohibited from activities it viewed as essential to technology transfer, such as investing in start-up companies and early-stage funding of development activities. In 1987, the corporation closed the Patent Management Division and transferred all of its activities to an independent for-profit organization, Research Corporation Technologies (RCT), whose purpose is "identifying, developing, and commercializing inventions for universities, colleges, medical research organizations, and other non-profit laboratories" (1987 *Annual Report*, p. 20).

Although the RCT has the same mission as the corporation's former Patent Management Division, it uses retained earnings to fund technology transfer activities rather than scientific research. RCT received half of the Research Corporation's endowment (about $45 million in 1996 dollars) at the time of the spin-off, as well as the Research Corporation's patent portfolio and technology

82   transfer staff. The spin-off agreement stipulated that the Research Corporation would receive a portion of RCT's net royalty income until the $45 million transfer in endowment was paid back. Today, the Research Corporation focuses exclusively on research grants, which are funded from the returns on its endowment, the repayment by the RCT of its endowment grant, and philanthropic contributions.

The RCT's Cooperative Program allows academic institutions to use RCT to evaluate inventions, similar to the Research Corporation's Invention Administration Program. The RCT also operates the Benchmark Program, which allows universities and other institutions to use RCT services on an "as-needed" basis. According to Gilles (1991), the Benchmark Program is used primarily for evaluating the inventions of academic clients, with no commitment to managing any patents, and management of patenting and licensing for inventions in fields in which the university technology licensing offices lack expertise. Very few universities have used RCT's Cooperative Program, and both the Cooperative and Benchmark Programs are being phased out.

By some measures, the RCT remains a successful technology transfer organization: the Association of University Technology Managers's 1996 *AUTM Licensing Survey* (attachment E, p. 53) reports that its gross licensing income amounted to $70 million, more than any U.S. university in that year. About $45 million of this amount was distributed to the inventors and universities responsible for the inventions (see Research Corporation Technologies, 1996, "Corporate Update"). Nonetheless, the importance of RCT as a technology transfer agent has diminished considerably, and its activities differ significantly from those of the Research Corporation.

CONCLUSION

This brief history of the Research Corporation underscores the points made in Chapters 2 and 3 concerning the history of U.S. universities' patenting activities during the twentieth century. The Research Corporation played an important role in the growth of these activities during the middle years of this century and created a portion of the institutional and administrative infrastructure for the post-1980 upsurge in patenting and licensing by individual U.S. universities. Discussions surrounding the foundation of the Research Corporation, and much of the debate over its early years of operation, anticipated many of the contemporary comments and debates over the desirability and effects of university technology licensing. Indeed, Cottrell articulated the "prospect" argument (Kitch, 1977) for patenting of university inventions in his 1912 assertion that "some minimum level" of protection for the intellectual property resulting from academic research was necessary in order for industry to invest in its subsequent development and commercialization. But Cottrell was ambivalent about the effects on academic norms and behavior of locating the responsibility for management of these activities within the university, fearing the consequences of conflicts of interest and pressures by university administrators to increase the income flowing from patent licenses, an ambivalence that is notably absent today.

The Research Corporation's history illustrates other features of markets for intellectual property that manifest themselves in many U.S. universities' current patenting and licensing operations. Although there appear to be advantages to specialization in patent and license management that reflect the high fixed costs, benefits of portfolio diversification, and possibilities for efficiency gains through learning, the history of the Research Corporation suggests that these benefits are counterbalanced by significant limitations.

In particular, the requirements for specialized knowledge about individual technology fields and (of equal importance) about the market for licenses in a given technology field limit the applicability of know-how acquired from patenting and licensing in one technology field to other fields. The importance of geographic proximity in even arms' length licensing arrangements also limits the cost savings attainable through centralization of activities in a single site or organization. These factors contributed to the declining financial performance of the Research Corporation in the 1970s, and they are apparent in the operation of many contemporary university technology licensing offices. Licensing managers tend to focus on specific technology areas, rather than being generalists. A number of universities' patenting and licensing offices have been reorganized so as to decentralize their operations, while at least a few other universities have maintained independent licensing efforts in different organizational units, such as their medical and engineering schools.

The study also underscores the limits of "pure" licensing agreements to support the exploitation or commercialization of inventions. From its earliest days, the corporation had to invest in extensive applications engineering and in customization of its precipitation technologies, and it found it necessary to acquire an extensive portfolio of complementary patents. The Research Corporation also relied on investments in additional development and other complements to many of the academic patents that it sought to commercialize, driving up costs and reducing profits. Contemporary university licensing offices have also found it necessary to make additional investments, in some cases taking equity stakes in firms founded to exploit their inventions, in order to pursue commercial development. Needless to say, this expansion of their activities increases costs and risks.

84   Finally, the history of the Research Corporation illustrates the difficulty of managing a patent licensing portfolio solely with a view to maximizing income, another issue that has bedeviled the operation of many contemporary university technology licensing offices. Licensing income tends to be dominated by a small number of "home runs," often based on biomedical research. The appearance of such "home runs" is difficult to predict, they typically account for a small share of all inventions, and their contribution to licensing income is limited by the term of their patents. As a result, licensing income is unstable and difficult to forecast.

The high costs of patent management also limit the financial returns from patent licensing. Trune and Goslin (1998) estimate that only 41 percent of university technology transfer offices yield a positive net income for their institutions, and we believe that their estimate may be high. But many of these contemporary licensing offices pursue a broader set of goals, including the development of closer links with regional industry for the support of university-based research. The single-minded pursuit of licensing income above all other goals led the Research Corporation into a dispute with MIT over the terms of the license to IBM for MIT's Forrester memory patent. The dispute among the Research Corporation, MIT, and IBM over this license vividly illustrates the potential conflicts between the goals of the licensing agent, the Research Corporation, and its principal, MIT. Similar conflicts have emerged recently within U.S. universities that manage their patenting and licensing internally.

The history of the Research Corporation anticipates many contemporary challenges faced by U.S. universities in their efforts to manage licensing and research relationships with industry. The ultimate withdrawal of the Research Corporation from its major role in managing U.S. universities' intellectual property reflected shifting federal policies toward philanthropic organizations, as well as the Bayh-Dole Act. But this chapter has pointed out that the seeds of decline had been planted well before 1980 and were apparent in the growing deficits of the corporation during the 1970s. Indeed, the same factors that contributed to the withdrawal of the Research Corporation from its dominant role as a manager of patent licensing for U.S. universities may well produce cutbacks in the independent patenting and licensing offices of some of the U.S. universities that entered into these activities during the 1970s and 1980s. The university technology licensing operations that survive are likely to pursue a broader set of goals than royalty income alone.[35]

5

A POLITICAL HISTORY OF THE
BAYH-DOLE ACT OF 1980

The effects of the Bayh-Dole Act of 1980 on university patenting and licensing cannot be understood without some consideration of the political origins of the Act itself. The Bayh-Dole Act is rooted in a debate that extends back to the late 1940s over the disposition of intellectual property resulting from federally funded research. But an important factor in the drafting and passage of the Act in 1980 was the growing role of U.S. universities as patenters and licensors. Indeed, U.S. universities themselves played a significant role in the passage of the Act, which can be viewed in part as a response to increased academic patenting and licensing activity, even as it provided an impetus to expansion in these activities.

In the following section, we argue that the debates during the late 1970s over Bayh-Dole included little evidence that patents and exclusive licenses facilitate the transfer and commercialization of federally funded academic research. Moreover, in contrast to the debates about university patenting earlier in the century that were discussed in Chapter 3, the Bayh-Dole debates devoted little consideration to potential effects of expanded university patenting and licensing on "open science" and on academic research more generally.

The overriding concern of Bayh-Dole supporters was increased commercialization of university inventions, and numerous subsequent journalistic accounts of the "effects of Bayh-Dole," as well as a number of analyses from governmental agencies, argue that these goals have been met. As we point out later in this chapter, however, important questions about the positive and negative effects of Bayh-Dole, and about what might have happened in the absence of the Act, remain unanswered. Subsequent chapters in this volume address a number of these issues.

86   Partly because of the widespread journalistic and political portrayal of the Bayh-Dole Act as a success, a number of other industrial-economy governments are considering or have adopted similar policies. The penultimate section of this chapter considers foreign-government "emulation" of the Bayh-Dole Act. Although it is hardly an isolated example, the selective nature of foreign governments' emulation of Bayh-Dole could produce limited or even counterproductive results. These efforts at emulation overlook the fact that U.S. university-industry interactions incorporate many channels beyond those of patenting and licensing and predate Bayh-Dole, as we pointed out in Chapters 2–4.

A POLITICAL HISTORY OF THE BAYH-DOLE ACT

The Debate over Patent Rights for Federally Funded Inventions

Congress had debated the issue of ownership of patents resulting from publicly funded research for decades before the passage of Bayh-Dole, and federal patent policy was a central point of contention during the debates of the 1940s over the organization of postwar U.S. science and technology policy. One side of the debate over patent policy was represented by Senator Harley Kilgore (D-W.Va.), who argued that the federal government should retain title to patents resulting from federally funded research and place them in the public domain (Kevles, 1978). According to Kilgore, allowing private contractors to retain patents represented a "giveaway" of the fruits of taxpayer-funded research to large corporations, reinforcing the concentration of technological and economic power. The opposing position was articulated by the director of the wartime Office of Scientific Research and Development, Vannevar Bush, who argued that allowing contractors to retain patent rights would preserve their incentives to participate in federal R&D projects and to develop commercially useful products based on government-funded research.[1]

The postwar debate highlighted the central questions in government patent policy for the next three decades. Supporters of the retention of intellectual property rights by government agencies argued that allowing contractors, rather than government agencies, to retain title to patents resulting from federally funded research favored large firms at the expense of small business. Moreover, they asserted, such a policy would raise prices for the fruits of taxpayer-funded research. Supporters of allowing contractors to retain title to patents resulting from federally funded research argued that failure to do so would make it difficult to attract qualified firms to perform government research and that the absence of clear title to intellectual property resulting from

such research would reduce incentives to invest in commercial development
of these inventions.

Another contentious issue in these debates about government patent policy was the desirability of a uniform patent policy across all federal agencies. Each of the major federal R&D funding agencies had established its own patent policy following World War II, and the resulting mix of agency-specific policies created ambiguities and uncertainties for contractors and for government employees.[2] Despite numerous congressional hearings on this issue, no legislation was adopted during the 1950–75 period because of the inability of supporters of the opposing positions outlined above to resolve their differences. This legislative deadlock was reinforced by statements on federal agencies' patent policies issued by Presidents Kennedy and Nixon in 1963 and 1971, respectively. Both presidents' statements asserted that agency-specific differences in patent policy were appropriate and reflected differences in their missions and R&D programs.[3]

Government Patent Policy and University Research

The debates over federal patent policy largely ignored U.S. universities during the 1940s and 1950s. After all, U.S. universities have never been responsible for performance of more than 34 percent of federally funded R&D (excluding university-based Federally Funded Research and Development Centers [FFRDCs]) during the postwar period and their share of federally funded R&D exceeded 20 percent only after 1991.[4] Moreover, as we noted in Chapter 3, U.S. universities historically had limited their direct involvement in patenting and licensing activities.

Federal policy toward patents resulting from publicly funded university research became a topic of debate after the release in 1968 of reports on the National Institutes of Health's (NIH) Medicinal Chemistry program by the U.S. General Accounting Office (GAO) (1968) and by Harbridge House (1968a), a consulting firm that the Federal Council for Science and Technology (FCST) commissioned to conduct a study on government patent policy as part of a review of this issue by the FCST itself.[5] Both reports examined the effects of federal patent policy on research collaboration between U.S. pharmaceutical firms and academic researchers in medicinal chemistry. During the 1940s and 1950s, these pharmaceutical firms had routinely screened compounds developed by NIH-funded university researchers at no charge.[6] In some cases (depending on the patent policies of particular universities), these pharmaceutical firms received exclusive rights to develop and market the compounds. In 1962, the Department of Health, Education, and Welfare (HEW) notified

88   universities that firms screening compounds must sign formal patent agreements that prevented the firms from obtaining patents on technologies resulting from NIH funding (GAO, 1968, p. 10). Indeed, the HEW policy further
stated that firms could not obtain patents on inventions in the "field of research work" supported by NIH funds at a given institution.

The GAO and Harbridge House reports criticized HEW's patent policy,
arguing that pharmaceutical firms had stopped screening NIH grantees' compounds because of the firms' concerns that the HEW policies could compromise their rights to intellectual property resulting from their in-house research
(Harbridge House, 1968a, p. II-21; GAO, 1968, p. 11). Both reports recommended that HEW change its patent policy to clarify the circumstances under which rights reverted to the government and those under which universities could retain title to patents and issue exclusive licenses to firms.

HEW responded to these critical reports in 1968 by establishing Institutional Patent Agreements (IPAs) that gave universities with "approved technology transfer capability" the right to retain title to agency-funded patents.[7]
In addition, the agency began to act more quickly on requests from universities and other research performers for title to the intellectual property resulting from federally funded research. Between 1969 and 1974, HEW approved
90 percent of petitions for title, and between 1969 and 1977 the agency granted
IPAs to seventy-two universities and nonprofit institutions (Weissman, 1989).
The National Science Foundation (NSF) instituted a similar IPA program in
1973, and the Department of Defense (DOD) began in the mid-1960s to allow
universities with approved patent policies to retain title to inventions resulting
from federally funded research.

By the beginning of the 1970s, U.S. universities thus were able to patent the
results of federally funded research via agency-specific IPAs or similar programs at the DOD as well as through case-by-case petitions. Nevertheless, in
the late 1970s U.S. universities became concerned that HEW might limit their
ability to negotiate exclusive licenses in the department's IPA programs. These
concerns, along with growing dissatisfaction within Congress and the industrial community over the lack of uniformity in patent rights to inventions resulting from federally funded research, provided the immediate impetus for
the introduction in 1978 of the bill that eventually became the Bayh-Dole Act.

The Bayh-Dole Bill

As we noted above, HEW's 1968 revisions in its patent policy expanded the
number of IPAs negotiated with universities and other research institutions
and allowed more universities to obtain patents on NIH-funded inventions on
a case-by-case basis. U.S. universities had become more active in patenting

and licensing faculty inventions during the 1970s, especially in the biomedical field (see Chapters 3 and 4), and therefore welcomed these changes in HEW patent policies.

But these patent policies triggered considerable debate within HEW. In August 1977, HEW's Office of the General Counsel expressed concern that university patents and licenses, particularly exclusive licenses, could contribute to higher health-care costs (Eskridge, 1978). The department ordered a review of its patent policy, including a reconsideration of whether universities' rights to negotiate exclusive licenses should be curtailed.[8] During the ensuing twelve-month review by HEW of its patent policies, the agency deferred decisions on thirty petitions for patent rights and three requests for IPAs.

Thus, although Bayh-Dole is often regarded as being the catalyst for the growth of university patenting and licensing in the United States, in fact U.S. universities that were active in patenting and licensing, as well as other universities, lobbied for the introduction and passage of the bill. Broad (1979a, p. 476) notes that in response to HEW's review of its patent policies, "[u]niversities got upset and complained to Congress." And Heaton et al. (2000) note that a patent attorney from Purdue University and a congressional staffer who previously worked at the University of Arizona, both of which sought more liberal policies toward patenting publicly funded research, respectively asked Senators Birch Bayh (D-Ind.) and Robert Dole (R-Kans.) to introduce the bill. These and other university licensing officials also aided in drafting portions of what became the Bayh-Dole Act.[9]

In September 1978, Senator Dole held a press conference where he criticized HEW for "stonewalling" university patenting (commenting, "rarely have we witnessed a more hideous example of overmanagement by the bureaucracy") and announced his intention to introduce a bill to remedy the situation (Eskridge, 1978, p. 605). On September 13, 1978, Senators Bayh and Dole introduced S. 414, the University and Small Business Patent Act. The Act proposed a uniform federal patent policy that gave universities and small businesses rights to any patents resulting from government-funded research.[10] The bill lacked provisions that had been included in most IPAs, including the requirement that a participating university must have an "approved technology transfer" capability. In contrast to the language of some IPAs between universities and HEW, the bill imposed no restrictions on the negotiation by universities and other research institutions of exclusive licensing agreements.[11]

As we noted earlier, many members of Congress had long opposed any federal grant of ownership of patents to research performers or contractors (Broad, 1979b). The Bayh-Dole bill nevertheless attracted little opposition. The bill's focus on securing patent rights for only universities and small

90   business weakened the argument (à la Kilgore) that such patent-ownership policies would favor big business.[12] The bill's introduction in the midst of debates over U.S. economic competitiveness also proved crucial to its passage. An article in *Science* discussing the debate on the Bayh-Dole bill observed:

> The critics of such legislation, who in the past have railed about the "giveaway of public funds" have grown unusually quiet. The reason seems clear. Industrial innovation has become a buzzword in bureaucratic circles . . . the patent transfer people have latched onto this issue. It's about time, they say, to cut the red tape that saps the incentive to be inventive. (Broad 1979b, p. 479)

A number of universities, including Harvard University, Stanford University, the University of California, and MIT, lobbied for passage of the bill and throughout the debates were active in "commenting and helping to develop the final language" of the House and Senate versions of the bill (Barrett, 1980). Not surprisingly, witnesses from active institutional patenters (including Stanford, Purdue, and Wisconsin) testified in support of the bill, as did representatives from various university associations (including the American Council on Education, the Society for University Patent Administrators, and the National Association of College and University Business Officers) and the Research Corporation. The support of these groups was supplemented by positive statements from witnesses representing various small businesses and small business trade groups, like the National Small Business Association, the Small Business Legislative Council, and the American Society of Inventors.

Considerable testimony and commentary during these hearings focused on lagging U.S. productivity growth and innovativeness, suggesting that government patent policy contributed to these woes.[13] In their opening statements in the Senate Judiciary Committee hearings on the bill, Senators Bayh and Dole each pointed to two problems with federal patent policy as of 1979: (1) the "policy" in fact consisted of more than twenty different agency-specific patent policies; and (2) most federal agencies made it difficult for contractors to retain title to patents.

Witnesses supporting the Bayh-Dole bill cited another section of the 1968 Harbridge House report (1968b) in claiming that rates of utilization of government-funded patents were higher when contractors rather than agencies held title to these patents.[14] Another frequently cited statistic was drawn from the FCST's 1978 *Report on Government Patent Policy* (FCST, 1978), which concluded that fewer than 5 percent of the 28,000 patents owned by the federal government as of 1976 were licensed.[15] Legislators and witnesses used this finding to argue that giving patent rights to contractors would create incentives for development and commercialization that were lacking under the current system.

As Eisenberg (1996) has pointed out, however, the data in the Harbridge House and FCST reports did not support this conclusion. The patents examined in the Harbridge and FCST studies were drawn primarily from research funded by the DOD (83 percent of the patents from the Harbridge House sample and 63 percent of those from the FCST sample), an agency that readily granted patent rights to research performers. Since these defense contractors could and often did seek the rights to patents that they believed might result in profitable innovations, it is likely that the patents for which they did not seek ownership rights had limited commercial potential. It therefore is not surprising that these patents were not commercialized.

The data in these reports also were based primarily on patents resulting from government-funded R&D carried out by private firms. As such, they shed little light on the importance for commercial exploitation of patenting by universities of inventions funded by the federal government. It is likely, for example, that the characteristics of federally funded university inventions differ from those associated with federally funded inventions patented by contractors, reflecting the fact (among other things) that federally funded academic research typically includes more fundamental research and less development activity than do research contracts with industry.

In addition to citing this statistical evidence, supporters of the bill argued that the characteristics of university inventions made patents and exclusive licenses important for the commercialization of these inventions. According to these witnesses, most university inventions are embryonic when first disclosed, requiring significant additional development before they can be commercially useful. In this view, firms would not invest in these costly development activities without clear rights to the relevant intellectual property, something that in many instances would require an exclusive license.[16] Other witnesses suggested that giving title to universities would create incentives for inventors and institutions to become actively involved in the development and commercialization of embryonic inventions, anticipating arguments developed more formally by Jensen and Thursby (2001).[17]

The Bayh-Dole Act was passed overwhelmingly in both the House and the Senate in the winter of 1980 with minimal floor debate, and President Jimmy Carter signed the Act into law in December 1980.[18] The Act's provisions facilitated university patenting and licensing in at least two ways. First, they replaced the web of IPAs and case-by-case petitions with a uniform policy. Second, the Act expressed congressional support for the negotiation of exclusive licenses between universities and industrial firms for the results of federally funded research.

The broad political support for university patenting of intellectual

92   property, especially that resulting from federally funded research, that was expressed in hearings and floor debate on the Bayh-Dole Act contrasts with the
widespread expressions of concern by university administrators and others in
the debates of the 1930s over university patenting and licensing that were discussed in Chapter 3. For example, none of the witnesses in these hearings discussed the potential risks created by university patenting and licensing for the
"disclosure" and other norms of academic science, nor were any potentially
detrimental effects of patenting and licensing for other channels of university-
industry technology transfer considered.[19] Nor did the hearings and floor debate over Bayh-Dole discuss the political risks for universities of direct involvement in the management of patenting and licensing that loomed larger
in the debates of the 1930s and 1940s.

In many respects, the central justifications for the Bayh-Dole Act elevated
to the national level the "taxpayer benefit" arguments that were widely used
during the 1920s and 1930s to justify state universities' involvement in patenting and licensing. These arguments were especially salient in the economic
environment of the late 1970s, when U.S. global competitiveness (or the lack
of same) had become an important political issue in domestic debate. In a
global economy in which scientific and technological knowledge moved
across national boundaries and could be exploited more easily by non-U.S. enterprises than in previous decades, supporters of the Bayh-Dole Act argued
that U.S. taxpayers would benefit from federal support of academic R&D only
if the results of this research were commercialized, an outcome widely believed to be more likely if these results were patented.

This argument repeated the justifications of the prewar period for the widespread involvement of public universities in patenting and licensing — patenting was essential to the capture by state taxpayers of the benefits of their universities' research activities. But the majority of the inventions whose
licensure was debated during the 1930s had been funded by industrial or state
government sources rather than by the federal government. The invocation by
supporters of Bayh-Dole of these justifications at the national level reflected
the rise to dominance of federal agencies as sources of academic research support during the postwar period and implied that both private and public universities faced a similar "public service" obligation to patent and license faculty inventions in the wake of Bayh-Dole.

The Bayh-Dole Act

The Bayh-Dole Act became effective on July 1, 1981, creating a uniform federal patent policy for universities and small businesses that gave them the
rights to any patents resulting from grants or contracts funded by any federal

agency. The federal government retained a nonexclusive royalty-free license to any such patents and retained "march-in" rights to compel licensing or to utilize the invention itself when contractors' licensing policies failed to promote utilization or where doing so is necessary for public health or safety. The Act and subsequent implementing regulations also incorporated policies governing the timetable for disclosures of inventions to the funding agency and for filing patent applications.[20] These regulations required that universities share any licensing royalties with inventors and mandated a preference for small businesses in the award of licenses by universities and other research performers. The Act also limited the duration of any exclusive licenses that universities could negotiate with large businesses.

The Act's limitations on the rights of large firms to obtain title to patents resulting from federally funded research were subsequently nullified. In 1983, President Ronald Reagan circulated an Executive Memorandum to agencies instructing them to allow large businesses as well as universities and small businesses to retain title to federally funded patents, and he issued an Executive Order to this effect in 1987.[21] In 1984, an amendment to Bayh-Dole removed the time limits on the length of exclusive licenses universities could offer to large businesses.[22]

The Bayh-Dole Act was one part of a broader shift in U.S. policy toward stronger intellectual property rights during the 1980s.[23] Among the most important of these policy initiatives was the establishment of the Court of Appeals for the Federal Circuit (CAFC) in 1982. Established to serve as the court of final appeal for patent cases throughout the federal judiciary, the CAFC soon emerged as a strong champion of patentholder rights. Even before the establishment of the CAFC, however, an important U.S. Supreme Court decision in 1980, *Diamond v. Chakrabarty*, upheld the validity of a broad patent in the new industry of biotechnology, opening the door to patenting the organisms, molecules, and research techniques emerging from biotechnology. The origins and effects of Bayh-Dole must be viewed in the context of this larger shift in U.S. policy toward intellectual property rights, and the effects of the Act are easily confounded with those of these other intellectual property initiatives.

THE EFFECTS OF BAYH-DOLE

During the late 1990s and early twenty-first century, many commentators and policymakers portrayed the Bayh-Dole Act as the critical catalyst to growth in U.S. universities' innovative and economic contributions. Indeed, the Organization for Economic Cooperation and Development (OECD) went so far as to argue that the Bayh-Dole Act was an important factor in the remarkable

94   growth of incomes, employment, and productivity in the U.S. economy of the late 1990s.[24] Implicit in many if not all of these characterizations is the argument that university patenting and licensing were indispensable to these asserted increases in the economic contributions of U.S. university research. For example, a recent article in the *Economist* opined that:

> possibly the most inspired piece of legislation to be enacted in America over the past half-century was the Bayh-Dole Act of 1980. Together with amendments in 1984 and augmentation in 1986, this unlocked all the inventions and discoveries that had been made in laboratories throughout the United States with the help of taxpayers' money. More than anything, this single policy measure helped to reverse America's precipitous slide into industrial irrelevance. Before Bayh-Dole, the fruits of research supported by government agencies had gone strictly to the federal government. Nobody could exploit such research without tedious negotiations with a federal agency concerned. Worse, companies found it nigh impossible to acquire exclusive rights to a government owned patent. And without that, few firms were willing to invest millions more of their own money to turn a basic research idea into a marketable product.

But after Bayh-Dole,

> Overnight universities across America became hotbeds of innovation, as entrepreneurial professors took their inventions (and graduate students) off campus to set up companies of their own. Since 1980, American universities have witnessed a tenfold increase in patents they generate. ("Innovation's Golden Goose," p. T3)

Similar characterizations of the effects of the Bayh-Dole Act have been articulated by the president of the Association of American Universities,[25] the commissioner of the U.S. Patent and Trademark Office,[26] and the *Technology Review*, edited and published at MIT.[27]

Remarkably, none of these characterizations of the positive effects of the Bayh-Dole Act cite any rigorous evidence in support of their claims. This cavalier treatment of evidence, of course, is not unprecedented in the political history of the Act. We noted above that the legislative debates over the bill's drafting and passage relied on little if any evidence that patents and licenses are necessary for the commercialization and development of university technologies.

Scholarly research on the effects of Bayh-Dole has been slower to appear, reflecting the need for evidence to support such empirical research. We discuss this research in greater detail in subsequent chapters as part of our empirical investigation of U.S. university patenting and licensing before and after 1980. Here, we simply highlight the central findings and unresolved issues raised by this research.

There is little evidence of substantial shifts since Bayh-Dole in the content of academic research, a finding that is not surprising in view of the blurry lines between "basic" and "applied" research in the biomedical sciences that have been the focus of most of the increased university patenting and licensing since the 1970s. But current research, which remains quite preliminary in its findings on this issue, provides mixed support for the argument that patenting and licensing are necessary for the transfer and commercial development of university inventions. Other scholarly work (for example, Louis et al., 2001) suggests that university patenting and licensing have negatively affected "disclosure norms" of academic research in specific fields, leading to higher levels of secrecy and less sharing among researchers of early results, but more research on this issue is needed. Finally, the effects on the research enterprise itself of any increased assertion by institutional and individual inventors of property rights over inputs to scientific research have only begun to receive serious scholarly attention.

Journalistic and policy-oriented accounts of the Bayh-Dole Act thus present little evidence in support of their claims, while scholarly research on the Act's effects by other scholars and ourselves reaches a much more tentative and guarded verdict on the Bayh-Dole Act. Nevertheless, the limited evidence on the Act's effects (both positive and negative) has not prevented a number of other OECD governments from pursuing policies that closely resemble the Bayh-Dole Act.

INTERNATIONAL "EMULATION" OF THE BAYH-DOLE ACT

A recent OECD survey reports "a general trend across OECD countries to emulate the Bayh-Dole patent legislation that allows performers of government research, including universities and small businesses, to patent and license inventions" (OECD 2002, p. 10). These initiatives are based on the belief that Bayh-Dole was essential to increased university-industry interaction and technology transfer in science-based industries in the United States. But as the review above suggests, these attempts are based on a misreading of the limited evidence concerning the effects of Bayh-Dole and on a misunderstanding of the factors that have encouraged the long-standing and relatively close relationship between U.S. universities and industrial innovation.

International interest in and emulation of the Bayh-Dole Act are hardly unique to this policy initiative. Such emulation has been especially widespread in the field of technology policy, most notably in the area of collaborative R&D policies. Research collaboration was cited by U.S. and European policymakers during the 1970s and 1980s as a key policy underpinning Japan's rapid technological advance. Accordingly, both the European Union and the

96   U.S. during the 1980s implemented policies and programs to encourage such collaboration, with mixed results. One of the best-known examples of such R&D collaboration is the SEMATECH (Semiconductor Manufacturing Technology) R&D consortium established in Austin, Texas, in 1987 with public and private funding. In response to the perceived success of the SEMATECH collaboration, Japanese managers and policymakers initiated publicly and privately funded research consortia (ASET and SELETE) in the late 1990s. Japan, which initially provided the model for emulation by the United States and the European Union, now is emulating the programs that allegedly were initially based on Japanese programs.

International policy emulation of this sort is characterized by two key features: (1) the "learning" that underpins the emulation is highly selective; and (2) the implementation of program designs based on even this selective learning is affected by the different institutional landscape of the emulator. Both of these characteristics of international emulation are readily apparent in the case of SEMATECH. They are even clearer in the international emulation of the Bayh-Dole Act that began during the 1990s.

The policy initiatives that have been debated or implemented in most OECD economies have either sought to shift ownership of the intellectual property rights for inventions resulting from publicly funded research from the government funding agency or inventor to the entity performing the research, or in some cases from the government to the academic inventor. In university systems such as those of Germany or Sweden, researchers have long had ownership rights for the intellectual property resulting from their work, and debate has centered on the feasibility and advisability of shifting these ownership rights from the individual to the institution. In Italy, legislation adopted in 2001 shifted ownership from universities to individual researchers. In Japanese universities, ownership of intellectual property rights resulting from publicly funded research is determined by a committee, which on occasion awards title to the researcher. No single national policy governs the ownership of intellectual property rights within the British or Canadian university systems, although efforts are under way in both nations to grant ownership to the academic institution rather than to the individual researcher or the funding agency. In addition, the Swedish, German, and Japanese governments have encouraged the formation of external technology licensing organizations, which may or may not be affiliated with a given university.

These foreign-government emulation initiatives differ from one another and from Bayh-Dole itself. The policy proposals and initiatives display the classic signs of international emulation described above — selective borrowing from another nation's policies for implementation in an institutional context that differs significantly from that of the nation being emulated.

But patenting and licensing were only one of many channels through which U.S. universities contributed to industrial innovation throughout the twentieth century, and the surveys of industrial managers discussed in Chapter 2 suggest that these channels are not the most important ones in most technological fields. Inasmuch as patenting and licensing are of secondary importance in most fields, emulation of the Bayh-Dole Act is insufficient and perhaps even unnecessary to stimulate higher levels of university-industry interaction and technology transfer. Instead, reforms to enhance interinstitutional competition and autonomy within national university systems, as well as support for the external institutional contributors to new-firm formation and technology commercialization, such as venture capital funding, labor mobility, and other important catalysts for technology commercialization, appear to be more important.

Moreover, the impact of Bayh-Dole on the other channels of knowledge and technology transfer remains unclear, as we have argued above. There are potential risks to the university research enterprise that accompany increased involvement by university administrators and faculty in technology licensing and commercialization, and uncritical emulation of Bayh-Dole in a very different institutional context could intensify these risks.

CONCLUSION

The Bayh-Dole Act of 1980 was an effect as well as a cause of increased university patenting and licensing in the United States. The debates leading to passage of the Act included little if any of the substance of previous debates among university administrators over the desirability of direct institutional involvement in patenting and licensing. Nor did parties to the debate over the Bayh-Dole Act draw on the lengthy controversy within the U.S. Congress over the appropriate policy toward ownership of the intellectual property rights created in federally funded research programs. The relatively noncontroversial character of the bill and the limited debate surrounding it both seem to have reflected the broad bipartisan concern within the Congress and executive branch in the late 1970s over "international competitiveness," as well as the rising tide of faith in the role of strong intellectual property rights to strengthen the United States in international competition.

A remarkable feature of the debate over Bayh-Dole and much of the celebratory "analysis" of its effects in the popular press and elsewhere is the lack of hard evidence to support the claims of proponents and opponents. This evidentiary vacuum, however, has not prevented the widespread adoption or serious consideration of similar policies by other industrial-economy governments.

98   In the following chapters, we analyze the effects of the Bayh-Dole Act, arguing that much of what has occurred since 1980 in U.S. university patenting and licensing might well have occurred without the Act. The surge in university patenting and licensing is as much a result of the long-standing relationships between U.S. universities and industry, the broader shift toward stronger intellectual property rights during the 1980s in the United States, and the transformation of biomedical science as it is a result of the Bayh-Dole Act. Moreover, the Act's proponents have exaggerated the necessity of patenting and licensing to support such interactions and technology transfer, even as they have overlooked potential risks for U.S. universities and for the broader economy flowing from increased patenting of university research results.

6

THE BAYH-DOLE ACT AND PATENTING AND
LICENSING AT THE UNIVERSITY OF
CALIFORNIA, STANFORD UNIVERSITY,
AND COLUMBIA UNIVERSITY

Although the Bayh-Dole Act of 1980 is widely cited as the central factor in the growth of U.S. academic patenting and licensing during the 1980s, its effects on U.S. research universities and on the U.S. innovation system have been the focus of little empirical analysis (Henderson, Jaffe, and Trajtenberg 1998a,b, are important exceptions). In this chapter, we examine the patenting and licensing activities of three academic institutions that were the leading recipients of licensing and royalty income for much of the 1990s: the University of California (UC), Stanford University, and Columbia University.[1] A combined analysis of data from these three universities allows us to consider the effects of these new federal policies on universities such as Columbia, which became large-scale patenters and licensers only after 1980, and universities that were active in patenting and licensing well before 1980, such as the University of California and Stanford. Chapter 7 complements this analysis of individual institutions with an examination of the characteristics of the patents issued to all U.S. universities before and after 1980.

THE EFFECTS OF THE BAYH-DOLE ACT: EVIDENCE
FROM THE UNIVERSITY OF CALIFORNIA, STANFORD
UNIVERSITY, AND COLUMBIA UNIVERSITY

The University of California

Unlike Columbia, the University of California established policies requiring faculty disclosure of potentially commercially useful research results long before Bayh-Dole. Mechanisms for supporting the commercial exploitation of any resulting patents were put in place in 1943, and assignment by faculty of

100   their inventions to the university was determined on a case-by-case basis. Patenting and licensing were the responsibility of the UC General Counsel's office, which oversaw the creation and gradual growth of the UC Patent Office. The UC Board of Regents established the University Patent Fund in 1952 to invest the earnings from university-owned inventions in the UC system's General Endowment Pool: earnings from the fund also supported the expenses of UC patenting activities and faculty research.[2] In 1963, the UC Board of Regents adopted a policy stating that all "[m]embers of the faculties and employees shall make appropriate reports of any inventions and licenses they have conceived or developed to the Board of Patents."[3]

In 1976, the Patent Office was reorganized into the Patent, Trademark, and Copyright Office (PTCO). Only in 1980, however, was the PTCO staffed with experts in patent law and licensing, as part of a broader expansion in UC patenting and licensing activities. The Board of Patents was abolished in 1985, and new policies allowing for sharing by campuses in patent licensing revenues were adopted by the Office of the President and the campus chancellors in 1986. Staff employment in the PTCO grew from four in 1977–78 to forty-three in 1989–90, and the PTCO was renamed the Office of Technology Transfer (OTT) in 1991. In 1990, however, UC Berkeley and UCLA established independent patenting and licensing offices, relying on the systemwide Office of Technology Transfer selectively for expertise in patent and licensing regulations. By 2002, six UC campuses (UC Berkeley, UCLA, UC San Diego, UC Irvine, UC Davis, and UC San Francisco) had established independent licensing offices.[4]

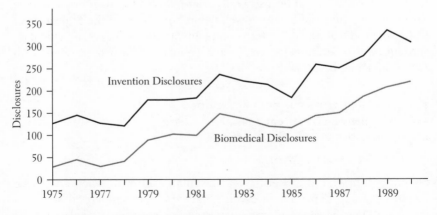

FIGURE 6.1   University of California invention disclosures, 1975–90

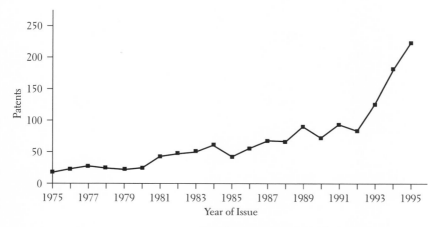

FIGURE 6.2   University of California patents by year of issue, 1975–95

Since the University of California was active in patenting and licensing well before the passage of the Bayh-Dole Act, a comparison of the 1975–79 period (prior to Bayh-Dole) and 1984–88, following the passage of the bill, provides a "before and after" test of the Act's effects. The average annual number of invention disclosures during 1984–88 is almost 237, substantially above their average level (140 annual disclosures) for the 1975–79 period. Similarly, the average annual number of patents issued to the University of California in the earlier period is 22, compared to 58 for 1984–88. The period following the Bayh-Dole Act thus is associated with a higher average level of annual invention disclosures and patents (confirmed in Figures 6.1 and 6.2); but the timing of the increase in annual disclosures suggests that more than the Bayh-Dole Act affected this shift.

The increase in the average annual number of invention disclosures in Figure 6.1 predates the passage of the Bayh-Dole Act; indeed, the largest single year-to-year percentage increase in disclosures during the entire 1974–88 period occurred in 1978–79, before the Act's passage. This increase in disclosures may reflect the important advances in biotechnology that occurred at UC San Francisco during the 1970s or other changes in the structure and activities of the UC patent licensing office that were unrelated to Bayh-Dole. For example, the Cohen-Boyer DNA splicing technique, the basis for the license that accounted for more licensing revenues than any other invention at either the UC system or Stanford University, was disclosed in 1974, and the first of several patent applications for the invention was filed in 1978, well before Bayh-Dole (this patent issued in 1980).

TABLE 6.1

Selected Data on University of California, Stanford University, and Columbia University Licensing Income, FY1970–95

Institution	Fiscal Years					
University of California	FY1970	FY1975	FY1980	FY1985	FY1990	FY1995
Gross income (1996 dollars: 000s)	1,245.0	1,605.6	2,329.6	4,273.3	14,454.6	63,925.8
Gross income from top 5 earners (1996 dollars: 000s)	982.4	1,173.4	1,182.3	2,025.1	7,892.8	42,211.4
Share of gross income from top 5 earners (%)	79	73	51	47	55	66
Share of income of top 5 earners associated with biomedical inventions (%)	34	19	54	40	91	100
Share of income of top 5 earners associated with agricultural inventions (%)	57	70	46	60	9	0
Stanford University	FY1970	FY1975	FY1980	FY1985	FY1990	FY1995
Gross income (1996 dollars: 000s)	196.9	919.9	1,183.8	5,339.4	16,110.8	39,119.1
Gross income from top 5 earners (1996 dollars: 000s)		632.4	1,023.7	3,669.1	12,230.0	33,062.7
Share of gross income from top 5 earners (%)		69	86	69	76	85
Share of income of top 5 earners associated with biomedical inventions (%)		87	40	64	84	97
Columbia University	FY1970	FY1975	FY1980	FY1985	FY1990	FY1995
Gross income (1996 dollars: 000s)				591.7	7,536.6	34,705.6
Gross income from top 5 earners (1996 dollars: 000s)				584.7	6,950.5	32,681.0
Share of gross income from top 5 earners (%)				99	92	94
Share of income of top 5 earners associated with biomedical inventions (%)				81	87	91

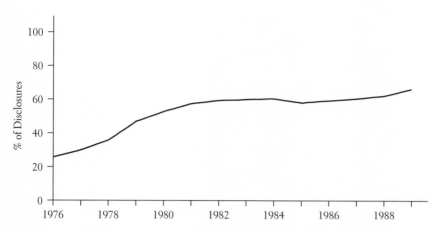

FIGURE 6.3   University of California biomedical disclosures as a percentage of total disclosures, 1975–90 (3-year moving average)

Since biomedical inventions account for the lion's share of UC patenting and licensing after 1980, our assessment of trends before and after Bayh-Dole focuses on biomedical inventions, patents, and licenses. Figure 6.3 reveals that the shares of biomedical inventions within all UC invention disclosures began to grow in the mid-1970s, before the passage of Bayh-Dole. Moreover, these biomedical inventions accounted for a disproportionate share of the patenting and licensing activities of the University of California during this period: biomedical invention disclosures made up 33 percent of all UC disclosures during 1975–79 and 60 percent of patents issued to the University of California for inventions disclosed during the period. Biomedical patents accounted for 70 percent of the licensed patents in this cohort of disclosures, and biomedical inventions accounted for 59 percent of the UC licenses in this cohort that generated positive royalties. Biomedical inventions retained their importance during 1984–88, as they accounted for 60 percent of disclosures, 65 percent of patents, 74 percent of the licensed patents from this cohort of disclosures, and 73 percent of the licenses for this cohort of disclosures with royalty income.

Growth in the number of biomedical disclosures, which dominated UC patenting and licensing throughout 1975–90, thus predates the passage of the Bayh-Dole Act. Additional evidence on the shifting composition of the UC technology licensing portfolio is displayed in Table 6.1 and Figure 6.7. The UC data in Table 6.1 reveal the high concentration of licensing revenues among a small number of inventions before and after the Bayh-Dole Act and highlight the remarkable growth (more than fifty-fold) in constant-dollar gross revenues during 1970–95. The share of gross licensing revenues accounted for by the UC system's "top five" inventions actually decreases throughout the 1970–95 period, from nearly 80 percent in fiscal 1970 to 66 percent in fiscal 1995, having reached a low point of 47 percent in fiscal 1985.

Equally remarkable is the illustration in Table 6.1 of the shift in the UC system's "top five" inventions from agricultural inventions (including plant varieties and agricultural machinery) to biomedical inventions. Among the three universities in this comparative analysis, only the University of California maintained a large-scale agricultural research effort. During the 1970s, agricultural inventions accounted for a majority of the income accruing to the "top five" UC money-earners. Beginning in fiscal 1980, however, this share began to decline, and by fiscal 1995 100 percent of the UC system's licensing income from its "top five" inventions, accounting for over $40 million in revenues (in 1996 dollars), was derived from biomedical inventions, up from 19 percent in fiscal 1975. Moreover, and consistent with the discussion of the previous paragraph, this share increased before the passage of Bayh-Dole in late 1980: the share of "top five" licensing revenues associated with biomedical inventions jumped from less than 20 percent in fiscal 1975 to more than 50 percent in fiscal 1980. The depiction in Figure 6.7 of the share of UC licensing agreements accounted for by biomedical inventions during 1975–95 as a three-year moving average similarly shows an increase in this share before the effective date of Bayh-Dole to a higher level that is sustained through much of the 1980–95 period.

Stanford University

As we noted in Chapter 3, Stanford University's Office of Technology Licensing (OTL) was officially established in 1970, following the success of Niels Reimers's "experiment" with direct management of patenting and licensing, and Stanford was active in patenting and licensing throughout the 1970s. Stanford's patent policy, adopted in April 1970, stated that "except in cases where other arrangements are required by contracts and grants or sponsored research or where other arrangements have been specifically agreed upon in writing, it shall be the policy of the University to permit employees of the University, both faculty and staff, and students to retain all rights to inventions made by them" (Stanford University Office of Technology Licensing, 1983, p. 1). Disclosure by faculty of inventions and their management by Stanford's OTL thus was optional for most of the OTL's first quarter-century.

In 1994, Stanford changed its policy toward faculty inventions in two important aspects. First, assignment of title to the university of inventions "developed using University resources" was made mandatory.[5] Second, the university established a policy under which "[c]opyright to software developed for University purposes in the course of employment, or as part of either a sponsored project or an unsponsored project specifically supported by University funds, belongs to the University" (Stanford University Office of Technology Licensing, 1994a).[6]

Faculty disclosure of inventions to university administrators thus was no more mandatory at Stanford before 1994 than at Columbia before 1984. Nevertheless, especially during the 1970–80 period, Stanford operated a much more elaborate administrative apparatus for the patenting and licensing of inventions than did Columbia. The expanding scale of Stanford's licensing operations during the 1970s and 1980s suggests that a substantial share of faculty inventions were disclosed to the OTL.

Data from the Stanford OTL provide some insight into the patenting and licensing activities of a major private research university before and after Bayh-Dole. And similar to the situation at the University of California, these data suggest that the growth of Stanford's patenting and licensing activities reflected influences other than Bayh-Dole. Figure 6.4 displays trends during 1975–90 in Stanford invention disclosures. The average annual number of disclosures to Stanford's OTL increased from 74 during 1975–79, prior to Bayh-Dole, to 149 during 1984–88. Figure 6.5 shows the number of patents issued to Stanford during the 1975–95 period; the average annual number of issued patents also increased from thirteen during 1975–79 to forty-two during 1984–88. Although the evidence of a "Bayh-Dole effect" in the annual number of disclosures (such as the jump in disclosures between 1979 and 1980) is stronger in the Stanford data than in the UC data, the increase in disclosures between 1977 and 1978 indicates that the annual number of invention disclosures was growing prior to Bayh-Dole.

The data in Figures 6.4 and 6.6 also suggest that the importance of biomedical inventions within Stanford's invention portfolio advances had begun to expand before the passage of Bayh-Dole. Figure 6.4 indicates that the annual number of biomedical invention disclosures began to increase sharply during the 1978–80 period, and the share of all disclosures accounted for by biomedical inventions (see Figures 6.4 and 6.6) increased steadily from 1977 to 1980, leveling off after 1980 and declining after 1983. The magnitude of these increases in biomedical inventions prior to Bayh-Dole is more modest than at the University of California, but the trend is similar.

The Stanford data in Figure 6.7 highlight trends in licensing agreements that resemble those for the UC system during the same period; biomedical inventions increased as a share of Stanford's (nonsoftware) licenses during

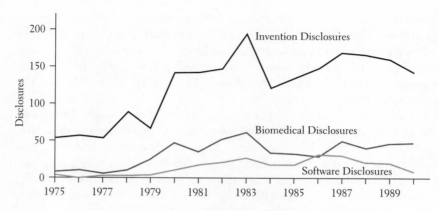

FIGURE 6.4   Stanford University invention disclosures, 1975–90

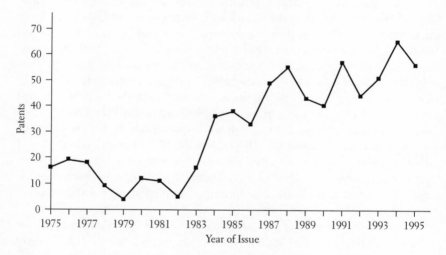

FIGURE 6.5   Stanford University patents by year of issue, 1975–95

1975–90, although the upward trend was less pronounced and fluctuated more widely than in the UC data.[7] Table 6.1 indicates that as of fiscal 1980, slightly more than 40 percent of the income from Stanford's "top five" inventions was attributable to biomedical inventions, suggesting the considerable importance of these inventions prior to Bayh-Dole. This share increased to more than 96 percent by fiscal 1995. Stanford's licensing revenues grew by almost 200-fold (in constant dollars) during 1970–95, and its "top five"

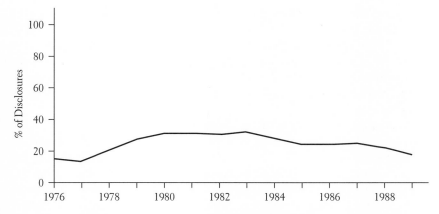

FIGURE 6.6   Stanford University biomedical disclosures as a percentage of total disclosures, 1975–90 (3-year moving average)

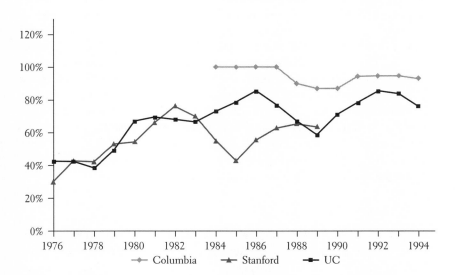

FIGURE 6.7   Biomedical technology share of Columbia, Stanford, and University of California license agreements, excluding Cohen-Boyer and software licenses, 1975–95 (3-year moving average). Columbia shares reported for 1983–95 (100% of licenses at Columbia were for biomedical technologies in 1981, but Columbia did not execute any licenses in 1982). Stanford shares reported for 1975–90.

108   inventions accounted for a larger share of gross income for the 1980–95 period
        than do the "top five" UC inventions.

        Both Stanford and the UC system thus experienced a shift in the composi-
        tion of their invention and licensing portfolios in favor of biomedical inven-
        tions prior to Bayh-Dole. Bayh-Dole was an important but not a determinative
        factor in the growth and changing composition of patenting and licensing ac-
        tivity at these institutions.

        In contrast to the data from the University of California, Stanford's inven-
        tion disclosures include a number of software inventions, which account for
        10–15 percent of annual disclosures. As is the case at Columbia during the
        1980s, most of these inventions were not patented and therefore cannot be
        traced through annual patent counts. The importance of software disclosures
        in Stanford's licensing activity expanded during the 1970s and 1980s. Only two
        of the forty-one inventions disclosed during 1974–79 (less than 5 percent) that
        were licensed within eight years of their disclosure were software inventions,
        but this figure increased to more than 20 percent for the 1984–88 period.
        Many of these software inventions (for example, the WYLBUR operating sys-
        tem) were licensed on a nonexclusive basis to academic institutions through
        Stanford's Software Distribution Center during the 1980s. The majority of
        these licenses involved a small, one-time payment by the licensee institution.[8]
        Partly because of the large number of such "site licenses," the coverage by our
        data of Stanford software licensing agreements is spotty, and our estimate of
        the share of all Stanford licensing agreements accounted for by software is less
        accurate. Nonetheless, like Columbia University, a significant portion of Stan-
        ford's licensed inventions (at least 10–20 percent of annual licensing agree-
        ments and a smaller share of gross revenues) covered nonpatented inventions
        during the 1980s, Bayh-Dole notwithstanding.

        Columbia University

        The essence of Columbia's pre-Bayh-Dole patent policy is contained in the
        University's 1944 "Statement of Research Policy and Patent Procedures"
        (Trustees of Columbia University, 1944).[9] This policy prohibited patents on
        the results of research (regardless of the source of funding for such research)
        at the medical school, although other faculty members at the university were
        free to patent inventions resulting from their research. In many cases, non-
        medical faculty turned to the Research Corporation for assistance in patent-
        ing and administering their inventions. The 1944 policy remained substan-
        tially intact until 1975, when the stipulation against patenting medical
        inventions was dropped. Discussions within Columbia's administration and

faculty over institutional assertion of rights to faculty inventions began in the late 1960s and gained momentum in the 1970s but produced no formal change in policy until the passage of Bayh-Dole (for a fuller discussion, see Crow et al., 1998).

Columbia's laissez-faire policy toward patenting the results of faculty research during the three decades following World War II meant that the university had no administrative structure for managing patent matters. Beginning in the late 1970s, however, the university expanded its involvement in patent transactions between its inventors and the Research Corporation, created a central archive of potentially patentable inventions, and petitioned government agencies for title to faculty inventions resulting from federally funded research. Indeed, Columbia filed a patent application on the Axel cotransformation invention, which accounted for the largest share of its licensing revenues during the post-1981 period, before the passage of Bayh-Dole or the establishment of a technology transfer office (see Chapter 8 for a more extensive discussion of the Axel cotransformation invention and patent). Nevertheless, fewer than ten patents were issued to Columbia University during 1975–81.

Columbia changed its policies toward faculty patents and created an administrative apparatus for managing their prosecution and licensing only after the passage of Bayh-Dole. A new patent policy, which took effect on July 1, 1981 (the effective date of Bayh-Dole), stated that Columbia could assert rights to faculty inventions created within university laboratories or research facilities, mandated the disclosure of such inventions to the university, and provided for royalty sharing with the inventor and his or her department. In 1984, this policy was published in the university *Faculty Handbook*. In 1989, Columbia's policy on reserving rights to the university for faculty inventions was extended to cover software. Inventions were to be disclosed to Columbia's technology transfer office, the Office of Science and Technology Development (OSTD), which was founded in 1982. OSTD was renamed the "Columbia Innovation Enterprise" in 1994, and in 2001 its name was changed again, to "Science and Technology Ventures."

Figure 6.8 shows the rapid "ramping up" of Columbia invention reports during the 1980s. Since most academic research programs change only gradually, the initial surge of invention reports may reflect increased identification by university administrators (based on a more intensive canvassing of the faculty) of potentially valuable inventions derived from research projects already under way. Almost 75 percent of the 877 invention reports disclosed between 1981 and 1995 are biomedical technologies (that is, biotechnology, medical devices, pharmaceuticals, and biochemical compounds), and biotechnology

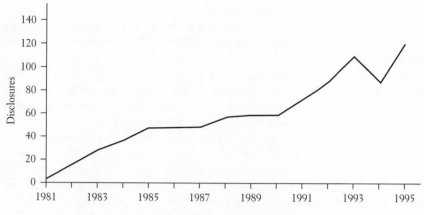

FIGURE 6.8   Columbia University invention disclosures, 1981–95

inventions accounted for 60 percent of these biomedical invention reports.[10] Although our Columbia data on inventions and patenting do not extend back into the pre-1980 period, the timing of the changes in this university's patent policies, as well as the filing of a patent application in 1980 by Columbia administrators on a major biotechnology invention, suggests that the growth of Columbia's post-1980 patenting and licensing activity in biomedical technologies was caused by more than the passage of Bayh-Dole.

Outside of the medical school, Columbia's inventive activity was concentrated in a few departments and research institutes that, like the medical school, rely heavily on federal R&D funding. During the 1981–95 period, over 60 percent of the nonbiomedical invention reports and over 65 percent of the patenting associated with nonbiomedical invention reports originated in two departments, electrical engineering and computer science, and two research centers, the Center for Telecommunications Research and the Lamont-Doherty Earth Observatory. Software inventions accounted for a significant share of Columbia faculty disclosures, increasing to more than 10 percent of disclosures by the 1990s; software inventions also account for a large share of Columbia licensing agreements. The data in Figure 6.9 suggest that increased invention reports generated increased patenting with a slight lag.

As the comparative data in Table 6.1 indicate, Columbia University's technology licensing activities were associated with a surge in constant-dollar gross licensing revenues, which grew almost sixty-fold in the decade between 1985 and 1995. This income was highly concentrated among a small number of inventions: the "top five" accounted for more than 90 percent of gross revenues throughout this period. Biomedical inventions accounted for more than

80 percent of the revenues of the "top five" inventions during the 1985–95 period (Table 6.1).[11] Moreover, biomedical technologies accounted for most of
the nonsoftware licenses at Columbia between 1983 and 1995 (Figure 6.7).

In assessing the effects of Bayh-Dole on Columbia University, we lack a
compelling counterfactual: what would have happened in the absence of this
federal law, given the other trends operating in university finances and research after 1980? We believe industrial interest in Columbia's research results, especially in the biomedical area, combined with the prospect of large
licensing revenues, would have led Columbia to develop some administrative
machinery for patenting and licensing in the absence of the Bayh-Dole Act.
Indeed, as we noted earlier, Columbia appears to have been moving in that direction before Bayh-Dole. Nevertheless, the change in federal policy embodied in Bayh-Dole may well have catalyzed a more dramatic change in policies,
procedures, and rules than would otherwise have occurred.

Another piece of evidence relevant to an assessment of the effects of Bayh-
Dole at Columbia concerns the significant role of software in Columbia's post-
1980 licensing activities. Virtually all of the software inventions licensed by
Columbia during the 1980s were protected by copyright, a form of intellectual
property never affected by Bayh-Dole, rather than by patents, the focus of this
federal law. Software licensing was a new form of technology marketing that
resulted from the university's creation of a technology marketing operation

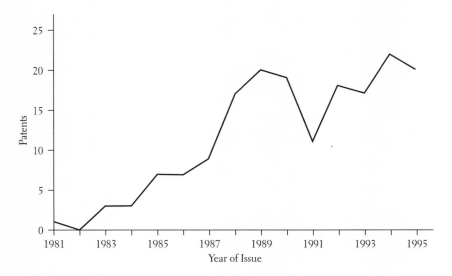

FIGURE 6.9   Columbia University patents, 1981–95

and (like biomedical research) from exogenous changes in the academic research agenda, rather than from the specific policy shifts embodied in Bayh-Dole. Moreover, although the arguments for Bayh-Dole stressed the importance of exclusive licensing in effective technology transfer and commercialization, many of Columbia's licensed inventions, including its biggest single source of revenues, have been licensed widely on a nonexclusive basis.

Comparing Invention Disclosures and Licenses at All Three Universities in the Late 1980s

In addition to comparing the periods before and after Bayh-Dole for two of these three universities, we compared data on the disclosure, patenting, and licensing activities of all three universities for the 1986–92 period to assess interinstitutional similarities and differences after the passage of the Bayh-Dole Act.[12] The data in the top panel of Table 6.2 suggest considerable similarity among these three universities in the characteristics of their invention disclosures, though a larger share of Stanford University's disclosures are licensed and a larger share of Stanford's invention disclosures yield positive licensing income than is true of either Columbia or the University of California.[13] Restricting the focus to biomedical inventions does little to change the conclusions of this comparison among our three universities (the second panel of Table 6.2).

The comparison of software inventions for the two universities within our sample (Stanford and Columbia) that have been active licensors of these technologies suggests that software licenses rarely involved patented inventions in the early post-Bayh-Dole period: 100 percent of the software inventions disclosed at Stanford during 1986–90 and 83 percent of Columbia's software inventions disclosed during this period that were licensed within six years of disclosure were not patented.

Another issue for consideration in our comparative evaluation of licensing in the post-Bayh-Dole era at these three universities concerns the share of inventions that were licensed through "exclusive" contracts, which we define here as contracts that are globally exclusive or that contain specific field-of-use or market restrictions. A relatively high percentage of all inventions that are licensed—as high as 90 percent for UC licenses and no less than 58.8 percent for Stanford licenses of "all technologies" during this period—are licensed on an exclusive basis under this definition, and these shares are similar for biomedical inventions. Perhaps because of the weaker formal protection for this technology (during much of this period, the lack of patent protection), software inventions are less frequently licensed on an exclusive basis: 46 percent

TABLE 6.2

Comparative Evidence on Invention Disclosures and Licenses at Stanford University, Columbia University, and the University of California, 1986–90

Technologies	Institution		
	Stanford	Columbia	UC
1986–90 (6-year "trailing window"): All Technologies			
% of disclosures yielding patents	23.2	18.6	20.4
% of disclosures that are licensed	33.2	16.4	12.3
Disclosures with licensing income			
>0/all disclosures (%)	22.4	12.3	7.4
Licensed disclosures with licensing income			
>0/number of disclosures that are licensed (%)	67.4	75.0	60.6
% of licensed disclosures that are licensed exclusively	58.8	59.1	90.3
1986–90 (6-year "trailing window"): Biomedical Technologies			
% of disclosures yielding patents	17.5	15.3	15.7
% of disclosures that are licensed	38.7	17.3	14.8
Disclosures with licensing income >0/all disclosures (%)	33.5	13.9	10.0
Licensed disclosures with licensing income			
>0/number of disclosures that are licensed (%)	86.6	80.0	67.2
% of licensed disclosures that are licensed exclusively	54.9	62.9	90.3
1986–90 (6-year "trailing window"): Software Technologies			
% of disclosures yielding patents	0	17.6	NA
% of disclosures that are licensed	53.6	35.3	NA
Disclosures with licensing income > 0/all disclosures (%)	45.5	23.5	NA
Licensed disclosures with licensing income			
>0/number of disclosures that are licensed (%)	84.7	66.7	NA
% of licensed disclosures that are licensed exclusively	46.3	16.7	NA

and 17 percent, respectively, of software invention disclosures at Stanford and Columbia were licensed exclusively during 1986–90.

Nevertheless, the licenses accounting for the largest share of revenues at all of these universities are nonexclusive licenses. The Stanford-UC Cohen-Boyer patents were licensed widely and nonexclusively.[14] Columbia University's Axel cotransformation patent also was licensed on a nonexclusive basis. Although many proponents of patent protection for university inventions during and after the debate over the Bayh-Dole Act argued that would-be commercial developers of these technologies needed exclusive title to this intellectual property in order to obtain a clear "prospect" for their significant investments in this activity, these cases suggest that for inventions of broad promise and potentially widespread use, nonexclusive licenses accommodated both universities' interest in revenues and the needs of commercial users

TABLE 6.3

University of California and Stanford University Invention Disclosures, Patents, and Licenses, 1975–79 and 1984–88 (8-Year "Trailing Window")

Indicator	University of California		Stanford (including software)		Stanford (excluding software)	
	1975–79	1984–88	1975–79	1984–88	1975–79	1984–88
Marketing Intensity Indicators						
1. (Disclosures resulting in issued patents)/(Invention disclosures)	20.2%	21.9%	14.9%	25.1%	15.5%	29.8%
2. (Disclosures generating patent applications)/(Invention disclosures)	24.0	31.2	NA	NA	NA	NA
3. (Disclosures licensed)/(Invention disclosures)	5.6	12.6	13.0	36.6	12.8	34.3
4. (Disclosures generating licenses with income > 0)/(Invention disclosures)	4.6	5.0	9.8	22.0	9.5	17.9
Marketing Yield Indicators						
5. (Patents issued)/(Patent applications)	62.1	43.6	NA	NA	NA	NA
6. (Patents licensed)/(Patents issued)	25.1	35.5	62.7	63.7	62.7	63.7
7. (Licenses with income > 0)/(Licenses)	84.1	47.1	91.4	90.7	90.0	76.2

for access to the essential intellectual property (see Chapter 8 for additional   115
discussion of the role of exclusive licenses in specific cases of university-
industry technology transfer).

The Yield of Patenting and Licensing at the University of California and Stanford, 1975–79 and 1984–88

In this section, we use the data on UC and Stanford disclosures, patenting, and licensing to discuss the technology marketing efforts of these universities before and after Bayh-Dole. The data in Table 6.3 provide measures for the 1975–79 and 1984–88 periods of (1) the intensity of these institutions' technology marketing efforts, reflected in their propensities to patent or license faculty invention disclosures, and (2) the yield of these marketing efforts, based on such indicators as the share of patent applications that result in issued patents, the share of issued patents that are licensed, and the share of licenses that generate positive income.[15]

The first row in Table 6.3 displays "before and after" data for the share of invention disclosures resulting in issued patents, which scarcely changes between the two periods at the University of California and increases from nearly 15 percent to slightly more than 25 percent (excluding software, from 15.5 percent to 29.8 percent) at Stanford. The second row of Table 6.3 shows that the UC system also increased its patent application rates in the wake of Bayh-Dole—the share of disclosures that generate patent applications rose from 24 percent to slightly more than 31 percent. But this increased tendency to file for patents was associated with a decline in the "yield" of these efforts, as the share of patent applications resulting in issued patents dropped from more than 62 percent in the 1975–79 period to less than 44 percent in 1984–88 (row 5 of Table 6.3). These data on marketing intensity and patent yield suggest that UC administrators intensified their efforts to protect and promote faculty inventions after the Bayh-Dole Act. Their intensified efforts nevertheless appear to have produced a lower "yield," as measured by the share of applications resulting in issued patents. The increase in the share of Stanford disclosures yielding issued patents after 1980 is more difficult to interpret, since we lack data on patent applications that are comparable to those from the University of California. But this increase is broadly consistent with a more aggressive effort to patent faculty inventions.

Rows 3, 4, 6, and 7 in Table 6.3 provide additional evidence of change in the "intensity" and "yield" of the UC and Stanford technology-marketing efforts after Bayh-Dole. The share of UC disclosures resulting in licenses (row 3) increased from 5.6 percent in 1975–79 to 12.6 percent in 1984–88,

116   while the share of UC disclosures resulting in licenses that generated positive royalties (row 4) grew from 4.6 percent in 1975–79 to 5 percent in 1984–88. In contrast, the share of Stanford disclosures that were licensed nearly tripled between 1975–79 and 1984–88. The share of Stanford disclosures yielding positive licensing income more than doubled (growing from 9.8 percent to 22 percent) when software invention disclosures are included and nearly doubled when these are excluded (increasing from 9.5 percent to almost 18 percent).[16] At both the University of California and Stanford, the proportionate increase in the share of disclosures that were licensed after 1980 (a measure of the intensity of institutional technology marketing efforts) exceeded the proportionate increase in the share of disclosures yielding positive licensing income (an indicator of the yield of these marketing efforts). We interpret these data as indicating some decline in the yield of licensing revenues during the post-Bayh-Dole period in both universities' licensing operations.

Two additional measures of the yield of these institutions' technology marketing efforts, the share of issued patents that were licensed (row 6 of Table 6.3) and the share of these licenses yielding positive income (row 7 of Table 6.3), also suggest some decline in yield after the Bayh-Dole Act. The share of UC patents that were licensed grew from slightly more than 25 percent to more than 35 percent, but the share of these licenses yielding positive income dropped by almost half, from roughly 84 percent to 47 percent. The "before and after" data at Stanford reveal a similar trend. The share of issued Stanford patents that were licensed (an indicator that is comparable to the UC data only for the far-right columns that exclude software inventions) is essentially unchanged, increasing from almost 63 percent to almost 64 percent. The share of Stanford licenses yielding positive income[17] dropped from 90 percent in 1975–79 to roughly 76 percent in 1984–88 when software inventions are excluded (a more meaningful basis for comparison with the UC licensing effort).[18]

Overall, these data suggest an intensification in technology marketing activities after the passage of Bayh-Dole. The post-Bayh-Dole period of invention disclosures is associated with more extensive licensing of the patents resulting from these universities' disclosures. The more extensive licensing efforts of the post-1980 period also appear to have produced some decline in the "yield" of these licenses at both the University of California and Stanford, measured as the share of licenses yielding positive royalties. But these indicators of decline in the average productivity of the marketing efforts of the UC and Stanford technology licensing offices need not imply inefficient or economically irrational behavior—after all, the marginal, rather than the average, returns to licensing activities are most important in evaluating the returns to

these institutions' licensing activities. Moreover, our measure of the "yield" of
these universities' licensing activities does not capture the size of the revenue
streams associated with the average or the marginal license before and after
Bayh-Dole.[19] Nevertheless, these effects appear to be relatively small and suggest that Bayh-Dole had modest effects on the "technology transfer" activities
of these established academic patenters and licensors.

THE "IMPORTANCE" AND "GENERALITY" OF STANFORD, COLUMBIA, AND UC PATENTS, 1975–92

The data on the intensity and yield of the technology marketing activities at
the University of California and Stanford suggest that in the first decade after
the passage of the Act, these "incumbent" universities' technology transfer
efforts intensified moderately and their yield declined. Did these changes in
their patenting and licensing activities reflect a shift in the characteristics of
Stanford and UC research in response to the Bayh-Dole Act? The possible
effects of Bayh-Dole on academic research, especially on the mix of fundamental and more applied research activities within universities, has been the
focus of a growing body of empirical research.

One analysis of this issue by Thursby and Thursby (2002) used nonpara-
metric linear programming techniques to disaggregate the contributions to
growth in university commercial activity between 1994 and 1999 into those attributable to changes in the nature of academic research and those attributable to changes in other factors, including universities' propensities to file patent applications and firms' propensities to license university inventions. These
authors cannot reject the hypothesis that the content of faculty research
shifted during the 1994–99 period, but their analysis suggests that most of the
recent growth in university patenting and licensing is largely attributable to
other changes, particularly the increased propensity of universities to file for
patents, instead of some shift in academic research toward applied topics.

Another body of empirical work on university patenting and licensing compares the characteristics of individual researchers who do and do not patent. If
academic patenting has indeed "crowded out" basic research, faculty who are
relatively intensive patenters should have fewer (or fewer significant) publications in leading basic research journals. But the limited empirical research on
this issue reveals few such differences between faculty who patent and faculty
who do not. The analysis of fifty-five "star" academic scientists in biotechnology by Zucker, Darby, and Armstrong (1994) found that faculty with patents
were the authors of a significantly larger number of publications that were
cited by other papers (and therefore deemed more scientifically important)

118   than faculty who did not patent. Similar results for faculty in nonbiomedical research are reported by Agrawal and Henderson (2002) in their analysis of patents and publications by faculty members in two MIT engineering departments. Agrawal and Henderson found no evidence of a negative relationship between the extent of patenting and publication by the faculty members in their sample. Indeed, the number of patents obtained by an individual faculty member was positively related to the quality of his or her publications, as measured by the number of times they are cited in subsequent publications. Preliminary work by Stephan et al. (2002), based on data from a 1995 National Science Foundation survey of doctoral-degree recipients, also finds a positive relationship between the number of patents and publications by individual faculty members.

Still other scholars have examined various characteristics of academic patents to determine any changes in the content of academic research activities after the Bayh-Dole Act. The analysis of post-1980 academic patenting by Henderson, Jaffe, and Trajtenberg (1995, 1998a) found that these intensified post-Bayh-Dole efforts to market faculty inventions were associated with the issue to U.S. universities of patents that were less "important" and less "general," based on the patterns of citations to these patents. Moreover, these scholars also found that experienced academic licensors' post-1980 patents declined somewhat in quality, as measured by the "importance" and "generality" (defined below) of these patents. As Henderson, Jaffe, and Trajtenberg (1995) argue, these changes in the characteristics of U.S. universities' post-1980 patents "may reflect changing motives within the university research community or shifts in the focus of university research from basic to more applied work" (p. 1; see also Foray and Kazancigil, 1999).

Our analysis of this issue in this chapter follows the approach of Henderson, Jaffe, and Trajtenberg (1995, 1998a) and Trajtenberg, Henderson, and Jaffe (1997) in examining the importance and generality of UC and Stanford patents before and after Bayh-Dole and comparing these characteristics of UC, Stanford, and Columbia patents after 1980. Although we examine a similar set of characteristics of these universities' patents, we employ a slightly different "control population" of patents (see below). Our "before and after" analysis of UC and Stanford patents uses the year in which the invention was first disclosed as the key datum in classifying faculty disclosures and any associated patents as falling into the pre-Bayh-Dole or post-Bayh-Dole eras. We further categorize patented disclosures by the date of the patent application. Our data for the University of California and Stanford thus contain: (1) disclosures and patents for which the disclosures and patent application occurred

during and after 1970 and the issue of the patent occurred before 1981 (the year $\qquad$
during which the Bayh-Dole Act went into effect); (2) disclosures and patent
applications that occurred during or after 1981 and before 1993; and (3) inventions disclosed after 1970 and prior to 1981, for which patent applications were
filed during or after 1981 and before 1993.[20]

We also include Columbia University patents in our analysis of the post-
Bayh-Dole era. Although we define Columbia as an "entrant" academic
patenter, reflecting the fact that this university developed an active patenting
and licensing policy only after 1980, as mentioned earlier, Columbia did
accumulate a modest portfolio of fewer than ten patents during the 1975–80
period.

Henderson and colleagues use patent-citation measures in their analysis of
university patents. When the U.S. Patent and Trademark Office grants a patent, the patent examiner includes a list of all previous patents constituting
"prior art." This list is made public as part of the publication of the patent at
the time it issues. The examiner is aided in compiling this list by the patent
applicant, who is legally bound to provide with the application a list of all
"prior art" of which he or she is aware. Citations of prior patents can thus serve
as an indicator of the technological lineage of new patents, much as bibliographic citations indicate the intellectual lineage of academic research.

Our analysis of UC, Stanford, and Columbia patents focuses on "forward
citations" to these patents, defined as the number of citations received by each
patent following its issue. Citations to patents typically peak four to five years
after the date of issue of the cited patent. As a result, data on citations to more
recently issued patents will be "right-truncated," that is, more recent patents
will be underrepresented in the citations data. In order to address this problem, our dataset includes only citations to patents that occurred within six
years of the year of issue of the patent, and our sample includes only patents
issued between 1975 and 1992. Our dataset also includes a control sample of
nonacademic patents for each of these three universities, spanning the same
time period and replicating the distribution of the UC, Stanford, and Columbia patents among patent classes. We matched one nonuniversity patent
with each university patent, based on the patent class and application date of
the relevant university patent.[21] Citations to patents in the control sample also
are restricted to those occurring within six years after the year of issue.

We used the number of citations to a patent during the six years following
its issue as a measure of the importance of the patent, based on the assumption that citations form an index of the influence over subsequent inventive
activity of the cited patent. The number of observations for our UC, Stanford,

TABLE 6.4

Number of Patents in the University of California, Stanford, and Columbia Datasets

	Overall			Biomedical			Nonbiomedical		
	UC	Stanford	Columbia	UC	Stanford	Columbia	UC	Stanford	Columbia
Patent application 1970 ≤ & <1981; patent issued 1975 ≤ & < 1981	97	110	—	43	23	—	54	87	—
Disclosed < 1981; patent application ≥1981 & ≤1992	32	30	—	23	10	—	9	20	—
Disclosed & patent application ≥1981 & ≤1992	245	377	112	154	93	63	91	284	49

and Columbia samples of patents is displayed in Table 6.4 (because Columbia has very few pre-1981 patents, we exclude this university from the pre-1981 data). We also divide the Columbia, UC, and Stanford patents into biomedical and nonbiomedical categories in order to test for differences in the effects of Bayh-Dole between these broad technology classes.[22] Clearly, for some cells of the dataset (for example, Stanford biomedical patents in the "disclosed before 1981 and patented during or after 1981" subset), the number of observations is small (far smaller, for example, than the university patent samples for individual years in Trajtenberg, Henderson, and Jaffe, 1997). Because of the small number of observations within each, the standard errors for these subsamples are large, and the statistical significance of our tests is low. Nevertheless, we believe that measures of the importance and generality of this category of our patents are worth computing and analyzing separately and therefore have retained these small subsamples in the results that follow.

The upper panel of Table 6.5 displays means and standard errors for the number of citations to the UC, Stanford, and Columbia patent samples and their disaggregated subsamples. We also present means and standard errors for the control patent samples and subsamples corresponding to each of the UC, Stanford, and Columbia categories in the lower panel of Table 6.5. Without exception, the number of citations received in the six years following issue by the patents of all three universities is larger than those received during the identical period by the control samples of patents, for all time periods and disaggregated categories. There is no apparent time trend in the absolute magnitude of differences between the number of citations received by the Stanford and UC patents and those in the control sample. With the exception of biomedical patents in the second and third of our three subperiods, the mean number of citations received by the Stanford patents exceeds the mean number of citations received by UC patents, although these differences frequently are small. With one exception (Stanford biomedical patents), UC and Stanford patents also are more heavily cited than Columbia patents during the post-1980 period.

The upper panel of Table 6.5 also reports the results of tests for the statistical significance of differences between the mean values of forward citations to the UC, Stanford, and Columbia patents and forward citations to patents in our control samples.[23] We find no evidence of a statistically significant decline in the importance of Stanford and UC patents, relative to the control samples, after 1980 (columns 2 and 3).[24] Tests for the significance of the difference in mean citations between the Columbia patents and the Columbia control sample, however, indicate that the difference is significant only for the overall Columbia patent sample at the 10 percent level. The absence of significantly

TABLE 6.5

Mean Values for "Forward Citations"; University of California, Stanford, and
Columbia Patents and Corresponding Control Group Samples

Samples	Overall			Biomedical			Nonbiomedical		
	UC	Stanford	Columbia	UC	Stanford	Columbia	UC	Stanford	Columbia
University patents									
1. Patent application ≥1970 & <1981; patent issued 1975 ≤ & <1981	3.96 (7.56)	5.65** (8.75)	—	3.30 (3.50)	6.74 (13.17)	—	4.48 (9.66)	5.36** (7.23)	—
2. Disclosed <1981; patent application ≥1981 & ≤1992	5.91** (7.33)	7.43** (6.96)	—	5.43* (5.16)	4.10 (3.67)	—	7.11 (11.53)	9.10** (7.66)	—
3. Disclosed & patent application ≥1981 & ≤1992	5.21** (6.14)	6.92** (7.35)	4.45* (6.44)	4.50** (6.22)	4.42 (3.75)	4.49 (7.61)	6.42** (5.83)	7.73** (8.02)	4.39 (4.62)
Control Group patents									
Patent application ≥1970 & <1981; patent issued 1975 ≤ & <1981 (matched to University patents group 1)	2.92 (4.73)	2.28 (2.87)	—	3.02 (4.47)	2.39 (2.37)	—	2.83 (4.96)	2.25 (3.00)	—
Patent application ≥1981 & ≤1992 (matched to University patents group 2)	2.53 (3.87)	3.00 (3.40)	—	2.96 (4.32)	2.40 (2.32)	—	1.44 (2.18)	3.30 (3.85)	—
Patent application ≥1981 & ≤1992 (matched to University patents group 3)	3.15 (3.79)	3.97 (4.97)	3.24 (4.19)	2.99 (3.70)	3.45 (5.17)	2.92 (4.64)	3.43 (3.92)	4.14 (4.91)	3.65 (3.52)

NOTES: Standard errors in parentheses. Unequal variances assumed. Asterisks denote significance in difference in means tests (t-statistics) between university and corresponding control group samples: ** $p > 0.05$; * $p > 0.10$.

greater citation rates for Columbia patents could reflect a less selective approach to patenting during the early years of Columbia's licensing activities, reflecting its limited experience in patenting in the early years of the Office of Science and Technology Development.[25] We discuss the possible effects of entry following the Bayh-Dole Act by inexperienced institutional patenters on post-1980 overall academic patent "quality" in Chapter 7.

The results of our tests for the significance of differences between the mean citation rates of the UC and Stanford biomedical patents and their respective nonacademic patent control samples indicate that the higher citation rates for these academic patents are statistically significant (at the 5 percent level) in the post-1980 period only for the University of California (the higher number of citations to UC biomedical patents for the "middle period" is weakly significant, at the 10 percent level). The mean number of forward citations for Stanford nonbiomedical patents significantly exceeds that for their control samples for all three periods, while the citation frequencies for UC nonbiomedical patents are significantly greater (at the 5 percent level) than those in the control sample only once, for the post-1980 period.[26] The results for Columbia during the post-1980 period indicate no significant differences in citation frequencies with the patents in the Columbia control sample, but there is no evidence that these Columbia patents are significantly less heavily cited than those in its control sample.

These results must be interpreted with considerable caution, in view of the small number of observations for some time periods. The fact that significant differences in importance between the university and control sample biomedical patents' citations are relatively infrequent is interesting in view of the importance of biomedical patents within the patenting and licensing activities of Stanford and the University of California before and after Bayh-Dole. But these data provide no indication of any decline in the importance of these universities' patents, relative to our control samples of nonacademic patents, after the Bayh-Dole Act. If anything, these data suggest that the UC and Stanford patents' relative importance increased, rather than declined, after the Bayh-Dole Act. Although these results do indicate that the patents applied for during the 1980s by Columbia, a university that did not patent significantly prior to Bayh-Dole, were less "important," relative to all nonacademic patents, than those of Stanford and the University of California during this period, they do not suggest that Columbia's patents were significantly less important than those in its control sample.[27]

Table 6.6 presents data on the generality of UC, Stanford, and Columbia patents before and after Bayh-Dole. The more widely cited a patent outside of its "home" patent class, the greater its generality and, arguably, the more

TABLE 6.6

Mean Values for "Generality"; University of California, Stanford, and Columbia Patents and Corresponding Control Group Samples

Samples	Overall			Biomedical			Nonbiomedical		
	UC	Stanford	Columbia	UC	Stanford	Columbia	UC	Stanford	Columbia
University patents									
Patent application ≥1970 & <1981; patent issued 1975 ≤ & <1981	0.38 (0.42)	0.51** (0.44)	—	0.41 (0.44)	0.57 (0.41)	—	0.36 (0.40)	0.50* (0.45)	—
Disclosed <1981; patent application ≥1981 & ≤1992	0.62 (0.40)	0.56 (0.44)	—	0.59 (0.42)	0.27 (0.44)	—	0.69 (0.37)	0.70** (0.38)	—
Disclosed & patent application ≥1981 & ≤1992	0.56** (0.43)	0.61** (0.41)	0.54** (0.43)	0.52 (0.44)	0.49* (0.43)	0.51** (0.43)	0.63** (0.41)	0.64** (0.39)	0.57 (0.44)
Control Group patents									
Patent application ≥1970 & <1981; patent issued 1975 ≤ & <1981	0.41 (0.44)	0.36 (0.43)	—	0.39 (0.46)	0.36 (0.42)	—	0.42 (0.43)	0.36 (0.44)	—
Patent application ≥1981 & ≤1992	0.61 (0.44)	0.41 (0.46)	—	0.64 (0.45)	0.61 (0.44)	—	0.46 (0.42)	0.32 (0.45)	—
Patent application ≥1981 & ≤1992	0.42 (0.43)	0.45 (0.44)	0.37 (0.44)	0.43 (0.43)	0.37 (0.42)	0.34 (0.43)	0.42 (0.43)	0.47 (0.44)	0.41 (0.45)

NOTES: Standard errors in parentheses. Unequal variances assumed. Asterisks denote significance in difference in means tests (t-statistics) between university and corresponding control group samples: ** $p > 0.05$; * $p > 0.10$.

significant the advance in knowledge represented by the patent. Following
Henderson, Jaffe, and Trajtenberg (1995, 1998a), we compute generality as
follows:

$$GENERAL_i = 1 - \sum_{k=1}^{N_i} \left(\frac{NCITING_{ik}}{NCITING_i} \right)^2$$

where for patent i, k is the index of patent classes and N_i the number of different classes to which the citing patents belong. This measure can be computed
for only those patents with at least one citation, and the sample in Table 6.6
accordingly differs slightly from that in Table 6.5. As in our measure of importance, we restrict forward citations to those occurring during the first six
years following the issue of the patent. Higher values of $GENERAL_i$ indicate
that a patent is relevant to subsequent inventive activities in a broader range of
technological fields.

As a measure of "dispersion" of patent citations, $GENERAL_i$ is inherently
biased — the more citations a patent receives, the greater the likelihood that
these citations will be spread across a larger number of patent classes. Moreover, this bias is greater for patents with a small number of citations. Therefore, we employ the following correction (Hall, 2002):

$$\hat{G}_i = \left(\frac{N_i}{N_i - 1} \right) GENERAL_i$$

where N_i is the number of forward citations to patent i during the first six years
following the issue of the patent. All reported results for generality incorporate
this correction for bias.

The data in Table 6.6 indicate that the mean generality measures for overall UC, Stanford, and Columbia patents are higher than those for their respective control sample patents, with the exception of UC patents applied for
and issued before 1981.[28] There is no evidence in Table 6.6 of any decline in
generality, relative to the control sample of nonacademic patents, in the UC
and Stanford patents in the post-Bayh-Dole era. The differences in mean generality between the overall UC and Stanford patents and their respective control samples are statistically significant (at the 5 percent level) for the post-1981
period. The mean generality score of the post-1981 Columbia patents also is
significantly higher (at the 5 percent level of significance) than the similar
score for the patents in its control sample.

Overall, the results of this analysis of the importance and generality of Stanford, UC, and Columbia patents yield conclusions that differ from those of
Henderson, Jaffe, and Trajtenberg (1995, 1998a), who analyzed a larger sample
of U.S. university patents. Importantly, these scholars also found a decline in
the importance and generality of the patents assigned to the universities that

126   occupied the top decile of the post-1980 patent distribution (using patents from 1988), a group that included the University of California and Stanford as well as other U.S. universities with considerable pre-1980 patenting experience. Why do we find little or no evidence of declines in the importance or generality of these universities' patents after the Bayh-Dole Act? First, our sample of university patents is small, although this should limit the statistical significance of any differences between the university and nonacademic patent samples. Another possible explanation for the different results is the use by Henderson and colleagues of a shorter time series of forward citations than we use in this analysis. Their results thus may be affected more heavily by "truncation bias." [29] Our empirical results also ignore the effects of entry by other universities, other than Columbia, into patenting and licensing after the passage of the Bayh-Dole Act on the characteristics of the overall U.S. academic patent portfolio. Although Henderson, Jaffe, and Trajtenberg (1998a) acknowledge that entry into patenting by less experienced institutions could account for their results, they are not able to test for the effects of entry after 1980 by inexperienced universities on overall academic patent quality. We undertake such a test in the next chapter.

CONCLUSION

The effects of the Bayh-Dole Act on U.S. research universities have received extensive rhetorical attention but modest empirical analysis. In this chapter, we have used an invaluable byproduct of the Act, the systematic records of the faculty inventions, patents, and licenses compiled by three leading U.S. research universities, in an analysis of some of the Act's effects at these institutions. Our data on the University of California and Stanford University suggest that for universities already active in patenting and licensing, Bayh-Dole resulted in expanded efforts to market academic inventions. The Act also led Columbia University, along with many other research universities formerly inactive in this area, to enter into large-scale patenting and licensing of faculty inventions.

But several additional factors in addition to Bayh-Dole stimulated the post-1980 upsurge in patenting and licensing at U.S. research universities, and it is difficult to separate their effects from those of the Act. These additional factors were especially influential in biomedical research. In particular, by the mid-1970s, biomedical technology, especially biotechnology, had increased significantly in importance as a productive field of university research that yielded research findings of great interest to industry. The feasibility of technology licensing in biotechnology was advanced by the *Diamond v. Chakrabarty* deci-

sion, and broader shifts in U.S. intellectual property rights policy increased 127
the economic value of patents and facilitated patent licensing. The expanded
patenting and licensing activities of a number of U.S. universities during the
1970s provided an important political impetus for the drafting and passage of
the Bayh-Dole Act, as we pointed out in Chapter 5.

An array of developments in research, industry, and policy thus combined
to increase U.S. universities' activities in technology licensing, and Bayh-
Dole, while important, was not determinative. Even without the Bayh-Dole
Act, the evidence presented in this chapter suggests that U.S. universities
would have increased their patenting and licensing activities during the 1980s
and 1990s. Indeed, our data indicate such growth before Bayh-Dole at the two
universities in our study active in patenting and licensing before its passage. At
Columbia, internal discussions of the feasibility of expanded institutional
patenting of faculty research results were well under way by 1980, and a key
patent application was filed before the passage of Bayh-Dole. The act nevertheless hastened the entry into patenting and licensing by many universities
(such as Columbia) that had formerly avoided these activities.

By the end of the first decade of Bayh-Dole, these three universities display
remarkable similarities in their patent and licensing portfolios, as illustrated
by the data in Tables 6.1 and 6.2 and Figure 6.7. A very small share of all
patented inventions account for the majority of gross licensing revenues at all
three universities. Moreover, these leading earners are concentrated in the
biomedical area, a technology field characterized by relatively strong patents
that are economically significant (Levin et al., 1987). A second important area
of licensing at two of these three universities, however, is software, for which
formal patent protection is less important.

Our analysis of the effects of Bayh-Dole on the content of academic research and the importance of the patents assigned to the University of California and Stanford University produced no evidence of significant change in
the characteristics of the academic research disclosures received by these universities' technology licensing offices. Nor did our analysis of the pre- and post-
Bayh-Dole patents assigned to these two universities reveal any decline in the
importance or generality of these universities' patents after Bayh-Dole, in contrast to the findings of Henderson, Jaffe, and Trajtenberg (1995, 1998a) for a
larger sample of U.S. academic patents. The patents of a major post-1980 "entrant," Columbia University, also are no less important or general than those
within a matched sample of nonacademic patents.

How do we reconcile a finding that citation-based measures of UC and
Stanford patents reveal no decline in importance after Bayh-Dole with our
conclusion that both the University of California's and Stanford's technology

128   licensing operations appear to have experienced a decline in "yield," that is, a decline in the share of licenses yielding positive revenues? Fundamentally, these two sets of indicators measure different characteristics of the invention and patent portfolios of these universities. Along with other scholars, we interpret patent citations as measures of the importance of the contribution to inventive knowledge of a given patent. But this contribution may or may not be correlated with the willingness of an industrial firm to pay for a license for this patent. The extent of correlation between licensing revenues and patent citations remains an important question for future research.

A number of observers have expressed concern that the upsurge of patenting and licensing has been associated with significant change in the character of university research toward applied questions and away from basic research. As we noted in Chapter 3, however, the shift in U.S. universities' patenting activity toward biomedical research on its face cannot be interpreted as a shift away from fundamental research — after all, much of the research that generated these biomedical patents is fundamental in nature. In addition, the effects of any change in university research "culture" and norms wrought by Bayh-Dole appear to be limited to relatively few units of these research universities. Increased post-1980 patenting and licensing activity has affected a relatively small number of departments and institutes at Columbia University, the only one of our three universities for which we have data on the departmental origins of invention disclosures. Were they available, similar data from Stanford and the UC system would likely support a similar conclusion.

The Effects of Entry and Experience on U.S. University Patenting Before and After the Bayh-Dole Act

The preceding chapter's analysis of the effects of the Bayh-Dole Act on the patenting and licensing activities of the University of California (UC), Stanford University, and Columbia University found that the "importance" and "generality" of the post-Bayh-Dole patents of our two universities with considerable pre-1980 experience in patenting (Stanford University and the University of California) was stable after the Bayh-Dole Act, a conclusion that contrasts with the results of Henderson, Jaffe, and Trajtenberg (1995, 1998a). These different conclusions from similar analyses of university patenting motivate this chapter's analysis, which examines the effects on overall U.S. university patenting of expanded patenting by less experienced academic institutions after the passage of the Bayh-Dole Act in 1980.

Although Henderson, Jaffe, and Trajtenberg (1998a) suggest that increased patenting after 1980 by smaller institutions may have been partly responsible for declines after 1980 in the importance and generality of overall U.S. academic patents, they are not able to control explicitly for the effects of expanded patenting by such institutions after 1980. And one of the most important characteristics of U.S. university patenting during the 1980s was precisely the entry into these activities of many universities that had been inactive or minimally active patenters before 1980.

Since Chapter 6 suggests that Bayh-Dole had modest effects on the patenting activities of two leading "incumbent" institutions, this analysis of the effects of entry on overall U.S. university patenting enables us to consider an area in which the effects of Bayh-Dole may be more pronounced. This chapter also extends our analysis of the importance and generality of the patents assigned to experienced university patenters before and after 1980

beyond the two research universities discussed in Chapter 6 to a broader
sample of academic patenters.

Our analysis of this issue compares the importance and generality of patents assigned to universities with varying levels of experience in patenting before 1980. Parallel declines in the importance and generality of the post-1980
patents of both "incumbent" and "entrant" universities could suggest that the
Bayh-Dole Act affected the incentives of academic researchers and administrators to disclose and patent inventions of lower importance and generality in
all U.S. academic institutions, regardless of their pre-1980 experience in
patenting. But if the importance and generality of entrants' patents are significantly lower than those of more experienced institutional patenters after 1980,
a different interpretation of the effects of Bayh-Dole is plausible. For example,
inexperienced university patent offices may seek patents on a broad cross section of faculty discoveries and thereby accumulate a portfolio of less significant patents (some anecdotal evidence supports this characterization). But as
these entrants acquire experience in patenting and learn the complexities of
protecting and marketing intellectual property, they may become more selective in their patenting, reducing the gaps between the characteristics of their
patents and those of the experienced patenters.

The first interpretation of Bayh-Dole's effects emphasizes lasting changes
in incentives and behavior throughout U.S. universities, while the second one
views the 1980s as a period of learning and adjustment by entrants inexperienced in patenting and licensing. Needless to say, these explanations are not
mutually exclusive, and the development of U.S. academic patenting during
the 1980s may reflect both effects. But our empirical analysis allows for an assessment of the relative strength of these two effects.

Immediately below, we conduct a statistical examination of the characteristics of the patents assigned to a comprehensive sample of U.S. universities in
order to assess the effects on the overall importance and generality of U.S. academic patents of the entry of less experienced academic patenters after 1980.
Our findings indicate that less experienced academic patenters did indeed receive less important or general patents in the aftermath of Bayh-Dole. The initial effects of the Bayh-Dole Act on entry thus may underpin any observed
change in the importance and generality of overall U.S. academic patents after 1980.

Consistent with the second interpretation of the effects of Bayh-Dole on
patenting by U.S. universities, we find that the importance of entrant institutions' patents improved during the 1980s and 1990s, closing the gap with incumbents during a period in which the average importance of overall aca-

demic patents improved relative to nonacademic patents. The second part of
this chapter examines such "university learning" in greater detail, seeking to
understand whether and why the importance (based on citations to these patents) of the post-1980 patents issuing to less experienced academic patenters
has improved during the 1980s and 1990s.

We find little evidence of strong "learning curve" effects, as neither cumulative patenting nor the (relatively) early establishment of a technology transfer office explains these improvements. Links with the Research Corporation
during the pre-Bayh-Dole era also exercise little influence over changes during the 1980s and 1990s in these characteristics of incumbent and entrant institutions' patents. Inasmuch as these observable sources of learning exercise
little influence, we conclude that a broader process of learning, based on
spillovers among universities and the strengthening of professional networks
among university licensing officers, may account for the convergence in importance between the patents of incumbent and entrant universities.

ENTRY, IMPORTANCE, AND GENERALITY
IN U.S. ACADEMIC PATENTING, 1975–92

We first examine the characteristics of all U.S. university patents during 1975–
92 in an analysis of the effects on academic patenting of entry into patenting
activities after 1980 by universities with limited patenting experience. As in
Chapter 6, we use forward citations to U.S. university patents, defined as the
number of citations received by each patent following its issue. We include
only citations to patents that occurred within six years of the year of issue of
the patent and examine patents issued between 1975 and 1992. We also constructed a control group of patents that included one nonacademic patent for
each patent in our academic patent database. Each nonacademic control patent was chosen so as to match as closely as possible the corresponding academic patent's U.S. Patent and Trademark Office technology class (at the
three-digit level) and its date of application.[1] Citations to patents in the control sample were restricted to those occurring within six years after the year
of issue.

Our academic patent dataset includes all patents assigned to U.S. universities other than Stanford, the University of California, and Columbia during
1975–92. Within this dataset, we distinguished among three categories: (1) universities with at least ten patents that were applied for after 1970 and issued
during 1975–80 ("high-intensity" incumbents); (2) universities with at least
one but less than ten patents applied for after 1970 that issued during 1975–80

132   ("low-intensity" incumbents); and (3) universities with no patents issued during the 1975–80 period and at least one patent issued during 1980–92 that was
applied for after 1980 ("entrants"). Our definitions of "entrant" and "incumbent" universities are intended to separate the effects on patent importance
and generality of increased patenting after Bayh-Dole by active pre-1980
patenters from increased post-1980 patenting by other institutions.

Table 7.1 contains information on the annual number of patents issuing to
these three groups of universities during the 1975–92 period that were applied
for after 1970, demonstrating the shrinking share of the "high-intensity" pre-
1980 academic patenters after the passage of Bayh-Dole. The "high-intensity"
patenters' share declines from more than 85 percent during 1975–80 to less
than 65 percent by 1992. The "low-intensity" pre-1980 patenters, by contrast,
increase their share of all academic patents from 15 percent in 1981 to almost
30 percent in 1992. And entrants increase their share of overall academic
patenting from zero in 1980 to more than 6 percent by 1992.

Tables 7.2–4 present the results of separate regressions of importance and
generality for the patents assigned to academic institutions in each of these
three categories, covering 1975–91 for the "high-" and "low-intensity" incumbents and 1981–91 for the entrants.[2] Negative binomial regression results are
reported for models in which importance is the dependent variable. Our
analysis of generality uses a tobit specification, since the dependent variable
(generality) is truncated at a lower limit of zero and an upper limit of one.[3]
Each specification is estimated for a dataset covering the patents of the relevant academic institutions and those in the control sample of nonacademic
patents. We control for year effects and interact a dummy variable denoting
academic patents with a dummy for the application year — the reported coefficients are those for the interaction terms for 1975–91. We present results for
overall academic patents as well as for biomedical and nonbiomedical patents.

The results for our analysis of each of these three samples of academic patents display contrasting patterns of importance and generality.[4] The "high-
intensity" incumbents exhibit consistently more important and more general
patents, relative to nonacademic patents, throughout the 1975–91 period than
do the other two groups of universities (Table 7.2). Thirteen of the seventeen
interaction coefficients in column 2 for the overall patent sample associated
with this group of universities are positive and statistically significant at the
5 percent level, indicating that for most of this period (and increasingly so during the 1980s), these institutions' patents were cited more intensively than
those in the matched industrial sample. As was true in Chapter 6's analysis of
UC, Stanford, and Columbia patents, the differences in importance between

TABLE 7.1

Number of Patents by Year of Issue: "High-intensity incumbents," "Low-intensity incumbents," and "Entrants," 1975–92

Patent issue year	High-intensity incumbents (n = 51)		Low-intensity incumbents (n = 92)		Entrants (n = 81)		Total
	Number	% of total	Number	% of total	Number	% of total	
1975	213	86.9	32	13.1	0	0.0	245
1976	248	89.2	30	10.8	0	0.0	94
1977	243	88.4	32	11.6	0	0.0	239
1978	262	89.7	30	10.3	0	0.0	280
1979	193	86.9	29	13.1	0	0.0	216
1980	295	87.8	41	12.2	0	0.0	332
1981	291	84.6	53	15.4	0	0.0	344
1982	319	88.1	42	11.6	1	0.3	361
1983	259	80.9	58	18.1	3	0.9	320
1984	320	76.2	85	20.2	15	3.6	419
1985	332	71.4	111	23.9	22	4.7	465
1986	384	71.0	130	24.0	27	5.0	541
1987	477	72.4	154	23.4	28	4.2	659
1988	496	74.8	138	20.8	29	4.4	663
1989	743	68.4	281	25.9	62	5.7	1,086
1990	738	68.2	282	26.1	62	5.7	1,082
1991	819	67.2	307	25.2	92	7.6	1,218
1992	932	64.0	431	29.6	93	6.4	1,456
Total patents	7,564		2,266		434		10,264

NOTES: High-intensity incumbents have 10 or more issued patents applied for prior to 1981 and after 1970; low-intensity incumbents have fewer than 10 issued patents applied for prior to 1981 and after 1970; and entrants have no issued patents applied for prior to 1981 and after 1970.

the patents of these experienced academic patenters and the nonacademic patent control sample are most significant for the nonbiomedical patents.

A broadly similar pattern appears in the results of our specifications comparing the generality of the entire sample of patents accounted for by these "high-intensity" incumbents with those in the control sample — all of the interaction coefficients are positive wherever significant, and ten of the seventeen positive interaction coefficients are statistically significant at the 5 percent level. Once again, these differences in generality are more frequently significant for the nonbiomedical patents.

The results of our regressions for the "low-intensity" pre-1981 patenters (Table 7.3) reveal only five years of patents that are more intensively cited (at the 5 percent significance level) than those in the nonacademic control sample. The results of the regressions for generality of their overall patents for

TABLE 7.2

Regression Coefficients for High-Intensity Incumbent × Application Year

Year	Negative binomial model (dependent variable: Importance)			Tobit model (dependent variable: Generality)		
	Overall	Biomed	Nonbiomed	Overall	Biomed	Nonbiomed
1975	0.36**	0.27	0.39**	0.10	0.14	0.08
	(0.11)	(0.21)	(0.13)	(0.13)	(0.27)	(0.16)
1976	0.13	0.29	0.07	0.39**	0.28	0.42**
	(0.11)	(0.22)	(0.12)	(0.13)	(0.27)	(0.15)
1977	0.19*	0.19	0.19	0.15	0.21	0.13
	(0.11)	(0.19)	(0.13)	(0.12)	(0.23)	(0.04)
1978	0.19*	0.41**	0.09	0.30**	0.20	0.35**
	(0.11)	(0.19)	(0.13)	(0.13)	(0.23)	(0.15)
1979	0.27**	0.01	0.40**	0.17	0.38**	0.05
	(0.10)	(0.17)	(0.12)	(0.11)	(0.19)	(0.13)
1980	0.32**	0.20	0.38**	0.23**	0.19	0.23**
	(0.09)	(0.15)	(0.11)	(0.11)	(0.18)	(0.13)
1981	0.38**	0.26*	0.45**	0.45**	0.63**	0.37**
	(0.09)	(0.15)	(0.12)	(0.11)	(0.18)	(0.13)
1982	0.20**	−0.12	0.33**	0.12	−0.51**	0.52**
	(0.09)	(0.15)	(0.12)	(0.10)	(0.17)	(0.13)
1983	0.27**	0.17	0.35**	0.17*	0.00	0.30**
	(0.09)	(0.14)	(0.12)	(0.10)	(0.15)	(0.14)
1984	0.32**	0.04	0.54**	0.15*	0.22*	0.09
	(0.08)	(0.12)	(0.11)	(0.09)	(0.13)	(0.12)
1985	0.31**	0.02	0.54**	0.35**	0.22**	0.43**
	(0.08)	(0.12)	(0.10)	(0.09)	(0.13)	(0.12)
1986	0.37**	0.09	0.57**	0.28**	0.15	0.39**
	(0.08)	(0.11)	(0.10)	(0.08)	(0.13)	(0.11)
1987	0.20**	0.03	0.31**	0.22**	0.25**	0.19**
	(0.06)	(0.10)	(0.08)	(0.07)	(0.11)	(0.09)
1988	0.15**	−0.09	0.29**	0.25**	0.21**	0.27**
	(0.06)	(0.10)	(0.08)	(0.07)	(0.11)	(0.08)
1989	0.29**	0.24**	0.32**	0.17**	0.15	0.18**
	(0.06)	(0.10)	(0.08)	(0.07)	(0.11)	(0.08)
1990	0.28**	0.19*	0.32**	0.10	−0.01	0.15*
	(0.07)	(0.12)	(0.08)	(0.07)	(0.13)	(0.09)
1991	−0.06	−0.23	0.03	0.34**	0.67**	0.20
	(0.10)	(0.18)	(0.12)	(0.11)	(0.20)	(0.13)
Constant	2.10	2.54	1.73	0.22	−0.09	0.96
	(0.19)	(0.63)	(0.46)	(0.22)	(0.90)	(0.51)
Number of observations	15125	5569	9556	11716	4313	7403
Log likelihood	−36170	−13280	−22836	−12468	−4456	−7939
Pseudo R^2	0.02	0.01	0.02	0.01	0.01	0.01

NOTES: Standard errors in parentheses. Year dummies not reported. Sample excludes patents from the University of California, Stanford, and Columbia. ** $p < 0.05$ * $p < 0.10$

TABLE 7.3

Regression Coefficients for Low-Intensity Incumbent × Application Year

Year	Negative binomial model (dependent variable: Importance)			Tobit model (dependent variable: Generality)		
	Overall	Biomed	Nonbiomed	Overall	Biomed	Nonbiomed
1975	0.65**	0.38	0.71**	−0.30	−1.01	−0.15
	(0.32)	(0.77)	(0.34)	(0.35)	(0.84)	(0.38)
1976	−0.11	−0.49	0.24	0.84**	1.85**	0.23
	(0.33)	(0.55)	(0.42)	(0.39)	(0.69)	(0.49)
1977	0.63**	1.69**	0.45	0.36	—	0.19
	(0.30)	(0.67)	(0.34)	(0.33)		(0.37)
1978	0.01	0.18	−0.05	−0.29	−0.15	−0.35
	(0.27)	(0.47)	(0.32)	(0.29)	(0.57)	(0.33)
1979	0.66**	0.35	0.79**	0.62**	0.69	0.59*
	(0.25)	(0.45)	(0.30)	(0.29)	(0.54)	(0.34)
1980	0.35	0.13	0.51*	−0.01	0.23	0.14
	(0.24)	(0.38)	(0.31)	(0.25)	(0.41)	(0.31)
1981	−0.12	−0.15	−0.10	0.31	1.01**	0.00
	(0.20)	(0.34)	(0.26)	(0.22)	(0.40)	(0.27)
1982	−0.06	−0.21	0.10	0.38**	0.35	0.42*
	(0.18)	(0.25)	(0.25)	(0.18)	(0.25)	(0.26)
1983	0.16	0.50*	0.03	0.18	0.63**	0.02
	(0.15)	(0.27)	(0.18)	(0.16)	(0.32)	(0.19)
1984	−0.18	−0.25	−0.11	0.04	−0.13	0.19
	(0.15)	(0.22)	(0.20)	(0.16)	(0.24)	(0.22)
1985	−0.05	−0.04	−0.06	−0.07	−0.19	0.00
	(0.14)	(0.23)	(0.18)	(0.16)	(0.25)	(0.19)
1986	0.40**	0.38**	0.41**	0.41**	0.38**	0.43**
	(0.13)	(0.19)	(0.17)	(0.14)	(0.20)	(0.19)
1987	0.11	0.04	0.15	0.28**	0.06	0.40**
	(0.11)	(0.19)	(0.14)	(0.12)	(0.20)	(0.15)
1988	0.17*	0.02	0.24**	0.15	0.15	0.16
	(0.10)	(0.17)	(0.12)	(0.10)	(0.18)	(0.12)
1989	0.38**	0.22	0.46**	0.29**	0.26	0.29**
	(0.10)	(0.17)	(0.11)	(0.10)	(0.18)	(0.12)
1990	0.15*	0.17	0.14	0.20**	−0.05	0.29**
	(0.09)	(0.18)	(0.11)	(0.10)	(0.18)	(0.11)
1991	0.11	−0.19	0.28	0.53**	0.38	0.57**
	(0.16)	(0.30)	(0.18)	(0.16)	(0.31)	(0.19)
Constant	1.10	2.30	−16.41	0.69	0.67	0.20
	(0.38)	(1.13)	(3661.49)	(0.38)	(1.01)	(0.52)
Number of Observations	4535	1627	2908	3528	1242	2286
Log Likelihood	−10980	−3893	−7056	−3745	−1285	−2436
Pseudo R^2	0.01	0.01	0.01	0.01	0.02	0.01

NOTES: Standard errors in parentheses. Year dummies not reported. Sample excludes patents from the University of California, Stanford, and Columbia. ** p < 0.05 * p < 0.10

this group of institutions yield positive and statistically significant (at the 5 percent significance level) year-coefficients for eight of the seventeen years. Finally, the results for 1981–91 for the entrant population of institutions also indicate lower levels of importance (only one year interaction is positive and statistically significant at the 5 percent level in Table 7.4) and generality (also one significant interaction coefficient), relative to nonacademic patents, than those accounted for by the "high-intensity" pre-1981 patenters.

These results broadly corroborate our findings in Chapter 6 concerning the

TABLE 7.4

Regression Coefficients for Entrant University × Application Year

Year	Negative binomial model (dependent variable: Importance)			Tobit model (dependent variable: Generality)		
	Overall	Biomed	Nonbiomed	Overall	Biomed	Nonbiomed
1981	0.39	0.51	0.18	0.38	0.35	
	(0.51)	(0.81)	(0.68)	(0.57)	(0.78)	—
1982	0.80	1.56*	0.11	−0.81	−0.42	−1.09
	(0.56)	(0.86)	(0.72)	(0.54)	(0.77)	(0.74)
1983	0.18	0.53	−0.20	−0.53	0.18	−0.95**
	(0.36)	(0.60)	(0.44)	(0.34)	(0.52)	(0.44)
1984	−0.19	−0.28	−0.03	−0.11	0.00	−0.22
	(0.32)	(0.44)	(0.45)	(0.32)	(0.39)	(0.49)
1985	−0.03	−0.63	0.11	0.06	−0.72	0.33
	(0.35)	(0.65)	(0.40)	(0.35)	(0.61)	(0.45)
1986	0.23	0.12	0.29	0.28	0.49	0.13
	(0.29)	(0.48)	(0.35)	(0.28)	(0.42)	(0.37)
1987	−0.16	−0.62**	0.50*	0.35	0.33	0.37
	(0.23)	(0.31)	(0.31)	(0.22)	(0.27)	(0.33)
1988	0.19	−0.20	0.46*	0.37*	0.30	0.43
	(0.23)	(0.34)	(0.29)	(0.21)	(0.31)	(0.28)
1989	0.51**	0.11	0.85**	0.51**	0.56**	0.44
	(0.19)	(0.26)	(0.25)	(0.18)	(0.3)	(0.27)
1990	0.26	0.10	0.47**	0.19	0.27	0.10
	(0.20)	(0.28)	(0.28)	(0.20)	(0.26)	(0.29)
1991	0.32	0.53	0.24	0.38	0.31	0.42
	(0.32)	(0.55)	(0.38)	(0.20)	(0.50)	(0.38)
Constant	1.70	1.32	0.25	−0.52	1.36	1.46
	(0.83)	(0.59)	(0.52)	(0.42)	(0.67)	(0.80)
Number of Observations	868	367	501	666	284	382
Log Likelihood	−2105	−919	−1163	−700	−290	−399
Pseudo R^2	0.01	0.02	0.02	0.03	0.04	0.04

NOTES: Standard errors in parentheses. Year dummies not reported. Sample excludes patents from the University of California, Stanford, and Columbia. ** $p < 0.05$ * $p < 0.10$

importance and generality of post-1980 patents issuing to the University of California and Stanford University. Taken together, these results indicate that any deterioration in the importance and quality of overall U.S. academic patents after 1980 may have resulted from the Bayh-Dole Act's encouragement of entry into patenting by academic institutions with relatively little experience in this activity.[5]

INSTITUTIONAL EXPERIENCE, LEARNING, AND THE CHARACTERISTICS OF UNIVERSITY PATENTS, 1981–92

Why might universities with less experience in patenting and licensing tend to receive patents that are less heavily cited? Conversations with licensing officers at several research universities and other field research suggested the possibility that inexperienced universities adopted an indiscriminate policy toward patenting as they entered into this activity after passage of the Bayh-Dole Act. In this view, many entrant universities sought patents for faculty inventions with little evaluation of the market for licenses for these inventions. As these entrant institutions encountered rising costs and stagnant licensing revenues, many of them became more selective in their patenting activities. Other research showing a correlation between licensing revenues and citations for licensed university patents (Sampat and Ziedonis, 2003, and the work cited therein discuss the links between citations and other measures of the private economic value of patents) suggests that patents that are more heavily cited are more likely to yield positive licensing revenues.

Accordingly, the analysis in this section tests the possibility that entrant universities, possibly motivated by the prospect of higher licensing revenues, gradually became more selective in their patenting activities, effectively "learning to patent." Any such increase in the selectivity of their patenting should be revealed in shifts in the patent portfolios of entrant universities to include more heavily cited patents. Our analysis in this section examines post-Bayh-Dole patents issued to all institutions designated as Research or Doctoral Universities in the Carnegie Commission on Higher Education's 1973 and 1993 reports (Carnegie Commission on Higher Education, 1973, 1993). Specifically, our dataset includes the 10,881 patents issued to these universities that were applied for between 1981 and 1992 and granted before 1994. We compare these patents to one another and to a matched control sample of patents, constructed as in the previous section.[6] Our analysis tests for any narrowing during the 1981–92 period in the gaps in importance between the patents of more and less experienced pre-1980 academic patenters.

138   We construct measures of the "importance" of these patents based on counts of citations to these patents appearing within five years of their issue dates. Limiting the citation window to five years (rather than six years, as in the previous section) enables us to increase the number of "patent cohorts" in our analysis, which is desirable since "learning to patent" presumably takes time.[7] We also exclude "self-citations" (that is, citations by an assignee of its previous patents), which may be less accurate indicators of the importance of a patent than citations by others.

Specification

We first compare the number of citations to academic patents with the citations to patents in our nonacademic control sample. The count nature of the dependent variable makes it necessary to utilize a negative binomial specification in this and related analyses.[8] Our base specification includes dummy variables for application year cohorts (1981–83, 1984–86, 1987–89, and 1990–92), university patents applied for in these years ($UNIV_{8183}$, $UNIV_{8486}$, $UNIV_{8789}$, and $UNIV_{9092}$), and patent classes. The patent class dummy variables span the 303 classes in our sample.

The next step in our analysis is a comparison of the importance of academic patents with patents in our nonacademic control sample. Next, we test for differences in average citation rates of entrant universities' patents with those issued to incumbent universities and with our nonacademic control patents by inserting additional dummy variables denoting patents assigned to entrant universities in these application-year cohorts (ENT_{8183}, ENT_{8486}, ENT_{8789}, and ENT_{9092}). Finally, to assess whether our various "learning mechanisms" influence the characteristics of patents issued to entrant universities, we identify three characteristics of entrant universities: (1) the existence of a contractual relationship with the Research Corporation, (2) above-median levels of cumulative 1980–86 patenting, and (3) the assignment of at least a single half-time employee (0.5 FTE) to formal technology transfer activities during 1980–86. We also include a set of dummy variables indicating patents assigned to experienced entrants in each application-year cohort ($EXPENT_{8183}$, $EXPENT_{8486}$, $EXPENT_{8789}$, and $EXPENT_{9092}$) to compare the number of citations to the patents of entrant universities with each of these characteristics with those of patents assigned to entrants lacking these characteristics. A more detailed discussion of our econometric specifications is contained in the appendix to this chapter.

Table 7.5 reports results of negative binomial regressions for the full sample of university and control group patents. Table 7.6 reports similar results for biomedical patents only, and Table 7.7 reports results for nonbiomedical patents. In each table, Model 1 represents the base specification, which includes application year and class dummies, as well as the *UNIV* dummy variables ($UNIV_{8183}$–$UNIV_{9092}$). Model 2 adds the *ENT* dummy variables, and Models 3–5 separately add each of the sets of *EXPENT* dummy variables. Table 7.8 reports results from Wald tests of entrant university patent importance relative to control group patent importance for Model 2 (see the appendix for the description of these tests). For expositional clarity, we do not report coefficients for the application year and patent class dummy variables.

We first compare the importance of patents assigned to incumbent and entrant universities during the early post-Bayh-Dole period (1981–86) and separately examine biomedical and nonbiomedical patents from these universities during this period. We then analyze changes in the importance of patents issued to entrant universities during the 1980s and consider sources of learning that could explain observed improvements.

Do Post-1980 Entrants Have Less Important Patents Than Incumbents During 1981–86?

We assess incumbent-entrant differentials in patent importance by examining the coefficients for *ENT* reported in Model 2 of Table 7.5. In this section, we compare the importance of incumbent-university patents with that of entrant-university patents for patents applied for during 1981–86. The negative and significant coefficients in Table 7.5 for 1981–83 and 1984–86 suggest that entrant universities received less important patents than incumbent universities in the early 1980s. The point estimates of the ratio of citations to entrants' patents to citations to incumbents' patents are 0.82 and 0.80 in 1981–83 and 1984–86, respectively, indicating that incumbent-university patents applied for during 1981–83 and 1984–86 received 20 percent and 25 percent more citations than entrant-university patents applied for during these periods.[9]

Biomedical patent results are reported in Table 7.6, and nonbiomedical patent results are reported in Table 7.7. The coefficients in Model 2 of Table 7.6 indicate that entrants' biomedical patents did not receive a significantly different number of citations than incumbents' patents applied for during 1981–83 and 1984–86.[10] Thus, for biomedical technologies, there is little evidence that incumbents received more important patents than entrants in the first six years following Bayh-Dole.

The analysis of nonbiomedical patents, however, reveals significant differences in importance between entrant- and incumbent-university patents

TABLE 7.5

Regression Coefficients for All Patents (1981–92 Sample):
Negative Binomial Model, Dependent Variable = Number of Citations

Variables	Model 1	Model 2	Model 3	Model 4	Model 5
			Add EXPENT$_T$ to Model 2		
	Base model	Add ENT$_T$ to base model	For entrants who were active RC clients	For entrants with above median patenting in 1981–86	For entrants with early establishment of TLOs
UNIV$_{8183}$	0.237	0.262	0.262		
	(5.31)**	(5.66)**	(5.66)**		
UNIV$_{8486}$	0.207	0.246	0.246		
	(5.56)**	(6.25)**	(6.26)**		
UNIV$_{8789}$	0.193	0.188	0.188	0.189	0.189
	(6.78)**	(6.13)**	(6.13)**	(6.14)**	(6.15)**
UNIV$_{9092}$	0.261	0.249	0.249	0.255	0.255
	(9.98)**	(8.73)**	(8.73)**	(8.94)**	(8.94)**
ENT$_{8183}$		−0.190	−0.095		
		(2.07)*	(0.46)		
ENT$_{8486}$		−0.218	−0.166		
		(3.19)**	(1.22)		
ENT$_{8789}$		0.022	−0.161	0.104	0.172
		(0.47)	(1.55)	(1.63)	(2.83)**
ENT$_{9092}$		0.044	0.134	0.110	0.021
		(1.07)	(1.26)	(2.02)*	(0.42)
EXPENT$_{8183}$			−0.116		
			(0.52)		
EXPENT$_{8486}$			−0.068		
			(0.45)		
EXPENT$_{8789}$			0.217	−0.183	−0.368
			(1.95)	(2.22)*	(4.46)**
EXPENT$_{9092}$			0.102	−0.157	0.038
			(0.91)	(2.20)*	(0.52)
Constant	0.834	0.818	0.806	1.384	1.351
	(3.20)	(1.47)	(1.50)	(1.82)	(1.35)
N	21,455	21,455	21,455	14,554	14,554

NOTES: Absolute value of z-statistics in parentheses. Application year dummy variables and patent class dummy variables included in all specifications (not reported). Coefficient for UNIV$_T$ is β_T; coefficient for ENT$_T$ is δ_T; coefficient for EXPENT$_T$ is ϕ_T (see appendix). * significant at 5% level ** significant at 1% level

applied for during the 1984–86 period. In Table 7.7, entrants' patents receive significantly fewer citations than incumbents' patents in each of the two cohorts of patents applied for before 1987 (see below for more discussion of improvements in the importance of entrants' patents during the later 1980s).[11]

The fact that incumbents enjoy a greater "importance advantage" for

TABLE 7.6

Regression Coefficients for Biomedical Patents (1981–92 Sample):
Negative Binomial Model, Dependent Variable = Number of Citations

Variables	Model 1 Base model	Model 2 Add ENT_T to base model	Model 3 For entrants who were active RC clients	Model 4 For entrants with above median patenting in 1981–86	Model 5 For entrants with early establishment of TLOs
			Add $EXPENT_T$ to Model 2		
$UNIV_{8183}$	0.175	0.153	0.153		
	(2.24)*	(1.86)	(1.87)		
$UNIV_{8486}$	0.070	0.092	0.092		
	(1.14)	(1.40)	(1.40)		
$UNIV_{8789}$	−0.004	−0.007	−0.007	−0.014	−0.014
	(0.07)	(0.13)	(0.13)	(0.25)	(0.26)
$UNIV_{9092}$	0.220	0.193	0.194	0.195	0.195
	(4.69)**	(3.82)**	(3.82)**	(3.80)**	(3.79)**
ENT_{8183}		0.131	0.452		
		(0.88)	(1.41)		
ENT_{8486}		−0.105	0.091		
		(0.98)	(0.47)		
ENT_{8789}		0.015	−0.079	0.033	0.107
		(0.17)	(0.43)	(0.27)	(0.85)
ENT_{9092}		0.102	0.226	0.215	0.097
		(1.33)	(1.30)	(2.02)*	(0.91)
$EXPENT_{8183}$			−0.403		
			(1.16)		
$EXPENT_{8486}$			−0.270		
			(1.24)		
$EXPENT_{8789}$			0.112	−0.028	−0.152
			(0.58)	(0.18)*	(0.99)
$EXPENT_{9092}$			−0.148	−0.194	0.028
			(0.81)	(1.44)	(0.21)
Constant	0.920	0.925	0.924	1.135	1.133
	(4.14)	(3.01)	(4.15)	(3.85)	(3.85)
N	7,383	7,383	7,383	4,823	4,823

NOTES: Absolute value of z-statistics in parentheses. Application year dummy variables and patent class dummy variables included in all specifications (not reported). Coefficient for $UNIV_T$ is β_T; coefficient for ENT_T is δ_T; coefficient for $EXPENT_T$ is ϕ_T (see appendix). * significant at 5% level ** significant at 1% level

nonbiomedical technologies than biomedical technologies during the first six years after Bayh-Dole may indicate that patenting experience is less important in biomedical fields. This hypothesis receives modest support in Chapter 4, which argued that Research Corporation client institutions (all of whom had little experience in patenting) were more successful at "cherry-picking" biomedical patents than nonbiomedical patents. These results also are consistent

TABLE 7.7

Regression Coefficients for Nonbiomedical Patents (1981–92 Sample):
Negative Binomial Model, Dependent Variable = Number of Citations

Variables	Model 1 Base model	Model 2 Add ENT_T to base model	Model 3 For entrants who were active RC clients	Model 4 For entrants with above median patenting in 1981–86	Model 5 For entrants with early establishment of TLOs
			Add EXPENT$_T$ to Model 2		
$UNIV_{8183}$	0.268	0.315	0.315		
	(4.97)**	(5.64)**	(5.65)**		
$UNIV_{8486}$	0.290	0.333	0.333		
	(6.21)**	(6.81)**	(6.82)**		
$UNIV_{8789}$	0.286	0.280	0.280	0.282	0.282
	(8.39)**	(7.64)**	(7.65)**	(7.73)**	(7.74)**
$UNIV_{9092}$	0.286	0.279	0.279	0.288	0.288
	(9.10)**	(8.12)**	(8.12)**	(8.41)**	(8.41)**
ENT_{8183}		−0.418	−0.596		
		(3.54)**	(2.11)*		
ENT_{8486}		−0.274	−0.431		
		(3.06)**	(2.19)*		
ENT_{8789}		0.024	−0.198	0.114	0.163
		(0.43)	(1.56)	(1.54)	(2.37)**
ENT_{9092}		0.024	0.042	0.076	0.005
		(0.48)	(0.31)	(1.22)	(0.08)
$EXPENT_{8183}$			0.211		
			(0.69)		
$EXPENT_{8486}$			0.189		
			(0.88)		
$EXPENT_{8789}$			0.261	−0.224	−0.421
			(1.93)	(2.30)*	(4.23)**
$EXPENT_{9092}$			−0.019	−0.160	0.002
			(0.14)	(1.91)*	(0.03)
Constant	0.869	0.848	0.839	1.36	1.32
	(3.39)	(3.31)	(3.27)	(4.02)	(3.90)
N	14,072	14,072	14,072	9,731	9,731

NOTES: Absolute value of z-statistics in parentheses. Application year dummy variables and patent class dummy variables included in all specifications (not reported). Coefficient for $UNIV_T$ is β_T; coefficient for ENT_T is δ_T; coefficient for $EXPENT_T$ is ϕ_T (see appendix). * significant at 5% level ** significant at 1% level

with Chapter 6's analysis of citations to UC and Stanford biomedical and non-biomedical patents before and After Bayh-Dole.

Does the Importance of Entrant-University Patents Improve After 1986?

Our analysis thus far suggests that post-Bayh-Dole entrants into academic patenting received less important patents, on average, during the 1981–86 period than did more experienced incumbents. If their lack of institutional experience in patenting is responsible for the lower importance of entrant universities' patents, then expanded patenting by these universities could result in institutional learning that narrowed the differentials between more and less experienced institutional patenters. Learning by entrants could also improve the importance of entrants' patents relative to the control patents. Accordingly, in this section we test for changes during the 1980s and early 1990s in the "importance differential" between entrants' and incumbents' patents and between entrants' and control-groups' patents.

Within our overall sample (Table 7.5), the importance of entrants' patents was significantly lower than the importance of incumbents' patents for patents applied for during 1981–86 (Model 2), but these differentials are statistically insignificant for patents applied for during 1987–92. Nonbiomedical patents, where the incumbent-entrant importance differential was most pronounced during the 1981–86 period, display similar changes in importance (Model 2 of Table 7.7). These findings suggest that in nonbiomedical fields, where the initial post-Bayh-Dole patent importance differences were most significant, entrant institutions narrowed the gap in importance between their patents and those of incumbent institutions for patents applied for during 1987–92.

We also examined changes in the "importance differentials" between entrant university patents and control group patents and report these results in Table 7.8. The results in Table 7.8 suggest that entrant-university patents were not significantly more highly cited than control-group patents during the early post-Bayh-Dole period (Wald test statistics are not significant for the patents applied for in either the 1981–83 or 1984–86 period). Wald statistics also are not significant in separate tests for differences in importance between

TABLE 7.8

$(UNIV_T + ENT_T)$ Coefficients (1981–92 Sample): Negative Binomial
Model, Dependent Variable = Number of Citations

Sample	Full sample, controls	Biomedical patents, controls	Nonbiomedical patents, controls
1981–83	0.072	0.284	−0.103
	(.62)	(3.73)	(0.77)
1984–86	0.028	−0.013	0.059
	(.16)	(.02)	(0.43)
1987–89	0.21	0.008	0.304
	(21.27)**	(0.01)	(31.34)**
1990–92	0.293	0.295	0.303
	(54.05)**	(16.04)**	(41.10)**

NOTES: Coefficient for $UNIV_T$ is β_T; coefficient for ENT_T is δ_T. Chi-square statistics for Wald tests of $(\beta_T + \delta_T = 0)$ in parentheses (see appendix). * significant at 5% level
** significant at 1% level

entrants' and incumbents' biomedical patents and for these groups' nonbio-medical patents. But entrant-university patents applied for during 1987–89 and 1990–92 were more highly cited on average than the corresponding control group patents for both the overall sample and the nonbiomedical sub-sample. Entrant biomedical patents applied for during 1990–92 were also more highly cited than the corresponding control group patents.

Overall, these data suggest that the "importance" of incumbent-university and entrant-university patents applied for during the later 1980s and early 1990s converged to a considerable extent. Moreover, this convergence reflects improvement in the importance of entrants' patents, rather than declines in the importance of incumbents' patents.[12] Convergence is most marked for nonbiomedical technologies, where the differences between the importance of incumbents' and entrants' patents applied for during 1981–86 were greatest. In most of our specifications, the importance of entrants' patents also improved relative to that of the nonacademic controls in the later cohorts of patents (those applied for after 1986). Taken together, these results suggest that entrant universities do indeed seem to have learned to patent during the 1980s.

Sources of Entrant Learning

What factors influenced the ability of entrant universities to "learn to patent" after 1980? A number of post-1980 entrants into patenting had been clients of the Research Corporation prior to 1980, and by the 1960s the Research Corporation had begun to train its institutional clients to identify inventions that were the best candidates for patenting and licensing (see Chapter 4). We therefore tested the hypothesis that "active" clients of the Research Corporation in the 1970s (that is, those that submitted five or more disclosures to the Research Corporation in any one year during that decade) received more important patents than other entrants during the first six years after the passage of the Bayh-Dole Act.

Another potential source of improvement in the importance of entrants' patents in the post-Bayh-Dole period is learning from cumulative institutional experience in patenting. If the relevant learning results from higher volumes of patenting activity, then entrants that patented more intensively during 1981–86 might obtain more important patents, on average, after 1986 than would entrant institutions with less patenting experience during the 1981–86 period. To test this hypothesis, we analyzed differences in patent importance between entrants receiving more than the median number of entrant-university patents during the 1981–86 period and other entrants.

Finally, the establishment of a formal technology licensing office (TLO) and the hiring of licensing professionals may have contributed to improvements in the importance of entrant universities' patents after 1980. We tested the hypothesis that "early entrants" (institutions that established TLOs during the first six years after the passage of the Bayh-Dole Act) acquired "higher-importance" patents, on average, than entrants that were slower to establish formal TLOs. We compared the importance of patents assigned to entrants who reported that at least one 0.5 FTE was employed in technology transfer activities prior to 1986 with the importance of patents assigned to entrant universities that had not established such technology transfer offices by that date.

As we noted earlier, the coefficient for *EXPENT* measures the difference in importance between patents issued to experienced entrants and those issued to less experienced entrants in a given period. Model 3 in Tables 7.5–7 reports the *EXPENT* variables' coefficients for entrants who were active clients of the Research Corporation before 1980 and for other entrants in each period from 1981–83 to 1990–92. The existence of a contractual relationship with the Research Corporation before 1980 is not associated with improvement in the importance of entrants' patents during the 1980s. The *EXPENT* coefficients in Column 3 for the overall sample are not significant in any period (Table 7.5). Similarly, the biomedical and nonbiomedical subsamples (Tables 7.6 and 7.7) provide no evidence that entrants who were active clients have more important patents than other entrants after Bayh-Dole.

The reasons for the Research Corporation's lack of influence on improvement in client firms' patents after 1980 are unclear. One reason could be the lack of incentives for selectivity by client universities in their submission of inventions to the Research Corporation for patenting and licensing. Research Corporation client universities bore no costs under Invention Administration Agreements (IAAs) with the corporation (Chapter 4) and therefore lacked any incentives to select commercially promising inventions during the 1960s and 1970s. It is also possible that their "outsourcing" of patent management activities to the Research Corporation prevented client universities from acquiring these skills.

A second source of learning discussed above is cumulative patenting ("learning by doing"). In Model 4 of Tables 7.5–7, *EXPENT* is set equal to 1 for all entrants with an above-median number of patents within the entrant population applied for during the 1981–86 period.[13] *EXPENT* in Model 4 measures differences between the importance of patents applied for after 1986 by entrants that received an "above-median" number of patents during 1981–86 and the importance of patents applied for during these years by entrants with a "below-median" number of patents for 1981–86. Surprisingly, the post-1986 patents issued to entrants with greater patenting experience in the 1981–

86 period tended to receive fewer citations, on average, than did other entrants' patents.

For the full sample, patents issued to more experienced entrants during 1987–89 and 1990–92 received significantly fewer citations than did the patents issued to less experienced entrants during these periods (Model 4 of Table 7.5). Similarly, within the biomedical and nonbiomedical subsamples, there is no evidence that entrants with higher levels of pre-1987 patenting had more important patents after 1987, as the "learning curve" hypothesis would imply. These findings suggest that cumulative experience in patenting does not account for the improvements in importance of entrants' patents observed after the mid-1980s.

Finally, we examined the effects on the importance of entrants' patents of the establishment after 1980 of formal TLOs. Using Association of University Technology Managers (AUTM, 1994) data, we coded $EXPENT$ to equal 1 for entrant universities that had established a formal TLO (that is, reported allocating at least one 0.5 FTE to the management of technology transfer, patenting, and licensing activities) by 1986. The results of our analysis of the effects of establishing a TLO during 1981–86 on the importance of entrants' post-1986 patents are reported in Model 5 in Tables 7.5–7. Table 7.5 suggests that for the overall sample of patents, early establishment of a TLO did not improve patent importance relative to entrants that did not establish TLOs prior to 1987. The $EXPENT_{8789}$ coefficient is negative and significant in Table 7.5, and the coefficient for $EXPENT_{9092}$ is not significant. For biomedical technologies, the coefficient for $EXPENT_{8789}$ is not significant in Table 7.6. For nonbiomedical technologies, the $EXPENT_{8789}$ coefficient is negative and significant, and the coefficient for $EXPENT_{9092}$ is not significant in Table 7.7.

These results suggest that early establishment of a TLO after Bayh-Dole was not correlated with receiving more important patents during the 1987–92 period. Indeed, the establishment of a TLO during 1980–86 actually is associated with less important patents during the 1987–89 period. Although not definitive, these findings are consistent with anecdotal evidence that some universities initially assigned persons with little knowledge or skill in patent and licensing management to these activities when they established formal TLOs and that simply bestowing the title of technology licensing officer on an inexperienced administrator was not sufficient to generate important patents. In some cases, the establishment of a formal office of technology licensing may have been an outcome, rather than a cause, of "learning to patent."

Although we are not able to test for their effects, other forms of organizational learning may have enabled entrants to improve the importance of their patents. Organizations can learn from the experiences of others directly (for example, consulting, personnel transfer, and conferences) and indirectly (for example, monitoring of others and informal discussions with colleagues). Both of these channels appear to have been important means for entrant universities to learn to manage patenting and licensing. For example, Niels Reimers, founder of Stanford University's Office of Technology Licensing in 1969, served as a consultant to a number of entrant and incumbent universities' TLOs during the 1980s and disseminated information on procedures that were successful at Stanford to other institutions.

Anecdotal evidence of personnel transfer among universities suggests another channel for interinstitutional knowledge diffusion and learning. In the late 1980s, Columbia University recruited the former director of the technology transfer program at Iowa State University, an institution with a long history of patenting. The AUTM, founded in the mid-1970s, also appears to have disseminated information on "best practice" through its conferences and professional meetings of university technology transfer personnel.

Entrant universities also learned from informal communication and interaction within the broader community of technology licensing officials during the 1980s. Following an initial wave of less selective patenting during 1981–85, Columbia University adopted the practice of patenting only when a probable licensee could be located, based on guidance from other institutions with greater experience in patenting.[14] Columbia's adoption of this and other policies resulted from informal discussions with directors of other university TLOs. Similar informal communications and interactions may have contributed to improvements in the "quality" of entrants' patents during the 1980s and early 1990s.

Indeed, from the earliest days of their involvement in patenting and licensing, U.S. universities have drawn on and learned from the experiences of others in selecting the inventions they sought to patent and in the overall management of patenting and licensing activities (Chapter 3; Sampat and Nelson 2002). This trend appears to have continued after Bayh-Dole; Feldman et al. (2002) suggest that universities have emulated one another in the use of equity investments as part of their technology transfer strategies during the 1990s. Seen against these historical and contemporary accounts, it would be surprising if universities did not "learn to patent" via informal channels, professional networks, and other mechanisms.

CONCLUSION

This chapter's empirical analysis of overall U.S. academic patenting before and after 1980 yields conclusions that are consistent with the results of the

148   analysis of UC, Stanford, and Columbia patenting presented in Chapter 6. Specifically, we find no decline in the importance and generality of the post-1980 patents assigned to universities with substantial pre-1980 patent portfolios. But the patents of institutions with little or no previous history were not significantly more important or general than nonacademic patents. We also examined the changing characteristics of the patents assigned to entrant and incumbent university patenters during the post-Bayh-Dole period in an effort to determine the existence and scope of improvements in the importance of entrant universities' patents.

Our results provide little evidence to support an argument that change in U.S. universities' internal "research culture" after Bayh-Dole triggered a decline in the importance of academic patents, at least for the first fourteen years following the passage of the Act. This finding does not rule out the possibility, however, that such changes in the academic research culture may be occurring gradually and could eventually be revealed in declines in these measures of academic patents' importance.

Although our analysis seems to suggest that universities can indeed learn to patent, the sources of such learning are not clear. Cumulative patenting experience, historical relationships with the nonprofit Research Corporation, and the allocation of administrative talent to formally designated technology transfer activities all fail to explain improvement over time in the importance of the patents in this group of universities. All of these measures of sources of learning are flawed, but their lack of significance suggests that a more diffuse learning process may underpin our results.

Appendix

Derivation of the Econometric Specifications Used to Test for "Learning" in Academic Patenting

In this appendix, we describe in more detail the econometric specifications outlined in the section of the chapter dealing with "Institutional Experience, Learning, and the Characteristics of University Patents, 1981–92." The dependent variable in our analysis is the number of citations received by a patent. We utilize negative binomial regressions to work with this "count" dependent variable. The conditional mean of the negative binomial citation function for our basic specification is:

$$E(Citations|App_t, UNIV, Class_c)$$
$$= \exp\{\Sigma_t[\alpha_t App_t + \beta_t(App_t * UNIV)] + \Sigma_c \gamma_c Class_c\} \quad (1)$$

where App_t is a dummy variable that equals 1 for all patents with application year t, $UNIV$ is a dummy variable that equals 1 for all university patents, $Class_c$ is a dummy variable that equals 1 for all patents in patent class c, and α_t, β_t, and γ_t are coefficients. Our reported results aggregate the application year dummy variables into four groups: $t = 8183$, $t = 8486$, $t = 8789$, and $t = 9092$ for application years 1981–83, 1984–86, 1987–89, and 1990–92, respectively.[15] The patent class dummy variables span the 303 classes in our sample.

The conditional mean for the number of citations to the sample of non-academic control patents in year $t = T$ is:

$$E(Citations|Control\ Sample) = E(Citations|App_T = 1, UNIV = 0, Class_c)$$
$$= \exp(\alpha_T + \Sigma_c \gamma_c Class_c) \quad (2)$$

Similarly, the conditional mean for the number of citations to university patents in year $t = T$ is:

$$E(Citations|University\ Sample) = E(Citations|App_T = 1, UNIV = 1, Class_c)$$
$$= \exp(\alpha_T + \beta_T + \Sigma_c \gamma_c Class_c) \quad (3)$$

The ratio of equations (2) and (1) is the "proportional difference" between the number of citations to academic patents and the number of citations to the control patents in year T, or $\exp(\beta_T)$. We test for differences between the number of citations to university and control group patents in year T by testing whether $\beta_T = 0$. Such a test indicates whether academic patents applied for in year T received significantly more citations than the corresponding sample of nonacademic control patents applied for in that year.

To compare the importance of entrant universities' patents with those issued to incumbent universities and with our nonacademic control patents, we insert a dummy variable, ENT, that identifies entrant universities in equation (1), making the conditional mean function:

$$E(Citations|App_t, UNIV, ENT, Class_c)$$
$$= \exp\left\{ \begin{array}{l} \Sigma_t[\alpha_t App_t + \beta_t(App_t * UNIV) \\ + \delta_t(App_t * ENT)] + \Sigma_c \gamma_c Class_c \end{array} \right\} \quad (4)$$

where ENT equals 1 for all entrant universities and zero for incumbent universities and controls, and δ_t is the coefficient for the App_t*ENT interaction term. Equations (5–7), respectively, calculate the mean number of citations to patents in the entrant, incumbent, and control patent samples for the application year $t = T$:

$$E(Citations|Entrant)$$
$$= E(Citations|App_T = 1, UNIV = 1, ENT = 1, Class_c)$$
$$= \exp(\alpha_T + \beta_T + \delta_T + \Sigma_c \gamma_c Class_c) \quad (5)$$

$$E(Citations|Incumbent)$$
$$= E(Citations|App_T = 1, UNIV = 1, ENT = 0, Class_c)$$
$$= \exp(\alpha_T + \beta_T + \Sigma_c \gamma_c Class_c) \quad (6)$$

$$E(Citations|Control\ Sample)$$
$$= E(Citations|App_T = 1, UNIV = 0, ENT = 0, Class_c)$$
$$= \exp(\alpha_T + \Sigma_c \gamma_c Class_c) \quad (7)$$

Dividing equation (5) by equation (6) yields the proportional difference between the number of citations to issued patents applied for by entrants and citations to those applied for by incumbents in year $t = T$, or $\exp(\delta_T)$. Similarly, the ratio of equations (6) and (7) is the proportional difference in citations between incumbent and control patents $(\exp(\beta_T))$, and the ratio of equations (5) and (7) is the proportional difference in citations between entrants and control patents, or $\exp(\beta_T + \delta_T)$. Testing for the significance of the first two differences $(\exp(\delta_T)$ and $(\exp(\beta_T))$ requires a standard Z-test. We use a Wald test of the linear restriction $\beta_T + \delta_T = 0$ to analyze the difference in citation rates between entrant and control sample patents.

To assess whether our various "learning mechanisms" influence the characteristics of patents issued to entrant universities, we constructed three dummy variables, *EXPENT*, that each equal 1 for experienced entrants corresponding to: (1) the existence of a contractual relationship with the Research Corporation, (2) above-median levels of cumulative 1980–86 patenting, and (3) the assignment of at least one 0.5 FTE to formal technology transfer activities during 1980–86. Adding *EXPENT* and the coefficient ϕ_t to equation (4) yields the following conditional mean function:

$$E(Citations | App_t, UNIV, ENT, EXPENT, Class_c)$$

$$= \exp \left\{ \begin{array}{l} \Sigma_t [\alpha_t App_t + \beta_t (App_t * UNIV) \\ + \delta_t (App_t * ENT) \\ + \phi_t (App_t * EXPENT)] \\ + \Sigma_c \gamma_c Class_c \end{array} \right\} \tag{8}$$

The proportional difference in the number of citations to patents applied for by experienced entrants and those applied for by other entrants in year $t = T$ therefore is $\exp(\phi_t)$.

8

WHAT HAPPENS IN UNIVERSITY-INDUSTRY TECHNOLOGY TRANSFER?

Evidence from Five Case Studies

Robert A. Lowe, David C. Mowery,
and Bhaven N. Sampat

Thus far, much of our discussion of university-industry technology transfer in this volume has highlighted trends in various quantitative indicators of research collaboration and technology transfer. But these indicators are less revealing about the characteristics of the process of technology transfer between universities and industry. And as we have noted in Chapter 5 and elsewhere, the framers and supporters of the Bayh-Dole Act held specific assumptions about this process and, in particular, about the role of patents and licenses within it. In order to provide a richer and more detailed account of the technology transfer process, this chapter presents case studies of the technology transfer process for five inventions patented and licensed by Columbia University and the University of California (UC).

Supporters of the Bayh-Dole Act argued that the lack of clearly defined property rights for university inventions impeded the commercialization of these inventions, and some recent scholarly research presents results consistent with this assumption. A paper by Jensen and Thursby (2001), based on a survey of technology transfer officers at sixty-two major universities, reports that 48 percent of university inventions are "proofs of concept" at the time of licensing. Jensen and Thursby argue that this finding is consistent with the characterization by supporters of Bayh-Dole of university inventions as "embryonic," requiring substantial additional investment for commercial development. Their survey results also suggest that inventor involvement is common in the commercialization of such early-stage inventions.[1] Based on these results, the authors argue that by giving academic inventors a financial stake

in the commercial success of early-stage inventions, Bayh-Dole created incentives for inventor involvement in postlicense development and commercialization and thus facilitated university-industry technology transfer.

Although these survey findings are broadly consistent with the assumptions
about the characteristics of university technologies made by the drafters and
supporters of Bayh-Dole, they provide little information about the central argument for Bayh-Dole, that is, that patents and exclusive licenses are necessary to give firms incentives to develop and commercialize university inventions. Nor do the survey results provide much detail on the importance of
patent-based incentives for inducing inventor involvement in the commercialization process or in the differences (if any) among fields of academic research in the technology transfer process.

The case studies in this chapter highlight the field-specific and invention-
specific differences in the technology transfer process and the role of patents
and licenses in this process. There is substantial variation across the cases in
the importance of patents and licenses, the role of the university, the importance and involvement of the academic inventor, and even the directionality
and characteristics of the knowledge flows between university and industry.

For example, Columbia University's patenting and licensing activities were
important to the development and commercialization of Xalatan, a glaucoma
treatment. University patents and licenses were less important to transfer and
commercialization, however, for two other inventions discussed in this chapter (the Axel cotransformation process and soluble CD4): firms learned about
the inventions through informal scientific and technological communities
and were willing to invest in commercialization without clearly established or
exclusive property rights to the inventions.

Two other inventions (gallium nitride and the Ames II Tests) were licensed
by inventor-founded start-ups after established firms had elected not to license
the inventions. These inventor-founders argued that protection for their intellectual property was important to the foundation of their firms, but it remains
unclear whether patent protection was in fact necessary for the commercial
development of their inventions.

Previous scholars have noted the importance of inventor cooperation in
developing embryonic technologies (Jensen and Thursby, 2001) and inventions associated with considerable know-how or tacit knowledge (Lowe, 2002;
Shane, 2002). These five cases, however, reveal considerable contrast in the
role of the university inventor in technology commercialization. In three of
the five cases, inventor-founded start-up firms played a central role in commercialization, and inventors necessarily were heavily involved. In the fourth

154   case, the efforts of established firms to exploit the university invention were aided by the inventor. In the fifth case, by contrast, the licensees required no assistance from the inventor.

The heterogeneity within this small sample of cases underscores the need for caution in generalizations about the nature of the technology transfer process and the role of formal intellectual property rights in that process. This heterogeneity also highlights the importance of flexibility in the technology management policies and practices of universities — for example, techniques or policies that are effective in biomedical fields may be less effective in electronics.

METHODOLOGY

The five cases discussed in this chapter are not random samples of the population of inventions at Columbia or the University of California, reflecting their origins in separate research projects focusing on different aspects of the university technology transfer process (see Colyvas et al., 2002; Lowe, 2001). These five case studies are not a representative sample of the full array of technologies covered by either the patent portfolios or the "invention disclosure portfolios" of Columbia University and the University of California. Moreover, all of these five inventions were patented and attracted industrial interest from either established or start-up firms, something that is not true of the majority of inventions disclosed at either institution. The cases thus overrepresent relatively "important" inventions, patented inventions, and successful technology transfer efforts at both universities. Nonetheless, interviews with university licensing officers and inventors, as well as our previous analysis of university invention and patenting data, led us to conclude that these cases provide an accurate depiction of the university patenting and licensing process.

The three cases from Columbia are drawn from a broader project that over-sampled licensed inventions that produced positive licensing revenues (see Colyvas et al., 2002). Indeed, two of the three Columbia inventions discussed in this chapter have produced more licensing revenues than all but a few inventions licensed by any U.S. university since the passage of the Bayh-Dole Act. The Columbia sample thus is biased in favor of particularly successful patented inventions. All of the Columbia inventions also are in the biomedical field, which, as noted in Chapter 6, accounts for the majority of Columbia licensing revenues.

The two UC cases focus on inventions licensed by inventor-founded start-up firms and are drawn from a sample of inventions that was selected randomly to match the distribution of all inventor-founded start-ups at the University of California in three dimensions: technology field, inventor's campus, and date of founding (see Lowe, 2001). These UC cases include one bio-medical and one electronics invention. By construction, therefore, our UC cases include only inventions with a high level of involvement by inventors in the technology transfer process.

Information for each case was collected from university records; interviews with inventors, licensing officers, and others involved in the process; and secondary sources. Each case study begins with a brief summary of the tech-nology, followed by a history of the research leading up to the invention, in-cluding research efforts both within and outside university labs. We then describe the state of development of the invention at the time a patent appli-cation was filed. Included in this discussion are the factors considered in the inventor's decision to disclose the invention and the university's decision to pursue patenting and promote the commercial development of the invention. Following this description, we discuss the role of the inventor in the technol-ogy transfer process and conclude with a summary of the current status of the technology, including products, product sales, and royalties paid to the university.

The five case studies are the following:

1. *Cotransformation:* a process to transfer genes into mammalian cells (Columbia University).
2. *Gallium Nitride:* a semiconductor with both military and commercial applica-tions (University of California).
3. *Xalatan:* a glaucoma treatment (Columbia University).
4. *Ames II Tests:* a bacteria assay for testing potential carcinogenic properties of pharmaceuticals and cosmetics (University of California).
5. *Soluble CD4:* a prototype for a drug to fight AIDS (Columbia University).

THE CASE STUDIES

Cotransformation

Cotransformation is a process that allows for the transfer of genes into mam-malian cells. Researchers use the cotransformation process to identify regula-tory sequences controlling gene transfer, to define mechanisms of gene ex-pression, and to understand gene function. Biotechnology firms also use the process to produce protein-based drugs. Columbia University's patents on the cotransformation process and resulting products were based on research by Richard Axel of Columbia's College of Physicians and Surgeons and have been among the most profitable academic inventions during the past two decades, producing more than $370 million in gross royalties since 1983

156   (1996 dollars). The cotransformation patents have been licensed by many firms and are used to produce an array of important genetically engineered pharmaceuticals.

Research History

Research on gene transfer techniques dates back to the 1940s, but the field was revolutionized in the 1970s with the development of recombinant DNA methods by researchers at Stanford and the University of California. Using these methods, researchers could for the first time control precisely which genes were transferred from one cell to another. Recombinant DNA technology also allowed researchers to tailor DNA to examine gene expression. Prior to recombinant DNA, little was known about the regulatory sequences controlling gene expression (Marx, 1980).

Progress in gene transfer research in the 1970s was impeded by the fact that relatively few cells took up the genes transferred into them by these methods, making it difficult to pinpoint the transformed cells. A major contribution to the transfer problem was provided in a series of papers published between 1977 and 1979 by Axel and colleagues that described the "cotransformation process" for inserting genes into mammalian cells.[2] The method involved transferring a gene of interest together with a marker gene that could be used by researchers to identify and isolate certain cells as the cells attached to the DNA, enhancing the efficiency of mammalian gene transfer. The Axel cotransformation process was widely viewed as a major advance in gene transfer (Marx, 1980).

University Patenting and Licensing

Although much of the research in gene transfer was motivated by a desire to understand gene expression, the scientific and technological community recognized that such methods could also be used to produce large amounts of proteins and therefore had significant applications in commercial drug production. Production of proteins with the cotransformation method had distinct advantages over the prevailing method of protein production, which used bacterial (prokaryotic) systems (Fox, 1983).

Axel discussed the commercial potential of cotransformation with the dean of Columbia's College of Physicians and Surgeons, who urged Axel and his team to disclose the invention to the Office of the General Counsel at Columbia University.[3] The university filed a patent application on the invention in February 1980, before the passage of the Bayh-Dole Act. In April 1980, Columbia petitioned the National Institutes of Health (NIH), which had supported Axel's research, for title to any patents that might be granted and requested the authority to grant an exclusive license. The NIH granted Columbia's petition for title but denied the university authority to negotiate an exclusive license.

As we noted in Chapter 6, Columbia established the Office of Science and
Technology Development (OSTD) in 1981, and OSTD assumed control of administration of the Axel patent application in 1982. The first of five patents on
cotransformation was issued in 1983, well after the publication of Axel's papers
describing cotransformation, and Columbia's patents eventually covered the
process, the production of specific proteins, and the use of specific markers.

Academic researchers and firms had been using Axel's cotransformation
process in their labs since the publication of his first paper on the topic in 1977
(Fox, 1983). Accordingly, the research community was not pleased when Columbia was granted a patent. Harvard University molecular biologist James
Barbosa noted in 1983:

> The [cotransformation] patent's process has been in use all over the academic world
> since '77 . . . It's been such a boon in getting mammalian cell gene transfer off the
> ground that it has almost become a laboratory reagent . . . that the process has been
> patented just doesn't seem right. And as far as policing industry's use of it, I don't see
> how Columbia will do it. The way a company makes a product is proprietary infor
> mation. ("Axel Patent Claims Mammalian Cell Transfer," 1983, p. 5)

Columbia initially sought to compel firms already using the technology to
negotiate a license with the university. Columbia licensing personnel examined the patents, end products, and scientific publications of industrial firms
to identify potential users of the Axel process and informed these firms that if
they were using the cotransformation process to produce proteins, they must
pay royalties to Columbia. In 1984, the assistant director of OSTD at Columbia announced in a biotechnology trade journal that "we understand from the
published literature, and from our own sources, that the process is being used
in research laboratories. Commercial corporations would have to license or
else be in infringement of the patent" and further noted that "Columbia's position is to defend the patent, taking legal action if necessary"("Axel Patent
Claims Mammalian Cell Transfer," 1983, p. 5).

Columbia's technology licensing office communicated the essence of its
views in letters to at least seventy-five companies by early 1984. But the credibility of Columbia's threats was undercut by the difficulties inherent in monitoring the use of specific processes by firms to produce proteins. Many firms
did not respond to the letters, either because they were not using the Axel process or did not believe that Columbia could prove that they were doing so.
Ten firms did respond by June 1984 and agreed to a license. Despite the

158   uncertainty over Columbia's ability to enforce the patent, these firms opted to license the cotransformation technology because of the relatively low royalty rates offered by Columbia, whose licensing officers stated that the university pursued a relatively low royalty rate "in order to encourage the use of the technology" ("Columbia University rDNA Patent Licensing," 1984, p. 4).[4] Another series of warning letters produced more licensees, and by December 2000 thirty-four firms had licensed the Axel cotransformation technology.

Commercialization and Development

Cotransformation was an embryonic technology, and its use for the production of specific proteins of commercial quantity and quality required additional experimentation and research. These development efforts continued after the invention was licensed on a nonexclusive basis. Exclusivity was not necessary to induce firms to commercialize a product based on the university technology, perhaps because drugs produced with the cotransformation process could themselves be patented.

Another interesting feature of the exploitation of this technology is the lack of interaction between the inventor and Columbia's licensees. Each of the licensee firms employed scientists whose training and research experience enabled them to understand and exploit cotransformation based on the description of the process in Axel's published papers. As a result, the inventor did not have to work with licensees to transfer his know-how or to otherwise convey important tacit information on the characteristics and applications of cotransformation. The invention's technical details were sufficiently codified, the papers by Axel and colleagues communicated enough of these details, and the "absorptive capacity" of industrial firms (Cohen and Levinthal, 1990) was sufficiently well developed for industrial researchers to pursue the commercial development of cotransformation without direct involvement by Axel or colleagues.

Since 1984, Columbia's cotransformation licensees have used the process to produce pharmaceuticals used in the treatment of a wide range of diseases, some of which have approached blockbuster status. Columbia has earned over $370 million (1996 dollars) in gross royalties on the cotransformation patents since 1983, making cotransformation one of the highest-grossing university inventions in the post Bayh-Dole era.

Summary

The history of the licensing and commercial exploitation of the cotransformation patents suggests that patents and exclusive licensing agreements are not always necessary to achieve commercialization of university inventions. In the case of cotransformation, firms had the capabilities and incentives to use the process for their own research and drug production in the absence of exclusive rights to the invention. Indeed, it appears that technology transfer occurred in spite rather than because of the patents, licenses, and involvement of the university technology transfer office. The university patent produced significant income for Columbia, but no evidence suggests that the patent and associated nonexclusive licenses facilitated commercialization. Columbia's nonexclusive licensing agreements for the Axel cotransformation patent, like the equally renowned (and lucrative) Cohen-Boyer patent jointly licensed by the University of California and Stanford University, do not appear to have accelerated or otherwise made feasible the commercial development of this invention. Instead, these licensing agreements were used by Columbia to levy a tax on the commercialization of an invention that was published in the scientific literature and whose commercial development in the absence of licensing almost certainly would have occurred on the basis of the technical information and demonstration of feasibility provided by the publication.[5] The Axel cotransformation case also suggests that heavy involvement by the university inventor in the commercialization process is less crucial when potential users possess sufficient "absorptive capacity" to exploit the invention.

Gallium Nitride

Gallium nitride (GaN) is a wide bandgap semiconductor; that is, a semiconductor that emits light across a wide spectrum of colors. GaN allows for colors, such as bright blue and green, not available from other materials used in light-emitting diodes (LEDs).[6] The technology has a number of other attractive features, and its commercial potential has long attracted the interest and investment of industrial and academic researchers. For example, GaN emits light at an intensity not available from traditional LED materials such as gallium arsenide (GaAs) and silicon (Si). Like other LEDs, GaN is more energy efficient (that is, less energy is lost to heat production in the process of converting electricity to light) than other lighting technologies. GaN semiconductors also provide greater transmission power with more efficiency than do traditional technologies used in mobile phones, military radar, and communications satellites.

Because of its unusual characteristics, industrial researchers in large U.S. firms began to invest in GaN-related R&D in the 1960s. Research on GaN has throughout its history included efforts by large corporate labs, small start-up firms, and universities, all of which have made important technical contributions. University research on GaN in many cases followed major advances

160   from industrial researchers, and much of the technology transfer in this case
flowed from industry to the research university, rather than vice versa.

Research History

Research on GaN first began in the late 1960s in the laboratory of a prominent
researcher at RCA's Princeton labs, Jacques Pankove. Recognizing considerable potential for GaN, major industrial firms such as IBM, Bell Labs, and
Matsushita had initiated research on GaN and related semiconductors by the
early 1970s, and a number of patents issued by the mid-1970s to these corporations. By the early 1980s, however, many of these corporate research efforts had
been abandoned because of limitations in the materials that could be used for   .
substrates, among other technical problems (Kahaner, 1995). Further basic research on new materials for substrates and new crystal-growing processes was
necessary to develop GaN technology for commercial applications. These
technical hurdles, combined with reductions by several of these industrial
firms in their central corporate research laboratories during the 1980s, reduced
industrial interest in the family of Class III-V semiconductors to which GaN
belonged.

As GaN projects were being dropped elsewhere, two Japanese researchers,
Isamu Akasaki of Matsushita and Shuji Nakamura of Nichia Chemical, continued work (independently of one another) on GaN, receiving over fifty U.S.
patents on GaN and related research through July 2002. Akasaki had worked
for a number of years on related research at Matsushita's research labs. After
meeting Pankove at conferences and visiting Pankove's lab, Akasaki launched
a GaN research program at the Matsushita Research Institute, where he was
the head of the Fundamental Research Laboratory and general manager of
the Semiconductor Department. Akasaki continued his work on GaN after
moving to a faculty position at Nagoya University in 1981. Nakamura, who
was employed by Nichia Chemical, a small Japanese maker of phosphors for
cathode-ray tubes and fluorescent lighting, began research on GaN in the
mid-1980s. He initiated his work on GaN at a time when researchers at large
electronics firms and several universities had begun work on zinc selenide–
based semiconductors, which seemed to have considerable potential for blue-
LED applications and were better understood than GaN.

Although zinc selenide materials were similar in structure to GaN and
were believed to be more feasible to produce, researchers in corporate labs
and U.S. universities failed to produce LEDs based on these materials that
could last longer than a few hundred hours, making them impractical for commercial use. These failures in zinc selenide R&D meant that Akasaki's and

Nakamura's successes with GaN renewed the interest of several companies
and university scientists in GaN by the early 1990s. But Nakamura had a substantial technological lead and produced the first modern prototype GaN-
based blue LED in his lab in 1994.[7]

Figure 8.1 presents data on the assignees for GaN patents granted between
1972 and 1998 in order to depict the relative importance of industrial, academic, and independent inventors during this period in the development of
GaN technology. The most interesting finding from the figure is the important role of industrial, rather than academic, researchers as patentees during
the first decade of this technology's development. Of 14 GaN-related patents
issuing during 1972–82, 11 were assigned to corporations, 2 were assigned to individual inventors, and only 1 was assigned to an academic institution.[8] During the later 1980s and 1990s, however, this picture changed somewhat; 29
of the 105 GaN patents issued during 1983–98 were assigned to universities.
Industrial patenting remained dominant during 1983–98, but the share of
GaN patents assigned to academic institutions roughly doubled, from 14 percent to nearly 28 percent. It is hardly surprising that industry dominated GaN

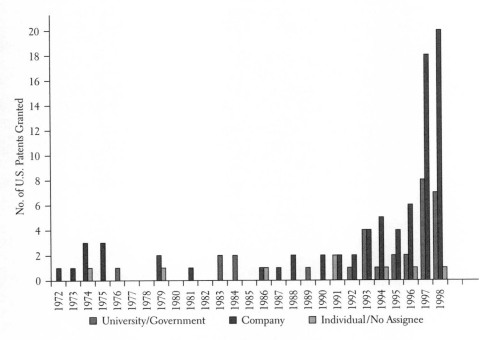

FIGURE 8.1   Assignees for U.S. GaN-related patents, 1972–98

patenting throughout the development of this technology, but the timing of the expansion in academic patenting is surprising. Rather than dominating the early stages of GaN patenting, patenting by academic researchers appears to have followed that of industrial researchers. The flow of knowledge and technology — in this case, at least — appears to have been as much from industry to universities as the reverse.

All but three of the GaN-related patents assigned to universities between 1983 and 1994 covered inventions by Akasaki at Nagoya University.[9] Two of the other three university patents were for inventions by Pankove, who had accepted a faculty position at the University of Colorado in 1985.[10] The flow of patentable research relevant to GaN into universities from industry during the 1980s thus was facilitated by the movement of Akasaki and Pankove from industry to academic positions.[11]

One industrial assignee for several of the GaN patents issuing in the early 1990s was Cree Research, a firm founded in 1987 that had licensed patents from North Carolina State University that covered silicon carbide materials for wafers and electronic devices. Cree Research, which played an important role in the exploitation of GaN patents developed at UC Santa Barbara (UCSB) (see below), had begun a research program during the 1990s to improve crystal growth methods and manufacturing processes that could be applied to GaN.

Nakamura's research and prototype attracted the interest of Steven DenBaars and Umesh Mishra of UCSB. DenBaars and Mishra began to investigate GaN applications in lasers and microwave transistors that had been overlooked by other researchers. As Mishra recounted during an interview:

> Akasaki and Nakamura were concentrating on a certain aspect, which of course is the commercially more important area: colored lighting. But then we decided to make some blue emitters, some lasers, and some microwave transistors [for wireless applications] . . . The first time we went to a conference, we went without a paper. We just went to listen. At the next conference, we had a substantial presence giving papers. (Mishra, 2001)

Established firms provided financial support for DenBaars and Mishra in their research on new applications for GaN in the mid-1990s. Hughes Electronics, which had a large research facility in Santa Barbara, had long maintained a close relationship with UCSB's engineering school. Although Hughes had for many years provided philanthropic support for the engineering school, the firm had never expressed interest in licensing the results of UCSB faculty research. Instead, Hughes used its philanthropic support of basic research to maintain a "window" on the research activities of UCSB faculty and to gain access to promising graduate students.

When Mishra and DenBaars decided to establish a laboratory at UCSB for   163
the study of GaN and related research, financial gifts from Hughes provided
"seed funding" for the lab, with no formal agreements governing the disposition of intellectual property produced by Mishra, DenBaars, or other researchers. Additional research funding was provided by grants from the National Science Foundation and the Office of Naval Research, as well as from
a Japanese LED manufacturer, Stanley Electric, that eventually took options,
but no licenses, on inventions from the UCSB lab.

University Patenting and Licensing

The UCSB research facility proved to be quite productive. During the 1995–
2001 period, Mishra and DenBaars published 223 papers and received twelve
patents on twenty-one invention disclosures based on GaN, GaAs, and related
projects in their laboratories. The dozen patents received by the UCSB researchers highlight the substantial commercial interest in their results, since
UC licensing officers at that time rarely filed patent applications without
strong signals of commercial interest in the technology, including a willingness by an industrial optionee or licensee to underwrite the patent prosecution costs.

Established firms funded at least a portion of the patent prosecution fees
for several of Mishra's and DenBaars's inventions. In other cases, industrial
firms (including some that had been active in GaN research in the 1970s)
signed "secrecy agreements" with the University of California that allowed
them to conduct technical evaluations of the inventions for which the University of California had filed patent applications. But the significant industrial interest in the UCSB research on GaN did not translate into licensing
agreements. In a recent interview, DenBaars (2000) stated that the lack of interest by established industrial firms in licensing the UCSB GaN patents reflected long-standing R&D practices in the electronics industry: "We were filing patents at the university, pretty aggressively at first . . . and the university
was marketing those patents, but our past experience has been with university
patents that large companies generally are not interested in licensing. They're
interested in doing it themselves."

In fact, few of Mishra's and DenBaars's inventions were licensed to established firms, although Siemens, Hewlett-Packard, Matsushita, Toshiba,
LumiLEDS (a joint venture between Agilent Technologies and Phillips), and
other large firms all had mounted substantial R&D programs by 2000 to develop GaN applications. Although twenty-three firms reviewed the UCSB
inventions, only one license (to Cree Research) had been executed as of

March 2002. Moreover, Cree negotiated its license with UCSB only after it had acquired a firm founded by Mishra and DenBaars (see below).

Part of the difficulty in marketing these patents was the early stage of development of the inventions. The UCSB patents covered processes that were small-scale prototypes of those needed for commercial production volumes, and considerable uncertainty remained about the "scalability" of the manufacturing processes used for their production. The UCSB researchers cited the importance of personal experience with the technology, rather than formal intellectual property, as the key source of competitive advantage. As DenBaars (2000) explained:

> Especially in the semiconductor business . . . the basic way big companies get at your technology, is to get the know-how, and that's done by hiring your students. Then [the technology] is in the public domain. The most important thing, at least in the semiconductor field, is know-how . . . and all of the amassed knowledge during the course of your Ph.D. So, the students are the most important resource we have. I'd say they're much more valuable than the patents.

As DenBaars's statement suggests, the lack of industrial interest in licensing the DenBaars-Mishra patents (including a lack of interest on the part of the inventors) appears to have been rooted in the characteristics of the "knowledge base" relevant to industrial innovation in semiconductor materials. In contrast to many fields of biomedical research, the codified technical information contained in the patent and licensing documents for the GaN inventions conveyed little of the critical know-how and related information necessary to translate the invention into commercial applications. At the same time, many of the firms active in this technical field had substantial related know-how and knowledge and needed little information beyond the demonstration of the feasibility of specific technical approaches in order to justify investment in their own R&D programs aimed at commercial applications. Finally, as was pointed out in Chapter 2, the strength and economic value of individual patents in a field such as semiconductors are widely acknowledged to be lower than is true of most biomedical patents, and industrial firms therefore may have seen less need to license relevant academic patents in order to pursue technical work in the area.

Development and Commercialization

Confronted with limited interest in licensing from large established firms, Mishra and DenBaars founded a firm to pursue further development of their inventions. Widegap Technologies, later renamed Nitres, was founded in 1997 by the two UCSB researchers and a former semiconductor industry executive,

Fred Blum, and hired several graduate students who had worked in the Mishra-DenBaars labs. After initial negotiations with the university, the inventors' new firm did not complete an option or license agreement for the GaN patents that were based on Mishra's and DenBaars's research.

Widegap Technologies/Nitres initially relied on funding from established firms and government grants. Hughes Electronics and General Electric, respectively, provided matching funds for a Small Business Innovation Research (SBIR) grant and a National Institute of Standards and Technology's Advanced Technology Program (ATP) grant. Widegap/Nitres also received federal research grants from the Air Force, the Office of Naval Research, the Defense Advanced Research Projects Agency, the Ballistic Missile Defense Organization, and the U.S. Army.

The uncertainty associated with the embryonic nature of the new firm's GaN technology appears to have limited funding for Nitres from venture capitalists or the equity markets. According to Blum (2000):

> We didn't even approach any VC's [venture capitalists] initially. We raised angel funding, but that was through my professional relationships with industry executives in the Los Angeles area. We didn't want VC money initially because they want to see a prototype too soon, and the technology was still too fragile. If they don't see a product coming up soon in the process, VC's get worried and can put unreasonable pressure on the company.

UCSB provided a valuable asset for Nitres's GaN research during the initial years by renting university "cleanroom" space to the firm. According to DenBaars and Mishra, the firm's financial constraints and the exorbitant costs of constructing or acquiring a "cleanroom" meant that Nitres would have been unable to operate without the UCSB research space.

Cree Research acquired Nitres in March 2000, after Nitres had developed commercial-level prototypes of some of its technology and had completed the development projects funded by its initial federal grants. By early 2002, Cree had released several GaN-based products, including green and blue LEDs for the commercial market, as well as applications for military and telecommunications. As of mid-2002, however, the University of California had yet to receive any royalty payments from Cree on the GaN licenses.

Summary

The GaN case, like that of the Axel cotransformation patents, is one in which patents per se appear to have been relatively unimportant for university-industry technology transfer. In both cases, the existence or absence of a patent on the key inventions did not affect the development by industry of

166   technological innovations based on the university invention. In contrast to the GaN patents, however, the Axel patents generated substantial income for Columbia University. The differences between these inventions and their licensing history reflect differences in the level of demand for the technologies they respectively supported, as well as underlying differences in the legal strength and economic value of patents in the biomedical and electronic fields. Another important contrast with the Axel case was the role of the inventors in such technology transfer as did occur with the UCSB patents—faced with limited interest from established industrial firms in their patents, the UCSB engineering faculty who had developed these technologies started their own firm. Finally, the history of GaN is characterized by a two-way flow of knowledge and personnel between industry and academia, rather than a one-way flow of knowledge and "prototypes" from universities to industry.

Xalatan

Xalatan is an eyedrop solution used to treat glaucoma, an eye disease associated with increased fluid pressure in the eye and damage to the optic nerve that can cause loss of vision or blindness. Xalatan uses a class of compounds called prostaglandins (PGs) to increase drainage and thereby reduce intraocular tension. Before the introduction of Xalatan, glaucoma was typically treated with beta-blockers, which often had serious side effects in patients with histories of cardiac problems. Xalatan has fewer side effects and now is the market leader among glaucoma therapies.

The transfer to industry and the commercial development of Xalatan appear to be consistent with the assumptions of the Bayh-Dole Act, in that the patents and exclusive license covering the drug were essential to its successful commercialization. In contrast to the Axel cotransformation process, however (and in a fashion reminiscent of the GaN case), Xalatan's academic inventor was centrally involved in its development and commercialization.

Research History

Laszlo Bito of Columbia University's College of Physicians and Surgeons began research on the effects of PGs on the eye in the early 1970s, funded by a series of grants from the National Eye Institute of the NIH. In the late 1970s, he published several papers demonstrating that small doses of PGs could decrease intraocular pressure in cats and rabbits (see, for example, Camras, Bito, and Eakins, 1977), and in 1981 he published a paper reporting similar results from experiments on primates (Camras and Bito, 1981).

University Patenting and Licensing

Bito had originally planned only to publish his research results and gave little thought to commercialization. But in the course of submitting a grant renewal application in 1982, he learned that Columbia's post-Bayh-Dole patent policy required him to report his research advances to the university's technology transfer office. Following discussions with the OSTD at Columbia, Bito filed an invention report in 1982 on "[t]he use of eicosanoids and their derivatives for the treatment of ocular hypertension and glaucoma," a disclosure based on the research that he had published in 1977 and 1981. Columbia applied for a patent on the use of PGs for treatment of ocular hypertension and glaucoma in 1982, and the patent issued in 1986. Columbia subsequently applied for and received two other patents on the technology.

Even before the first patent had issued, Columbia began to seek licensees for the invention. Despite a significant marketing effort by Bito and Columbia, however, there were no takers, perhaps because of the widespread view among industry experts that PGs were harmful to the eye. In a recent interview, Bito recalled that prospective industrial licensees were reluctant to contemplate the use of PGs in the human eye, arguing, "It's crazy. You can't put prostaglandins in the eye," and a leading eye expert called Bito's idea "next to ridiculous" (quoted in Gerth and Stolberg, 2000). Substantial additional research was required to determine whether and how the technology could be useful in humans, and few industrial firms saw significant commercial potential in Bito's research advance.

In 1983, however, the Swedish firm Pharmacia agreed to exclusively license the technology at the urging of a friend of Bito's who had developed a cataract treatment for the firm. Carl Camras, a student and colleague of Bito's who was instrumental in developing the invention, later noted that "if Lazlo Bito's friend hadn't done wonders for Pharmacia . . . no one would have picked it up" ("Columbia Innovation Enterprise: A Special Report," 1996, p. 1). The uncertainty surrounding the feasibility and commercial potential of Bito's treatment meant that the strong patent protection and exclusive licenses negotiated with Pharmacia were important in the commercialization of Xalatan.

Development and Commercialization

Bito played an important role in the development and commercialization of Xalatan. Inasmuch as he was one of the few individuals in the world who had used PGs to treat glaucoma, it is not surprising that Phamacia needed Bito's assistance to develop a drug based on his invention that was as effective as existing (non-PG) treatments for glaucoma. Some of the collaboration between

168 Bito and Pharmacia occurred in the firm's labs in Uppsala, Sweden, where researchers worked to understand the operation of PGs in treating glaucoma.
Bito also continued his research at Columbia with funding through a research
agreement between his university and Pharmacia.

By 1991, researchers at both Columbia and Phamacia had developed considerable confidence in the commercial prospects for the PG-based glaucoma
treatment, and by 1994 Pharmacia began to consider submitting its product to
the U.S. Food and Drug Administration (FDA) for clinical testing and approval. But the 1995 merger between Pharmacia and Upjohn, a large U.S.
pharmaceuticals firm, slowed the development of this technology. The new
management team did not assign a high priority to the project, and Bito noted
in a later interview that this "was a very stressful process, because after a good
team had brought the product to fruition, the new people in the management
of the merged company lacked familiarity with it" ("Columbia Innovation
Enterprise: A Special Report," 1996, p. 4).

By this time, a number of other pharmaceutical firms had approached Bito
and Columbia, expressing interest in obtaining a sublicense from Pharmacia
for the development of the PG-based glaucoma treatment for fields of use
other than those being pursued by the Swedish firm. Faced with evidence that
Pharmacia had scaled down its efforts to develop the glaucoma treatment since
its merger with Upjohn, Bito urged Columbia to require Pharmacia to permit
such a sublicense. The university conveyed Bito's sentiments to Pharmacia
and encouraged the firm to reinvigorate its commercialization efforts. Perhaps
because of this encouragement from its academic licensor, Pharmacia-Upjohn
began to move forward on commercialization of Xalatan, and the product obtained FDA approval in 1996. Sales of Xalatan grew rapidly following its commercial introduction and by FY2001 accounted for more than $740 million
(1996 dollars), making Xalatan the world's top-selling glaucoma medication. In
the last year (2000) for which data on royalties were available, Columbia
earned almost $20 million in gross royalties from Xalatan (1996 dollars).

Summary

The Xalatan case differs from the Axel cotransformation and GaN cases in that
patents appear to have been important to the transfer and commercialization
of this technology. In part, the importance of patents reflected the fact that this
invention resembled the "prototypes" discussed by Jensen and Thursby
(2001) — a lengthy and costly period of development was necessary to bring this
invention to market. And the inventor's know-how and involvement were indispensable to this development process, in contrast to the cotransformation
patents. But the Xalatan case illustrates another issue in exclusive licensing

agreements for university patents that also appears in the soluble CD4 case discussed below. Although a firm may be willing to sign an exclusive licensing agreement with the university (and although most such agreements include "due diligence" or "best efforts" clauses that commit a licensee to invest in the development of an invention), it is difficult for any licensor, let alone an academic licensor, to ensure that their licensee will undertake the costly process of technology development in a timely fashion.

The Ames II Tests

The Ames II Tests are an assay based on the Ames Tests that were developed in the late 1960s and early 1970s by Bruce Ames at UC Berkeley. The original Ames Tests were bacteria-based assays used to determine whether a test substance has mutagenic potential (the potential to cause mutation in cells). Mutagenic properties serve as simple proxies for the carcinogenic potency of the tested substance, and the original Ames Tests are widely used in the pharmaceutical, cosmetics, and food industries in basic product-safety testing. The Ames II Tests were based on research conducted by Pauline Gee and Dorothy Maron, two researchers in Ames's laboratory, two decades after the development of the original Ames Tests.

The commercialization of the Ames II Tests provides an interesting contrast with the commercialization of the original Ames Tests, developed before Bayh-Dole, which were not patented and were published in the scientific journals. As a result, firms and research labs were able to implement the Ames Tests without any licenses. In contrast, the Ames II Tests were published but also were covered by two patents and required licenses for their adoption. The research behind the Ames II Tests was published in the *Proceedings of the National Academy of Sciences* in 1994, one year after the first patent application was filed in October 1993 (Gee, Maron, and Ames, 1994) and three years before the filing of a second patent application on the invention by the University of California. The commercialization processes for the Ames and Ames II Tests also differed from one another in that inventor involvement was crucial to the development of the Ames II Tests, unlike the original Ames Tests. One of the Ames II Tests' inventors participated in the foundation of a firm devoted to commercialization of the tests and played an active role as an adviser to other firms seeking to apply this technology.

Research History

Bruce Ames publicly announced his original Ames Tests in 1975 and soon recognized the importance of his invention for academic and industrial research.

170   Although the original Ames Tests were not patented, the assays were available from the University of California's E. Salmonella Mutagenicity Test Resource Center for a small administrative fee.[12] According to the Mutagenicity Center's website, more than 3,000 industrial and academic labs have used the Ames Tests, and many firms and labs manufacture their own strains.[13] The standard version of the Ames Tests exposes a test substance, such as a pharmaceutical molecule, cosmetic, or food, to a strain of *Salmonella typhimurium* bacteria that has been chemically modified to no longer manufacture an amino acid, histidine, that is necessary for growth. Once mixed with the substance being tested, some of the strains of bacteria will mutate and grow, just as a nonmodified, or "wild type," bacteria would. Since only mutated strains of bacteria are able to manufacture histidine and grow, a count of the frequency of growing colonies of bacteria within the tested material provides a rough index of the material's mutagenic properties. If the test substance's interaction with the bacteria leads to considerable mutation and growth of the bacteria, the substance may have strong mutagenic properties and could be harmful to consumers.

      The original Ames Tests provided little information on the characteristics of the mutagenic properties of the tested substance. During the late 1980s, however, Gee and Maron began work on an enhanced version of the Ames Tests that utilized bacteria that had been genetically modified to produce specific mutations. By 1992, Gee and Maron had developed the Ames II Tests, which provided additional information on the mutagenic properties of a test substance by enabling researchers to determine which genes in the test bacteria were affected after exposure to a new material or substance.

University Patenting and Licensing

In compliance with UC policy, Gee and Maron submitted their invention, which included both the genetically engineered bacterial strains and the process through which they were produced, to the UC Office of Technology Transfer in 1993. The wide adoption of the original Ames Tests seemed to indicate that industrial interest in licensing Gee and Maron's follow-on invention would be substantial. Surprisingly, however, no established firms expressed interest in licensing the Ames II Tests for further development and commercialization. One biotechnology company expressed interest but did not pursue the invention with any formal agreement.

      Gee stated in a recent interview that at the time of her discovery, she had no intention of developing and commercializing the invention (Gee, 2001). Shortly after Gee and Maron's disclosure of their invention, however, Harvard professor Spencer Farr, a former postdoctoral fellow in the Ames laboratory, began discussions with Gee about commercializing her invention. Financed by two venture capitalists, Farr had founded a firm to develop and commercialize his own invention, a gene profiling assay, and he recognized considerable commercial potential for the Ames II Tests as a complementary product.[14] Farr invited Gee in 1993 to join his fledgling enterprise, Xenometrix, and Gee left academia to join the firm. Xenometrix licensed two patents related to her invention from UC.

Development and Commercialization

According to Gee, Xenometrix's licenses for the Ames II Tests patents aided the firm's efforts to raise capital, but the inventor's knowledge and experience with the invention were necessary to commercialize the Ames II Tests. As Gee (2001) recounted: "The value is not just the patent . . . My experience is intangible, whereas IP is tangible, and we can wrap legal language around the IP in our agreements. Clearly what you want is both, but the IP's protection is necessary in case someone tries to steal our technology."

The importance of Gee's knowledge and experience for development of the Ames II Tests was underscored by the efforts of Xenometrix's European distributor, Xenometrix GmbH, to replicate the Ames II Test strains. By the mid-1990s, Xenometrix GmbH was concerned about maintaining a sufficient supply of the bacterial strains and requested that Xenometrix train the distributor's scientists on the techniques used to grow the bacteria. The distributor's laboratory scientists spent a week at Xenometrix's U.S. headquarters, undergoing intensive training in the techniques and equipment needed to grow these bacterial strains. But after nearly a year of effort, the distributor's European scientists were unable to produce a supply of strains that met the company's specifications and could be sold to customers. In response, Gee spent several days at the distributor's European labs and produced roughly two years' supply of the bacteria.

By early 2001, the Ames II Tests had achieved limited commercial success. Xenometrix continued its development efforts, but Farr had departed to start another firm, Phase One. In early 2001, Discovery Partners International acquired Xenometrix to expand sales of the firm's two main product lines, Farr's profiling assay and the Ames II Tests. The University of California has earned almost $130,000 in royalties on its licenses for the Ames II Tests, although a substantial portion of the royalty payments (nearly $50,000) has been delayed or forgiven to ensure sufficient cash flow for Xenometrix to maintain operations (all in 1996 dollars).

Summary

The commercialization of the Ames II Tests presents some interesting similarities and contrasts with the GaN and Xalatan cases. Like GaN and Xalatan, inventor involvement was important and reflected the importance of tacit know-how for the inventions' applications. It seems likely that without the participation of the inventor, a license alone would not have sufficed to commercialize the Ames II Tests. But in contrast to GaN, patent protection for this invention and the exclusive licensing contract negotiated by its industrial commercializer proved to be important, just as was the case for Xalatan. Indeed, its license for the Ames II Test patents significantly enhanced the availability of venture finance for Xenometrix.

Soluble CD4

Soluble CD4 is a prototype for an AIDS drug that inhibits viral entry and infection. Since CD4 is a receptor for HIV (the virus that causes AIDS), a synthetic, soluble CD4 can "mop up" HIV before it invades healthy cells. The idea of a soluble version of CD4 emerged from university and industrial laboratories in the mid-1980s, a period during which rapid growth in the number of AIDS cases in the United States created a strong demand for better AIDS treatments. Soluble CD4 was widely viewed as a product with considerable commercial potential. The *Boston Globe* referred to soluble CD4 as "one of the hottest — though still preliminary — ideas in AIDS treatment since AZT, the only AIDS drug so far approved" (Foreman, 1988, p. 41), and Anthony Fauci, a leading AIDS expert, noted at an NIH meeting: "We are all very interested in this. It works very well in the test tube, [and] there appears to be an excellent scientific basis to proceed" (Perlman, 1987, p. A1). Despite this enthusiasm, as of 2001 no soluble CD4–based AIDS treatment had been approved for commercial use.

Research History

The discoveries that made soluble CD4–based treatments a possibility were developed in the mid-1980s in the laboratory of Richard Axel at Columbia University. Axel was no stranger to commercialization activities, having previously invented the cotransformation process described earlier. In 1985, scientists in the United States, Great Britain, and France provided evidence that the cellular receptor for the HIV virus was the CD4 molecule, and in 1985 Axel's Columbia lab was the first to clone the gene that produces the CD4 receptor (Foreman, 1988). Together with several graduate students, he showed that the

HIV virus could be "decoyed" into attaching itself only to cells into which the $\quad$
CD_4 receptor had been inserted.

These experimental results were published in 1985 and led Axel and one of his graduate students, Paul Maddon, to consider the therapeutic benefits of a soluble form of genetically engineered CD_4. Although their discoveries generated enthusiasm among scientists and pharmaceutical firms, uncertainty remained about the feasibility of CD_4-based AIDS treatments. First, the effects of soluble CD_4 on the overall human immune system were unknown. A second concern was the possibility that the body would produce antibodies against the CD_4 decoys, provoking an autoimmune reaction. Third, some scientists were skeptical that CD_4 was the only receptor for HIV, since HIV is capable of infecting cells in the brain and immature blood cells in the bone marrow that lack CD_4 receptors. By the mid-1980s, soluble CD_4 treatments had not been tested in animals, let alone humans, and the invention was little more than an idea with significant but uncertain commercial potential.

University Patenting and Licensing

In March 1986, Axel and Maddon submitted two invention disclosures based on their CD_4 research to the OSTD at Columbia. The first disclosure covered isolation of the gene encoding CD_4, and the second disclosure dealt with the method for producing soluble CD_4. The university filed patent applications on both disclosures in August of that year, and patents issued in 1992. OSTD began discussions with potential licensees about the CD_4 invention in 1987, and at least six firms expressed interest in licensing the CD_4 technologies from Columbia.

The evolution of Columbia's licensing strategy for soluble CD_4 illustrates the costs and benefits of exclusive licensing arrangements for early-stage inventions. Significant additional research was needed to develop a soluble CD_4–based treatment, and any licensee therefore faced considerable risk and uncertainty about the ultimate commercial feasibility and financial returns associated with the technology. These high risks, as well as the need for significant additional investments to bring a CD_4-based treatment to market, meant that some form of exclusivity in licensing the CD_4 technologies might be necessary to attract an industrial licensee. But OSTD also faced great uncertainty about the performance and prospects for commercial success of prospective licensees, especially if any such license was an exclusive one. As a result, OSTD sought to license several firms and scientific teams that could pursue different approaches to development of a CD_4-based product.

Columbia originally planned to grant a coexclusive license to three firms:

174   Biogen, Genentech, and SmithKline Beecham, each of which had been working on soluble CD4–based treatments since shortly after Axel's successful
cloning of the CD4 receptor (Axel had participated in SmithKline Beecham's
work in this area). But before the final agreements with these three firms were
finalized, Paul Maddon, Axel's graduate student, founded a firm (Progenics
Pharmaceuticals) to develop a soluble CD4–based treatment and requested
that Columbia add him to the list of coexclusive licensees. Columbia convinced the other three licensees to modify the draft license agreements, and
Progenics Pharmaceuticals was added to the list of licensees in 1989.

Commercialization and Development

Following the publication by Axel and colleagues of their paper in 1985 con-
firming that they had cloned the CD4 receptor (Maddon et al., 1985) and before the Columbia license agreements were signed, numerous firms had begun
research on a soluble CD4–based HIV treatment (Foreman, 1988). In December 1987, scientists from Genentech published a paper in *Science* reporting positive results, and scientists from Biogen, SmithKline Beecham, the
Dana Farber Institute, and the Basel Institute of Immunology each published
papers on their respective research on soluble CD4 in *Nature* later that month.
A contemporary press article observed, "[T]he nearly simultaneous appearance of five major papers in such a novel area of research is a sign not only
of the intense competition in AIDS research, but also of the tremendous
commercial promise that drugs for AIDS portend"(Foreman, 1988, p. 41). By
the summer of 1988, researchers from several other firms, including Becton-
Dickinson, Genelabs, and Ortho Pharmaceuticals, had published research papers on soluble CD4–based treatments.[15] In September 1988, seven NIH researchers reported in *Nature* that they had developed a poison that, when
combined with CD4, latched on to HIV and killed it; later that year they announced plans to license this technology (known as "CD4 – PE") exclusively to
Upjohn Pharmaceuticals ("Licensing Plan for AIDS Drug Draws Fire," 1988).

By 1989, the first year in which Columbia's license agreement was in effect,
the race to develop soluble CD4 was well under way and involved numerous
firms and labs other than the Columbia licensees. The presence of several
nonlicensee firms in the race indicates either that the scope of Columbia's patent was narrow and the firms believed that they were not infringing the
Axel/Maddon patents or that the returns to a commercially successful product based on infringement of the patents were so great that industrial developers believed that a mutually agreeable and profitable settlement with Columbia University could be negotiated in the event of litigation.[16]

The development activities of these nonlicensee firms also provide evidence that licenses for the Columbia/Axel patents were not necessary to support development efforts. Nonlicensee firms engaged in research on CD4 apparently believed that they had other means of appropriating the returns from their R&D, including patents on any products developed for clinical trials. It is also noteworthy that only two of the firms in the race to develop soluble CD4 (SmithKline Beecham and Progenics) enlisted the direct participation of the university inventors (Axel and Maddon, respectively) in their development efforts. In this case, like that of cotransformation, the university inventors evidently did not have a monopoly on the tacit knowledge needed to develop the invention, something that is further corroborated by the large number of papers on this topic that have been published by scientists in nonlicensee firms and in other research laboratories.

The enthusiasm surrounding soluble CD4 began to wane by 1990, the year after Columbia had signed the license agreements for the Axel/Maddon patents. Biogen's and Genentech's soluble CD4–based products showed little efficacy in Phase I clinical trials, and high development costs, along with predictions of high manufacturing costs, led these two firms and SmithKline to scale back their research on CD4. By 1995, each of these firms' licenses had been terminated by Columbia, and only the Columbia start-up licensee, Progenics, continued efforts to develop a soluble CD4–based treatment.

Before they dropped out of the commercialization race, Biogen, SmithKline, and Genentech had invested substantial funds in research on soluble CD4, and two of these firms had begun clinical trials. Ultimately, however, no commercial product was developed under the coexclusive license. In 1995, Progenics, which by this time was recognized as the leader in soluble CD4–based treatments, announced plans for clinical trials of its soluble CD4–based therapy.[17] In 1996, the firm renegotiated its license agreement with Columbia, acquiring exclusive rights for the development of a soluble CD4–based product. In 1996, Progenics disclosed the existence of a second receptor, CC-CKR-5, for the AIDS virus, a scientific discovery that meant that CD4 was necessary but not sufficient for HIV to bind to cells. Progenics currently has several drug candidates based on soluble CD4 and decoy CC-CKR-5 receptors in clinical trials.

Since the CD4 breakthrough was announced, an alternative approach, antiretroviral therapy, has been widely adopted for treatment of HIV-infected individuals. Nevertheless, interest in Progenics' drug candidates, and in "entry inhibitors" more generally, remains high.[18] As of December 1999, however, Columbia had earned less than $10,000 in sales-based royalties (1996 dollars) from the Axel-Maddon patents, since a CD4-based therapy has yet to be commercialized.[19]

Summary

The history of CD4's development process illustrates the commercial and technical uncertainties involved in bringing an embryonic invention, even one that appears to have great commercial potential, from laboratory to marketplace. This case also provides some evidence that exclusive licenses may not be necessary, even for embryonic inventions, if their potential profitability is sufficiently large and downstream innovations can themselves be patented. Moreover, the case highlights the risks associated with exclusive licensing agreements for such innovations, since it is often difficult for licensing professionals to determine which of several potential licensees (in the rare cases in which several firms are interested in pursuing licenses) is most likely to bring the invention to market successfully. Finally, this case (like the co-transformation case) suggests that in contexts where firms have strong links with the relevant scientific and technological communities, inventor involvement may be less critical for commercialization.

CONCLUSION

Chapter 5 pointed out that a key premise underpinning the Bayh-Dole Act is the belief that patenting and licensing are necessary to facilitate the development and commercialization of publicly funded university inventions. Although the Act does not mandate that universities follow any single specific policy in patenting and licensing faculty inventions, university administrators and technology licensing officers frequently assume that the technology transfer process is essentially similar in different technologies and industries. But these case studies reveal great heterogeneity within even a small sample of technologies. There are significant differences among these cases in the role of intellectual property rights in inducing firms to develop and commercialize university inventions, in the role of the inventor in postlicense development and commercialization, and in the relationship between academic and industrial research activities in different technical fields.

Patents and an exclusive license were important to successful commercialization in one of these five cases (Xalatan), but in at least two cases (cotransformation and GaN) it seems likely that development and commercialization would have gone forward without a patent on the university invention. In these cases, other means of appropriability, such as specialized knowledge or the prospect of a patent on downstream inventions, were sufficient to induce firms to invest in development and commercialization. The case of soluble CD4 also illustrates the difficulties that university licensing officers face in selecting among prospective licensees when the ultimate commercial prospects of the invention and the commercialization capabilities of the licensees are highly uncertain.[20]

The cases also reveal considerable differences in the extent of inventor involvement and the role of the inventor in development and commercialization. In at least two cases (soluble CD4 and cotransformation), one or more of the licensee firms had little or no interaction with the inventor, since firms had sufficient experience and internal expertise in the field of the invention or had strong relationships with external scientists with such experience. In these cases, the knowledge and know-how gap between the university inventor and a would-be industrial commercializer was relatively small, reflecting previous investments by the industrial firm in internal capabilities and external monitoring of scientific developments.[21] But two other inventions discussed in this chapter (GaN and Ames II) were developed and commercialized by start-up firms in which inventors played a central role.

The nature of feedback between industrial and academic research differs among these cases. Bayh-Dole was implicitly based on an assumption of a "linear model" of innovation, in which universities perform basic research with little concern for application and private firms invest in applied research and commercialization. In this view, patent-based incentives are essential to link universities, inventors, and industry in the commercialization process. As we pointed out in Chapter 2, however, this assumption does not accurately describe university-industry interactions, before or after Bayh-Dole, in many technical fields. Indeed, in most of the cases discussed in this chapter, there was considerable overlap between the scientific and industrial communities in the nature of research activities (including publication). Consistent with the work of Zucker and colleagues on biotechnology (Zucker, Darby, and Armstrong 1994), in these cases technology transfer from universities to firms took place via a range of channels, including labor mobility and research collaboration. Moreover, in two cases (GaN and CD4) university research itself built in part on research that originated in industry. There is also little evidence of significant delays in the disclosure or publication by academic researchers of their research advances. All of these inventions were the subject of published papers, and in a majority of the cases the publications appeared before patent applications were filed.

The research discussed in Chapter 2 highlights significant differences among industries in the influence of academic research on industrial innovation as well as in the channels through which these influences operate. This research also suggests significant interindustry differences in the importance of patents as vehicles for knowledge transfer among firms or between universities and industry and further reveals significant differences among industries

178   in the importance of patents and licenses as channels for the transfer of knowledge and technology between universities and industry. These case studies do
suggest, however, that patents may be important for start-up firms in their
search for financing. Consistent with previous studies, the evidence from our
small sample of cases suggests that university patenting and licensing were
more important for the biomedical inventions than for the one electronics invention we studied. But these cases also reveal considerable heterogeneity in
the technology transfer process among biomedical technologies.

These differences among inventions, industries, and technical fields can be
accommodated by flexibility in universities' patenting and licensing practices.
University licensing offices have at their disposal a number of contractual arrangements to facilitate technology transfer, including secrecy agreements,
options, licenses, material transfer agreements, and equity investments. To the
extent that universities choose among these instruments carefully, and with
the objective of facilitating use and commercialization rather than maximizing royalty income, patents and licenses can advance the mission of university-
industry technology transfer while maintaining the other important missions
of public and private universities in the United States.

9

CONCLUSION

In this concluding chapter, we summarize our argument concerning the Bayh-Dole Act and U.S. universities' role in economic growth and innovation and suggest some implications and cautions for U.S. policymakers and university administrators in the field of university patenting and licensing. We believe that much of the current discussion of the economic role of U.S. research universities and the contributions of U.S. universities to the economic boom of the 1990s exaggerates the role of Bayh-Dole. In fact, U.S. universities have been important sources of knowledge and other key inputs for industrial innovation throughout the twentieth century, and much of this economic contribution has relied on channels other than patenting and licensing.

Any assessment of the economic role of universities must recognize the numerous, diverse channels through which university research influences industrial innovation, and vice versa. This recognition is lacking in many of the current efforts of other nations to emulate Bayh-Dole in initiatives designed to enhance the contributions of their university systems to innovation and economic growth. U.S. policymakers and university administrators also must keep in mind these characteristics of university-industry interactions and technology transfer and should base policy and management decisions on a more nuanced and realistic view of the relationships between academic research and commercial innovation. University administrators in particular should heed the concerns raised by their predecessors during the 1930s and 1940s over the political risks created by any appearance of university "profiteering" from patenting and licensing.

The relationship between U.S. university research and innovation in industry is a long and close one. Indeed, organized industrial research and the U.S. research university both first appeared in the late nineteenth century and have developed a complex, interactive relationship. We pointed out in Chapter 2 that the unusual structure of the U.S. higher education infrastructure, which blended financial autonomy, public funding from state and local sources, federal research support, and substantial scale, provided strong incentives for university faculty and administrators to focus their efforts on research activities with local economic and social benefits. Rather than being exclusively concerned with fundamental scientific principles, much of U.S. university research throughout the late nineteenth and twentieth centuries focused on understanding and solving problems of agriculture, public health, and industry.

The massive increases in federal financial support for U.S. university research that began in the 1940s weakened research ties with local industry in many universities, but this federal funding was dominated during the postwar period by agencies with two clear missions: national defense and public health. As a result, much U.S. university research during the postwar period remained focused on "Pasteur's Quadrant," combining a quest for fundamental understanding with a focus on the use of that understanding for solutions to specific problems or missions (Stokes, 1997).

U.S. universities have made important contributions to industrial innovation throughout the past century, not least through providing both advanced research and education. The strong links between education and research sustained a close relationship between the evolving scientific research agenda and problems of industry or agriculture, while at the same time providing a powerful and effective channel (in the form of trained students) for the transfer and application of much of this knowledge to industry and other economic sectors. In addition, many university researchers in engineering and medical schools maintained close ties with the users of their research and their graduates in industry, medical practice, and agriculture.

The collaboration between university and industrial researchers, combined with the focus of many U.S. university researchers on scientific problems with important industrial, agricultural, or other public applications, meant that a number of U.S. universities patented faculty inventions throughout the twentieth century. Nevertheless, despite the adoption by a growing number of universities of formal patent policies by the 1950s, many of these policies, especially those at medical schools, prohibited patenting of inventions (see Chapter 3), and university patenting was less widespread than was true of the post-1980 period. Moreover, many universities chose not to manage patenting and licensing themselves. Chapter 4 discussed the role of the Research Corporation, founded by Frederick Cottrell, a University of California faculty inventor who wished to use the licensing revenues from his patents to support scientific research, in managing university patents and licensing during much of the period between 1935 and 1980. But even in these early decades of patenting and licensing, biomedical technologies accounted for a disproportionate share of licensing revenues for the Research Corporation and other early university licensors, such as the Wisconsin Alumni Research Foundation.

The decade of the 1970s, as much as or more so than the 1980s, represented a watershed in the growth of U.S. university patenting and licensing. U.S. universities expanded their patenting, especially in biomedical fields, and assumed a more prominent role in managing their patenting and licensing activities, supplanting the Research Corporation. Agreements between individual government research funding agencies and universities also contributed to the expansion of patenting during the 1970s. Private universities in particular began to expand their patenting and licensing rapidly during this decade.

Expanded interest by U.S. universities in patenting and licensing academic inventions and growing concern over U.S. economic competitiveness during the late 1970s combined to produce the Bayh-Dole Act of 1980, which also was influenced by a broader federal effort during this period to rationalize and simplify policy governing the disposition of patent rights resulting from federally funded research. As we noted in Chapter 5, the Act did not legalize anything that previously had been prohibited by federal law or regulation, but it obviated the need for universities to negotiate agreements with individual agencies or petition for patent rights on a case-by-case basis and reduced uncertainty about the direction of government patent policy. Since the trend toward increased academic patenting and licensing (including patenting of government-funded research) predates the passage of Bayh-Dole, the Act's most important effect arguably was its provision of a congressional endorsement of patenting and licensing (including exclusive licensing) as appropriate activities for universities and public laboratories.[1]

The Bayh-Dole Act is widely credited (or blamed) for the growth in university patenting since 1980. As we have noted, U.S. university patenting had begun to grow before the passage of the Act, and the "patent propensity" of U.S. universities (patents per dollar of academic R&D spending) grew steadily throughout the post-1945 period with no sharp break in trend after 1980. The growth of university patenting during the 1970s and 1980s also was affected by

182   other developments, including advances in basic science, particularly molecular biology. Biomedical research advances during the 1970s and 1980s in turn
drew on an academic R&D infrastructure that had benefited from the growth
in federal funding of biomedical research since the 1960s. Expanded university patenting also was affected by judicial and patent office decisions that
clarified and broadened the range of patentable subject matter in the biomedical sciences. No evaluation of the causes and consequences of increased
university patenting since 1980 can overlook the influence of broader U.S. patent policy on such growth.

The Bayh-Dole Act did not dramatically affect the patenting and licensing
activities of universities that had long been active in this area, such as Stanford
University and the University of California. Indeed, the biomedical patents
and licenses that dominated these institutions' licensing revenues during the
1980s and 1990s had begun to grow before the passage of the Bayh-Dole Act. Columbia University, an institution with little experience in patenting and licensing before 1980 (and an institution that prohibited the patenting of inventions by medical faculty until 1975), also had filed for its first blockbuster patent
before the effective date of the Act. Nevertheless, the Act did increase patenting of faculty inventions at both Stanford and the University of California, although many of these patents covered inventions of marginal industrial value
and did not yield significant licensing royalties. And the Bayh-Dole Act drew
universities into patenting and licensing that previously had not been active in
these fields. Initially, this wave of entry was associated with the production by
many less experienced universities of relatively low-value patents. Over time,
however, entrants appear to have "learned to patent" and have begun to obtain
patents of greater technological (and potentially, economic) significance.

The analysis of U.S. university patenting and licensing before and after
1980 also highlights the high concentration of these activities in a relatively
narrow range of research fields, primarily the biomedical sciences. As we have
emphasized throughout our discussion of the topic, the biomedical sciences
differ from many fields of engineering and scientific research in the unusual
strength and economic value of patents and licenses for those patents. In addition, the advances in molecular biology that revolutionized the field during
and after the 1970s yielded scientific discoveries with significant applications
in the pharmaceutical and other industries, another aspect in which biomedical research seems to differ from other fields of academic enterprise. The concentration of patenting and licensing in a relatively narrow array of academic
fields means that the effects of increased patenting, before and after Bayh-
Dole, on U.S. universities' "research culture" cannot be described as perva-
sive. Instead, any such effects are concentrated in a few areas of research and

in a few academic departments in most universities. The other implication of these important differences among academic fields, of course, is the need to recognize that patent and licensing policies that may be appropriate for the biomedical sciences could well discourage university-industry collaboration in other fields, a point that we discuss in more detail below.

The entry and learning behavior of less experienced university patenters after 1980, which we discussed in Chapter 7, illustrate an especially interesting aspect of the long history of patenting and licensing by U.S. universities — the perspective that it provides on the operation of markets for intellectual property, a topic of considerable interest to economists and other students of the "knowledge-based economy." The mixed experiences of the entrants into patenting and licensing demonstrate the difficulty of developing institutional capabilities in managing markets for intellectual property. Successful university licensing officers must combine a deep understanding of a given technical field with considerable familiarity with industrial applications. Moreover, these licensing managers must establish and maintain close working relationships with faculty inventors whose estimates of both their own talent and the value of their inventions often are inflated, while negotiating complex contracts with industrial personnel who may have far more experience in a given field. In short, licensing officers draw on a set of talents that are not abundant within most university administrations, and it is hardly surprising that many universities found it difficult to establish a successful patenting and licensing organization in the immediate aftermath of the Bayh-Dole Act.

Did the Bayh-Dole Act and the growth in university patenting that characterized the 1970–2000 period increase the contributions of university research to the "New Economy" in the United States in the 1990s, as so many of the accounts cited in Chapter 5 suggest? The contributions of U.S. universities to economic growth and innovation during the 1980s and 1990s assuredly were important, but no evidence suggests that these contributions were more important than they were during the 1930s or 1950s. Nor does any evidence "prove" that Bayh-Dole substantially increased these contributions or that any such expansion would not have occurred in the absence of this Act. The nature of these contributions and the channels through which they have been realized before and after the Bayh-Dole Act have been complex and have included much more than patenting and licensing. But the factors underpinning these important economic and innovative contributions are rooted in the structure of the U.S. higher education system, which in many respects contrasts with those of other industrial economies. U.S. universities have been closely connected with the external groups that can benefit from their research and training. They have been relatively quick to expand new

184   fields and techniques of science in areas of interest to their constituents in agriculture, medicine, and industry. In some cases, university patenting has facilitated technology transfer. But in many cases, transfer does not depend on the possession by universities of intellectual property rights.

THE BENEFITS AND RISKS OF UNIVERSITY PATENTING AND LICENSING

The widespread belief held by many policymakers and university administrators in the United States and elsewhere that Bayh-Dole has been an unmitigated success and indispensable to the economic contributions by U.S. universities is based on little evidence. First, data on the growth of U.S. universities' patenting and licensing activities alone provide no basis on which to conclude that patenting and licensing are essential for technology transfer, since increased university patenting may cover technologies or inventions that previously were transferred via other channels. Second, increased academic patenting and licensing, as well as growth in other forms of university-industry collaboration, predate Bayh-Dole. Third, the "evidence" on low rates of commercialization before Bayh-Dole is weak, as we discussed in Chapter 5.

Any comprehensive assessment of the effects of Bayh-Dole, or the benefits of increased university patenting and licensing more generally, must consider the potentially negative effects of these activities on the academic research enterprise, on the access by industry to university research results, and on other channels of university-industry technology and knowledge transfer. We have uncovered little evidence that the expanded patenting and licensing activities of U.S. universities since 1980 have produced significant shifts in the orientation of academic researchers away from fundamental research toward more applied, short-term research activities that might be more easily patented and licensed. Moreover, as we have repeatedly noted, the concentration of patenting in a relatively narrow range of academic disciplines means that any such shift in the orientation of academic researchers would itself be highly concentrated in a few fields. It is also important to keep in mind the relatively utilitarian research orientation of many U.S. universities and academic researchers throughout the twentieth century. Moreover, our (limited) evidence on the characteristics of U.S. university patents before and after 1980 does not suggest a change in the research orientation of U.S. universities after Bayh-Dole.

Nor can one mount a convincing argument that patenting of the technological products of university research per se is likely to have detrimental consequences for innovation within the U.S. economy. Patenting, after all, involves the disclosure and publication of the details of a given invention and in some circumstances may reveal as much as a technical paper concerning the details of an invention.

There are two broad areas for concern over the effects of increased patenting by U.S. universities. The first deals with the extension of patenting since the 1970s to cover artifacts formerly viewed as "science": ideas, materials, and techniques that themselves represent important inputs into the scientific research process. We emphasize that this extension of the realm of patenting is only partially attributable to the Bayh-Dole Act; it reflects a set of broader changes in overall U.S. policy toward intellectual property rights. The second area for concern deals with the policies adopted by university patentholders toward the licensing of these patents. These policies can affect both the diffusion and use of important scientific and technological advances funded by public resources, and they may also pose significant political risks for universities of the sort discussed by university administrators in the debates of the 1930s and 1940s. We discuss each of these risks below.

Patents as Obstacles to Scientific Research

We have noted that much of university patenting comes out of research in fields in "Pasteur's Quadrant," where it is difficult to distinguish between a research result that enhances understanding in the field and points to further research and one that seems to point to practical future applications. It is these potential applications, of course, that makes these results potentially patentable. Nonetheless, the U.S. Patent and Trademark Office and the courts have in some cases granted broad patents on research results where any applications are highly uncertain and far in the future and whose principal near-term use is as an input to further research. Where this happens, the consequences for subsequent scientific research may be significant and negative.

Unlike the establishment of property rights over technological inventions, "privatization" of knowledge inputs that formerly were part of the "scientific commons" through patenting may impede the progress of research. Increased academic patenting also may enhance incentives for faculty or universities to delay publication, restrict sharing of research materials, and/or limit the sharing by faculty of their research results with the scientific community via conference presentations or informal communications (Dasgupta and David, 1994; Liebeskind, 2001). A survey of more than 2,000 biomedical faculty conducted in 1993 by Blumenthal et al. (1997) found that 20 percent of respondents had delayed publication of research results for at least six months. Nearly half of these faculty reported that they delayed publication of research results

186   in order to protect the patentability of these findings. This survey also found
       that 9 percent of respondents had denied other scientists' requests for access
       to their research results. In a follow-up survey by members of this research
       team conducted in 2000, 73 percent of respondents working in genetics indi-
       cated that difficulties in obtaining access to data or materials had slowed sci-
       entific progress in this field (Campbell et al., 2002).

       The study by Campbell et al. (2002) highlights another potential effect of
       academic patenting and licensing—greater restrictions on access by re-
       searchers to inputs for scientific research. If scientific research relies on access
       to many patented technologies held by different owners, that is, where there
       are numerous potential claimants to particular lines of product development
       or research, the transaction costs of obtaining access to these rights may slow
       research (Heller and Eisenberg, 1998). One indicator of these increased trans-
       actions costs is the growing reliance by universities and industry on formal li-
       censing contracts and material transfer agreements for the sharing of research
       materials (for example, Eisenberg, 2001; Rai and Eisenberg, 2003).[2]

       In these cases, the research outputs are important inputs to a flow of future
       research as well as useful inputs for those who are trying to solve practical
       problems. Accordingly, the economic benefits from such research advances
       are likely to be greater if they can be available to all those working to advance
       knowledge and practice in the area. Will such liberal dissemination eliminate
       any incentives for researchers to pursue such research, by reducing the ability
       of researchers to control or to profit from the use of their findings? We think
       not, since the primary reward mechanism for most publicly funded academic
       research is based on publication and priority of discovery (Dasgupta and
       David, 1994).

       Several changes in the U.S. patent system, rather than in the Bayh-Dole
       Act, might reduce impediments to scientific research resulting from increased
       university patenting. First, the U.S. Patent and Trademark Office could adopt
       a more skeptical policy toward patents on discoveries that largely cover natu-
       ral phenomena, for example, by requiring that the applicant make a strong
       case that the subject matter of the patent application or patent is "artificial."
       Although these distinctions are difficult to articulate at a general level and
       even more difficult to apply on a case-by-case basis, we believe that a more re-
       strictive policy on such patents could reduce any erosion of the "scientific
       commons."

       Second, a stricter interpretation of the meaning of "utility" or usefulness
       might limit patenting of inputs to science. This issue is particularly important
       for patent applications that argue that the research result in question can be
       employed to achieve something obviously useful—a case for usefulness once

removed. But the problem here is that the patented "invention" then is useful mainly as an input for future research and represents generic knowledge or technology that is most useful if kept in the public domain. A stricter interpretation here would require a more compelling demonstration of significant progress toward a particular practical solution than appears to be employed at present.

Third, patent applicants often make claims in their applications that are far broader than any results they actually have achieved. There are obvious advantages to the patentee of being able to control a wide range of possible substitutes to what has actually been achieved, but there are also advantages to society as a whole from limiting any obstruction of a field of technological innovation that may result from broad claims.

More extensive patenting by researchers from industry and academia alike of inputs to science, as well as the greater efforts of universities to support patenting and licensing of at least some research discoveries that previously would have been disseminated through publication, is creating a more complex landscape of intellectual property rights for scientific research. Indeed, the risks that academic researchers may knowingly or unknowingly infringe patents in the course of their fundamental research cannot be dismissed. Historically, academic researchers have been protected from exposure to infringement litigation or damages by the "research exemption." There is a long history of statements by judges that use of a patented invention or advance in pure research is not a violation of a patent. University researchers and administrators have relied on a de facto research exemption in opposing efforts by patentholders to threaten university researchers with infringement lawsuits, and U.S. industry historically has granted university researchers a de facto research exemption in many areas.

The research exemption has never been embodied in law, and the fact that much of U.S. university research is focused on practical objectives as well as on the goal of advancing basic understanding, has long complicated university administrators' arguments for a research exemption. But U.S. universities' recent efforts to seek patents and licensing agreements for research findings that previously were placed in the public domain also have changed the situation and may increase the reluctance of industry executives to maintain such a policy. In some fields, such as research materials and tools, university and industrial researchers now are competitors as much or more so than collaborators, and industry researchers are often required to obtain licenses to use patented university research results. Facing such demands from universities, industrial research managers see no reason why they should not make similar demands on universities (Eisenberg, 2001). Many of the obstacles to a research

188   exemption thus reflect the changes that have transformed universities from research collaborators to commercial competitors in some fields. As we note below, this shift in perceptions of the role of universities reflects their behavior with respect to licensing and litigation for the patents in their portfolios, rather than academic patenting per se.

An additional blow to the research exemption came from the 2002 decision of the Court of Appeals for the Federal Circuit in *Madey v. Duke*, which essentially denied the existence or validity of an academic "exemption" from patent infringement suits. The decision also hints at some change in the perception of university research by at least some members of the federal judiciary in response to the increased patenting and licensing activities of U.S. universities. Ruling on an infringement suit filed by an academic researcher against Duke University, the court argued that basic and applied research was part of the "central business" of a university. Since universities benefited financially and otherwise from their research activities, the court argued, it was reasonable under the law for a patentholder to require that the university take out a license before using patented material in research.

The *Madey v. Duke* decision has great potential to impede the progress of academic research in fields in which patenting has grown in frequency and has increasingly covered inputs to research.[3] If this decision is not overturned by the U.S. Supreme Court, legislation will be necessary to restore this exemption. As of mid-2003, however, neither a judicial reversal nor a legislative solution seems likely. Indeed, if Congress views universities as entities that profit from their research, both publicly and privately funded, the prospects for a legislative research exemption could be quite dim. Dreyfuss (2003) proposes granting a research exemption to university researchers who agree not to patent research results that rely on patented material. But the Dreyfuss proposal would require many universities to revise their policies toward patenting and licensing the results of academic research.

Another solution to the potential problems created by the patenting of scientific research tools has been proposed by Rai and Eisenberg (2001), who suggest that the Bayh-Dole Act be amended to strengthen federal agencies' discretion and ability to limit the patenting or restrictive licensing of critically important scientific discoveries. As the authors note, the National Institutes of Health (NIH) has on several occasions relied on exhortation to limit researchers' patenting of large strands of primary human genomic DNA, and the NIH has limited the restrictive licensing agreements for embryonic primate stem cells. Using amendments to the Bayh-Dole Act to create a more transparent mechanism for such intra-agency deliberations, including advice from a board of distinguished industry and academic scientific researchers for each agency, could improve the accountability and predictability of this process, while strengthening the legal basis for something that is presently an ad hoc procedure. But this proposal also may require considerable change in university licensing policies. Indeed, many universities might well oppose any proposal granting greater authority to federal research funding agencies to constrain their freedom in the field of licensing.

As we note in our discussion of licensing policies, U.S. universities may well encounter greater political or judicial hostility if they do not through their actions (as opposed to their rhetoric) recognize that as public institutions whose research is largely funded by the public, they have a responsibility for encouraging their research results to be used as widely as possible. The issues of "research freedom," universities' political standing, and licensing policies are intertwined, and no politically feasible solution to these problems can fail to address all of them.

University Licensing Policies

As the previous paragraph suggests, much of the responsibility for managing patenting and licensing in a fashion that preserves the integrity of higher education and maintains political support for the large public research budgets that have been devoted to U.S. universities' research activities since 1940 rests with universities. It is important that university administrators recognize that technology transfer and licensing are components of and subsidiary to their central institutional missions of education and research. Although there is abundant rhetorical recognition of this fact, university policies must be consistent with this understanding as well. A more sophisticated and nuanced approach to managing patenting and licensing activities is likely to benefit individual institutions as well as the overall institutional and political strength of U.S. research universities.

A critical first step in developing an institutional policy for patenting and licensing is recognition of the many objectives of any such policy and the trade-offs among these objectives. Among the goals of technology licensing that university administrators and licensing officers frequently emphasize are: (1) licensing revenues; (2) maintenance or expansion of industrial research support; (3) regional economic development; (4) faculty retention; and (5) technology commercialization. Earlier chapters cited examples of licensing policies (notably, those pursued by the Research Corporation) that sought to maximize licensing revenues, in spite of the risks posed by such policies to the maintenance of cordial relationships with corporate licensees who provide research support. Similarly, the use of licensing policies to retain faculty may involve more generous revenue-sharing with inventors or a licensing policy that favors new, faculty-founded start-up firms rather than established corporations. Regional economic development objectives also raise potential trade-offs with licensing revenues.

There is widespread rhetorical recognition of the multiple goals of university licensing policies. But the management of the complex trade-offs among these goals often is deficient. According to a recent survey of seventy-six major technology transfer offices, licensing income was the most important criterion by which technology transfer offices measure their own success (Thursby, Jensen, and Thursby, 2001). Licensing revenues are a legitimate objective of licensing policy (although it should not be the only one), but the limited profitability of technology licensing for most U.S. universities suggests that an exclusive emphasis on royalties at the expense of these other goals is ill advised.

A second important premise for institutional licensing and patenting management is the recognition that academic research flows to industrial applications (and as the case studies in this volume document, industrial research flows to academic applications) through a variety of channels, including the movement of faculty, students, and researchers between academia and industry; the publication of research articles; appearances by faculty and university researchers at conferences; and faculty consulting. All of these channels are important and often complement one another. A single-minded focus on patenting and licensing as the only important or effective channels for technology transfer is unrealistic and may produce policies that limit the effectiveness of other channels that are more important for knowledge transfer and exchange (Cohen, Nelson, and Walsh, 2002).

Institutional patenting and licensing policies also should recognize the significant differences among academic disciplines or research areas in the importance of patent-licensing agreements for technology transfer that we discussed in Chapters 2 and 8. Patent protection is strong and economically significant in biomedical research, and the dominance of licensing revenues by biomedical inventions reflects this fact. But in other areas, such as electronics, a commercial device may require access to dozens or hundreds of patents, and the average value of a patent often is much lower. Patent licenses typically are less important and valuable in these fields, and industrial firms often collaborate with academic researchers with little expectation of obtaining rights to key patents. Indeed, in such fields, the insistence by university administrators on extensive agreements covering intellectual property may serve as a source of friction rather than as a lubricant for research collaborations. It is important for university research administrators to adjust their intellectual property policies to accommodate these intersectoral differences, rather than conceptualizing all research collaborations as resembling those common in biomedical research. Once again, this recognition requires the pursuit of a broader and more flexible set of objectives through patenting and licensing policies, rather than focusing solely on licensing revenues.

Where exclusive licenses for patented academic inventions are not essential to commercial exploitation, exclusivity may reduce the societal benefits associated with an invention. In particular, restrictive licensing may excessively limit the diversity of further experimentation and development in a context when multiple, rivalrous development efforts may be more socially desirable (Merges and Nelson, 1994). Current evidence does not allow us to reach strong conclusions about the frequency of these cases or to estimate the magnitude of the associated social costs — they vary across technological fields and have surely changed over time. Because they involve counterfactuals (for example, "What would have happened without an exclusive license?"), these costs are difficult to measure systematically.

Nevertheless, the important public mission of universities and university researchers in the United States and elsewhere, as well as the fact that much of the research conducted within U.S. universities is supported by public funds, suggests that university licensing policies should favor relatively broad dissemination of the patented results of academic research. In our view, U.S. universities should pursue nonexclusive licensing agreements for the fruits of publicly funded research whenever possible. That is, the presumption should be broad dissemination: exclusivity should be employed in licensing agreements only when it is clear that the technology would not be commercialized without an exclusive agreement. Nonexclusive licensing agreements need not result in the sacrifice by universities of significant financial returns. As we have pointed out, some of the most important sources of licensing revenues for university licensors during the 1980s and 1990s were licensed on a nonexclusive basis to a large number of firms.

Ultimately, U.S. universities, no less than universities in other nations, will retain their privileged institutional status as entities that deserve extensive public financial support and prestige to the extent that they are seen by the public as serving its broad interests. The single-minded pursuit of revenue through patent licensing is not always consistent with this lofty position (indeed, this was one reason for the historical reluctance of many U.S. universities to assume a direct role in managing institutional patenting and licensing), and universities must take care to ensure that their core missions are not put at risk. The interinstitutional competition that has contributed to the remarkable dynamism and excellence of many U.S. universities must not be allowed

192   to produce a "race to the bottom," in which institutions focus on revenue-maximizing strategies to the detriment of education and research.

Our assessment of the Bayh-Dole Act emphasizes the role and responsibilities of universities, as well as those of public policymakers. U.S. universities must exercise considerable responsibility and political sensitivity in managing their intellectual property if the remarkable achievements of the past century are to be sustained in the new century.

NOTES

CHAPTER 2

1. Portions of this chapter draw on Rosenberg and Nelson (1994).

2. "[Federal] public policy tended to strengthen the competitive market in higher education by weakening any central authority that could substitute regulations and standards for competition. It accomplished this by driving decisions downwards and outwards, by giving more resources and discretion to the consumers of education and the institutions most responsive to them. It increased the power of the states in relation to the federal government, as in the defeat of the University of the United States and [passage of] the first Morrill Act; the power of the institutions in relation to state governments, as in the Dartmouth College case and the Hatch Act; and the power of the students in relation to their own institutions, as in the GI Bill and the Higher Education Act of 1972" (Trow, 1991, p. 274).

3. "[T]he absence of stable and assured support for our [U.S.] colleges and universities from the State or an established church has forced them to look for support from a multiplicity of other sources, notably student tuition and fees, contributions from alumni and other friends, and especially from wealthy benefactors and institutions. A constant concern for financial survival and resources for development and growth engendered a steady sensitivity to the needs and interests of this varied support community, reflected in the enormous diversity of activities and services that our institutions have provided" (Trow, 1991, p. 159).

4. "Unlike European universities, which often appointed their own star graduates for faculty posts and rarely recruited faculty from other universities, American universities competed in a diverse academic market. European universities featured great institutional loyalty and continuity of professional personnel. Senior faculty at the leading American universities, however, typically won their posts through participation in a competitive national academic marketplace" (Graham and Diamond, 1997, p. 20).

5. "Any chemical process, on whatever scale conducted, may be resolved into a coordinated series of what may be termed 'unit actions,' such as pulverizing, mixing,

194   heating, roasting, absorbing, condensing, lixiviating, precipitating, crystallizing, filtering, dissolving, electrolyzing and so on. The number of these basic unit operations is not very large and relatively few of them are involved in any particular process. Chemical engineering research . . . is directed toward the improvement, control and better coordination of these unit operations and the selection or development of the equipment in which they are carried out. It is obviously concerned with the testing and the provision of materials of construction which shall function safely, resist corrosion, and withstand the indicated conditions of temperature and pressure" (Little, 1933, pp. 7–8).

6. These paragraphs draw on Mowery (1999).

7. "To say that work like that of Durand and Lesley goes beyond empirical data gathering does not mean that it should be subsumed under applied science . . . It includes elements peculiarly important in engineering, and it produces knowledge of a peculiarly engineering character and intent. Some of the elements of the methodology appear in scientific activity, but the methodology as a whole does not" (Vincenti, 1990, p. 166).

8. Vincenti (1990, p. 158) astutely argues that "in formulating the concept of propulsive efficiency, Durand and Lesley were learning how to think about the use of propeller data in airplane design. This development of ways of thinking is evident throughout the Stanford work; for example, in the improvement of data presentation to facilitate the work of the designer and in the discussion of the solution of design problems. Though less tangible than design data, such understanding of how to think about a problem also constitutes engineering knowledge. This knowledge was communicated both explicitly and implicitly by the Durand-Lesley reports."

9. Aiken benefited from the financial and technical support of IBM in developing the "Mark I" computer, introduced in 1944. Aiken's device, which had powerful computational capabilities, nevertheless was still electromechanical, not electronic, in its basic design.

10. Hence Stokes's categorization of research with the dual aims of deep understanding and practical value in the physical sciences as well as in the medical sciences as research in "Pasteur's Quadrant" (Stokes, 1997).

11. Some of the large R&D programs that were mounted under the exigencies of war did generate huge societal benefits in the postwar years. A "crash" wartime program made penicillin, perhaps the greatest medical breakthrough of the twentieth century, widely available for the treatment of infectious diseases. Another large-scale program made low-cost synthetic rubber widely available and had lasting effects on the U.S. chemicals and petrochemicals industries. And wartime research in microelectronics, directed toward military goals such as improvement of radar systems, provided a rich legacy of enlarged technological capabilities to the postwar world.

12. This calculation includes reported performance by "universities and colleges" and "university FFRDCs" in the NSF "National Patterns of R&D Resources" tables. Since 1995, NSF data (National Science Board, 2002) indicate that the university share of total national basic research performance has declined to 49 percent in 2000. Mowery (2002) discusses these trends, which appear to reflect the sharp increase in industry-funded and -performed basic research in the late 1990s. This growth in

industry-funded and -performed basic research is likely not to be sustained through the economic downturn of 2000–2001, although no reliable current data are available as of this writing.

13. The best known of these was the GI Bill, which provided substantial financial support to all veterans who enrolled in college-level educational programs; others include graduate fellowships supported by NSF and AEC funds, training fellowships from the National Institutes of Health, and the National Defense Education Act fellowships.

14. See National Research Council (1982); Okimoto and Saxonhouse (1987). Sharp (1989) argues that the less prominent role played in scientific research by European universities has contributed to the slower growth of small biotechnology firms: "A researcher at a CNRS laboratory in France, or at a Max Planck Institute laboratory in Germany, is the full time employee of that institution. As such his/her prime responsibility is to public, not private science. Moreover, as a full time employee, he/she will not find it easy to undertake the 'mix' of research frequently undertaken by an American professor, who combines an academic post with consultancy in the private sector. Indeed the tradition of funding US academic posts for only nine months of the year, expecting the academic who wishes to carry out research in the summer to raise research funds to meet the remaining three months of salary, explicitly encourages the entrepreneurial academic. In stark contrast, his/her German opposite number at a Max Planck Institute will find all research costs, including staff and equipment, met as part of institutional overheads. The opportunity cost of leaving such a research environment for the insecurity of the small firm is all the greater since, once off the academic ladder in West Germany, it is more difficult to climb back on again. The same goes for the opposite number in France, and with the additional disincentive that French researchers are civil servants and dropping out of the system means *both* losing security of tenure/accumulated benefits *and* difficulty in re-entry should the need arise. In the circumstances, it is not perhaps so surprising that few spin-offs from public sector research arise, nor, for that matter, that in Europe most such spin-offs are to be found in the UK, where the organisation of academic science most closely matches that of the US. In the UK, it is notable that—with the exception of Celltech and the Agricultural Genetics Company (AGC)—most of the spin-offs from biotechnology have come from the universities" (pp. 12–13).

15. One might instead argue that the weakening of university-industry research linkages during a significant portion of the postwar period was the real departure from historical trends. Hounshell and Smith (1988) cite a 1945 memo from Elmer Bolton, director of what was to become the Du Pont Company's central research laboratory, that made a case for greater self-reliance by the firm in its basic research: "Three things were necessary: Du Pont had to strengthen its research organizations and house them in modern research facilities; the company's existing processes had to be improved and new processes and products developed; and 'fundamental research, which will serve as a background for new advances in applied chemistry, should be expanded not only in the Chemical Department but should [also] be increased in our industrial research laboratories and the Engineering Department.' Bolton stressed that it was no longer 'possible to rely to the same extent as in the past upon university research to supply this

196   background so that in future years it will be necessary for the Company to provide this knowledge to a far greater extent through its own efforts.' To 'retain its leadership' Du Pont had 'to undertake on a much broader scale fundamental research in order to provide more knowledge to serve as a basis for applied research'" (p. 355). Swann (1988, pp. 170–81) also argues that research links between U.S. universities and the pharmaceuticals industry weakened significantly in the immediate aftermath of World War II, in part as a result of vastly increased federal funding for academic research in the health sciences.

16. As we noted, the survey by Cohen, Nelson, and Walsh (2002) included queries about the importance of different channels for access to research within universities and government laboratories, issues not covered in the Yale survey. These differences between the surveys may produce some differences in responses to the Yale and Carnegie-Mellon surveys, although this issue merits further analysis.

CHAPTER 3

1. McKusick (1948) suggests that "at the beginning of the Depression decade . . . [t]wo different factors had turned university attention to the patent problem: first, a steady growth of research sponsored cooperatively by industry demanded a generally applicable policy toward resulting patents, and, secondly, spectacular inventions on university campuses demanded immediate concern with patent policy" (p. 212). He argues in addition that the frequency of such "spectacular inventions" increased dramatically over the 1930s. Sevringhaus (1932), Gregg (1933), Henderson (1933), and Gray (1936) all provide contemporary accounts of these debates.

2. The report, titled *The Protection by Patents of Scientific Discoveries*, deals with patents on "scientific discoveries" generally, not just discoveries made in universities. But most of the discussion is concerned with patenting by universities and other nonprofit institutions, as opposed to patenting by scientists working in firms or independently.

3. The committee's cautious language indicates an awareness that, in some instances, commercial development could proceed apace without patent protection, a distinction that was largely ignored in the debates that led to the passage of Bayh-Dole. See Eisenberg (1996) and Chapter 5 for further discussion.

4. The committee quoted Hoskins and Wiles (1921), who argued that "there is at large a type of engineer commonly called a 'patent pirate,' who thrives by monopolizing the practical applications of the abstract discoveries of others. The patent pirate is a menace to industry and a parasite on the community. Nothing would so hamper his activities as to have the real discoverer take out broad patents in every case" (p. 691).

5. The committee's report quoted Sevringhaus (1932, pp. 233–34): "The public is thereby protected against certain ruinous types of exploitation. Assurance can be gained that technical processes are used in dependable ways. Even the publicity may be kept on a satisfactorily high plane."

6. Specifically, the report discussed concerns "that patenting will involve scientists in commercial pursuits and leave little them little time for research" (p. 9), "that

patenting leads to secrecy" (p. 11), "that a patent policy will lead to a debasement of research" (p. 11), and "that the policy of obtaining patents will lead to ill feeling and personal jealousies among investigators" (p. 13).

7. The AAAS committee's report characterized the following argument by Zinsser (1927) as typical: "The invention of an improvement in the mechanism of automobiles, or of a shoe-buckle, concerns matters of convenience or luxury, and can be dispensed with easily by those who are forced to do without them. The relief of the sick and the prevention of unnecessary sorrow by the maintenance of individual and public health are matters in a different category. As soon as we are in possession of the knowledge of principles or methods which can contribute to these purposes their free utilization becomes a public necessity; and any procedure which inhibits their most rapid and effective application to the needs of the community would seem to us as unjustified as the cornering of the wheat market or the patenting of the process of making bread" (p. 154). The widespread reluctance to patent biomedical discoveries is especially paradoxical in view of the fact that biomedical patents proved to be one of the leading sources of licensing revenues for U.S. universities before and after the Bayh-Dole Act.

8. Citing the example of Frederick Banting and Charles Best of the University of Toronto, inventors of insulin-production techniques who patented their discovery, Steenbock noted that they sought patent protection for their inventions to ensure that "the public is protected against the manufacture of poor preparations and is also protected against the extortionate charges" and to "avoid the possibilities of misusing their discovery which not only would have retarded the further development and use of this product, but would also have resulted in causing untold suffering among diabetic patients" (cited in Apple, 1996, p. 36). Apple (1989) argues that Steenbock also wished to patent his invention in order to prevent margarine producers from acquiring the process, thus protecting the region's dairy interests (WARF was sued by the federal government in 1943 over its refusal to license margarine producers). Blumenthal, Epstein, and Maxwell (1986) conjecture that Steenbock was motivated by the experiences of his colleague Dr. Stephan Babcock, who had developed a method for determining the butterfat content of milk (see Chapter 2) and, as was then standard practice, did not file for patent protection on the invention. But the absence of a patent meant that Babcock could not prevent low-quality producers from flooding the market with "Babcock testers," eventually discrediting the method altogether.

9. Spencer (1939) reports that by 1936, the Steenbock patents had earned more than $6.7 million (in 1996 dollars) for WARF.

10. "During the last decade, the number of universities which have adopted well defined policies in regard to inventions made by their employees, or with the aid of university equipment, has steadily increased. Additionally, there are today many other universities actively considering the adoption of a 'Patent Policy' and it is likely that another ten years will see such a policy in every school in the country that offers scientific or engineering courses" (Spencer, 1939, p. 1).

11. Of these 85 policies, 3 were adopted prior to 1930; 6 between 1931 and 1935; 12 between 1936 and 1940; 19 between 1941 and 1945; 25 between 1946 and 1950; and 20 between 1951 and 1955.

12. Columbia's policy thus stated that "it is recognized, however, that there may be

198   exceptional circumstances where the taking out of a patent will be advisable in order
to protect the public. These cases must be brought to [the university administration]
for its consideration and approval" (cited in Palmer, 1962, p. 175).

13. The Research Corporation's actions reflected its declining financial viability, as
revenues lagged behind operating costs. As we note in Chapter 4, the corporation's activities in this area appear to have contributed to its eventual demise.

14. Entry is defined as the first year during which AUTM member institutions reported devoting at least one 0.5 FTE to officially designated "technology transfer" activities (see Chapter 7 for further discussion of this measure).

15. The population of university assignees includes the union of all assignees designated as "universities" in the Case Western–NBER U.S. Patents database (see Hall,
Jaffe, and Tratjenberg, 2001) and all institutions designated as Research or Doctoral
Universities in the Carnegie Commission's 1973 report. To collect patents assigned to
these universities, we searched the U.S. Patent and Trademark Office's annual reports
for patents assigned to these institutions from 1920 to 1965 (there were none in 1920,
other than patents assigned to the Research Corporation), the DIALOG Corporation's
Patents/CLAIMS database for patents from 1963 to 1980, and the Case Western–
NBER database for patents from 1975 to 1980. Searches of multiple sources for the
1963–65 and the 1975–80 periods produced similar results. Unless otherwise specified,
"university patents" refers to this entire sample of patents.

16. It is noteworthy that the increase in university patenting over the 1970s occurred
while overall U.S. patenting was decreasing. Indeed, U.S. universities' share of domestically assigned U.S. patents grew from 0.2 percent in 1963 to 0.7 percent in 1979, before the passage of the Bayh-Dole Act.

17. Data on total academic R&D were obtained from National Science Board
(2000), Appendix Table 4-4.

18. As we discussed above, two Ivy League institutions—Princeton and Columbia—signed IAAs with the Research Corporation by 1940. Some patents emanating
from these universities between 1940 and 1945 may have been assigned to the Research
Corporation.

19. Data in Fishman (1996) suggest that MIT generated more patents than any other
private university in 1940 and 1945, although under its IAA the patents were assigned to
the Research Corporation rather than to MIT.

20. Stanford signed an IAA with the Research Corporation in the early 1950s.

21. These calculations exclude Research Corporation patents.

22. To collect patents for these institutions, we classified multicampus universities
by the maximum ranking of any campus in the system, a procedure that is necessary
because patents are typically assigned at the university, not the campus, level. This procedure yielded 89 unique Research Universities (49 RU1s and 40 RU2s) and 73 Doctoral Universities. Within these groups, 79 of the Research Universities (all 49 of the
RU1s, 30 of the RU2s) and 40 of the Doctoral Universities had at least one patent during the 1948–80 period.

23. The basic trends discussed below for "incumbent" and "entrant" university
patenters are not affected by using different threshold values for the number of patents
in defining these groups.

24. Of the 40 universities that had IPAs during the 1970s, 23 had an IPA only with

HEW, 1 only with NSF, and 16 with both agencies.

25. The technological areas we use here are based on a concordance from U.S. patent classes to technological fields developed by Adam Jaffe and reported in Jaffe, Fogarty, and Banks (1998).

CHAPTER 4

1. Since Cottrell was a member of this committee, the similarity in views is not surprising.

2. In a 1911 speech before the American Chemical Society, Cottrell argued that without an entity charged with advertising, licensing, and developing academic inventions, such inventions might well fail to find any commercial applications: "[A] certain amount of intellectual by-products are going to waste at present in our colleges and technical laboratories all over the country. There is a great deal of work that is being developed to a practical or semi-practical standpoint that dies right there because the men . . . do not want to dip into the business side of technology and go out into practical fields and the work has not come to the point of economic usefulness that is desired" (quoted in Cameron, 1993, p. 166).

3. After 1912, Cottrell was no longer active as an inventor in the precipitation field. Beginning in 1911, he served as chief physical chemist at the U.S. Bureau of Mines, rising to become director of the bureau. He subsequently was director of the Fixed Nitrogen Research Laboratory of the U.S. Department of Agriculture during the 1922–27 period, where he oversaw the successful reverse engineering of the Haber-Bosch process that underpinned the synthetic ammonia industry (Mowery and Rosenberg, 1998). In 1935, Cottrell founded Research Associates to conduct research in other fields, but this endeavor collapsed in 1938. Cottrell devoted the last decade of his life to research on nitrogen fixation (Cameron, 1993).

4. From the "Correspondence A–Z: 1918" folder in the Research Corporation collection at the Smithsonian Institution Archives.

5. The corporation acted "as the intermediary between the inventor and the manufacturer, which can subject alleged discoveries inventions to practical tests and render a judicial opinion to the manufacturer which can be regarded as trustworthy" (*New York Sun*, July 24, 1917).

6. Nonetheless, the 1950 *Annual Report* noted that "although there was always the expectation that another precipitation business might evolve from these projects, none did so, and from a financial point of view at least, the operations were distinctly unsuccessful" (p. 39).

7. A 1922 report by a Committee of the Association of Land Grant Colleges on patent policies at Engineering Experiment Stations noted that "educational and research institutions are not in a position to do commercial business, such as would be involved in owning patents, to defend the patent owned, or even to negotiate successfully for the disposal of rights under patents. Unbusinesslike methods in handling patents by educational institutions would hinder rather than promote discoveries or inventions. It will be necessary to have some outside organization handle the details with reference to the

NOTES TO CHAPTER 4

disposition of the patents. The Research Corporation of New York has organized to handle the patents of those who are not in a position to exploit them" (Committee on Uniform Patent Policies in Land Grant and Engineering Experiment Stations, 1922, p. 234).

8. A September 3, 1937, letter from the Research Corporation's president, Howard Poillon, to the president of MIT, Karl Compton, notes that "our important precipitation patents are expiring, and we are trying to develop new activities of such type that will permit us to use all of our staff, when, due to competition, our precipitation business will be decreased" (MIT Archives, "Research Corporation" AC125, Folder 57-12).

9. This section is based on the discussions in Fishman (1996) and Etzkowitz (1994).

10. MIT Patent Committee Statement of Patent Procedure. MIT Archives, AC64, Box 1.

11. On the advice of Karl Compton, the Research Corporation opted not to handle patents resulting from National Defense Research Council (NDRC) and OSRD research. The first reason was fear of litigation: since much of the federal research effort during World War II funded parallel research efforts in specific technology fields by several research organizations, Compton predicted that "these particular fields will be the subject of some exceedingly active patent litigation after the war in order to untangle the various claims for priority." Second, because so much of MIT's wartime research centered around large Institute laboratories that were staffed by scientists and engineers from all over the world, at the end of the war "many of the inventors will scatter over the world and not be readily able to advise in case of Patent Office actions or other cases when their services are essential. In such cases the Corporation would be called on to employ others who may be expert in the subject, which will be both costly and time consuming" (MIT Archives, "Research Corporation" AC125, Folder 57-10). This latter concern anticipates some of the problems with centralized patent management that we discuss below.

The Research Corporation's reduced activities during wartime also reflected the fact that many of its staff members took leaves to aid in the war effort. An especially serious loss was the departure of the head of the Boston office, Carroll Wilson, who went to work at the Office of Scientific Research and Development as Vannevar Bush's chief of staff.

12. On the other hand, the Research Corporation–MIT relationship had not yielded significant returns to MIT either by this time. See Fishman (1996).

13. "Its further, and even larger responsibility, was to extend and expand this phase of the Corporation's activities, to further develop the concept of handling the patent problems of educational institutions, and to do so in a manner that would add funds available to the Corporation for its program of grants-in-aid, that is, operate at a profit" (1951 Annual Report, p. 40).

14. Similar concerns led several other Research Corporation client universities to administer their nonbiomedical patents in-house, rather than submit them to the corporation, during the 1950s.

15. From its commercial introduction in the mid-1950s until the expiration of the fi-

nal patent in 1975, nystatin was the Research Corporation's biggest single source of cumulative licensing income.

16. When revenues from hybrid seed corn, which during this period included payments of back royalties as a result of a legal settlement, are excluded from this calculation for 1970, the share of royalties accounted for by donated inventions declines to
82 percent.

17. Forrester's invention resulted from his involvement in the Whirlwind computer
project, originally funded by the U.S. Navy to produce a flight simulator.

18. According to its 1968 *Annual Report* (p. 37), the Research Corporation's policy
"requires that it resort to litigation when patents assigned are believed to be infringed,
and negotiation cannot bring about recognition of its rights." This commitment to litigation as a matter of policy (rather than discretion) reflects another cost of large-scale
patent administration: the need to defend all patents (even marginal ones) in order to
avoid developing a reputation of being "soft" and thus inviting future infringement.

19. Another example of such conflicts that involves a clash between university administrators and faculty is the recent litigation between two UC faculty inventors
(Jerome Singer and Lawrence Crooks) and the UC system over the terms of the licensing agreement for these inventors' MRI patents. Singer and Crooks filed suit
against the University of California, accusing the university of negotiating very low licensing fees with Pfizer Medical Systems in exchange for the firm's financial support
of UC research activities. The inventors were awarded $2.3 million in back royalties in
a 1996 jury verdict that was upheld on appeal in 1997 (Chiang, 1997).

20. The difficulty of transferring expertise across technology fields is seen in this
statement from the 1968 *Annual Report* (p. 6): "The evaluation of invention disclosures
is increasingly more complex each year. Not only is the available literature, both technical and patent, rapidly increasing, but technology itself is ever more complicated and
requires more concentrated study for proper understanding and evaluation. Only
through considerable use of outside consultants and patent attorneys were we able to
handle this volume. Even so the average time required to complete an evaluation and
the average number of disclosures in process at any given time was [*sic*] slowly increasing. The technological areas where these effects were most marked were in the mechanical and the electrical–electronic fields."

21. Legal costs here include expenditures on attorneys for evaluation services and
for patent prosecution, as well as litigation expenses. The latter category also contributed to the increased costs of patent management over the 1960s and 1970s.

22. This expanded visitation program was motivated by more than simply the corporation's desire to maintain close links with academic inventors. During this period,
the Research Corporation also was expanding its efforts to assist universities in adapt-
ing to changes in government patent policy, as we discuss below.

23. The corporation noted in 1966 that "the result from increased visitation program
and the wider dissemination of information about our patent assistance services has
been a steady increase in the number of inventions submitted for evaluation . . . In spite
of the addition of one associate in the past two years, this increased load has required a
substantial increase in the use of technical consultants and patent attorneys. It appears

202   certain that this activity will result in a substantial increase in retained income from inventions submitted under our agreements with institutions" (1966 *Annual Report*, p. 3).
These efforts also required more technical experts, and during 1968–73 the technical
staff of the invention administration program nearly tripled (1978 *Annual Report*, p. 25).

24. See also Jensen and Thursby (2001) on the importance of inventors' tacit knowledge for technology transfer. As Lowe (2002) points out, this need for inventor involvement also is an important reason for the foundation by university inventors of firms to
commercialize their inventions.

25. Lamoreaux and Sokoloff (2002) emphasize the importance of geographic proximity in the growth of invention intermediaries, who were concentrated in regions of
the United States with relatively high proportions of independent inventors in the late
nineteenth and early twentieth centuries. The analysis of data from the 1970s and 1980s
by Mowery and Ziedonis (2001) found that geographic proximity plays a more prominent role in the licensing of university patents than in the "knowledge spillovers" represented by citations to university patents.

26. The corporation noted that "responsibility for carrying out the procedures must
be assigned unequivocally to an individual or an office in the administrative branch of
the institution" (Marcy, 1978, p. 5).

27. The Research Corporation's 1968 *Annual Report* (p. 3) noted that "royalties received by Research Corporation from the institutional inventions is [*sic*] only about
one-third the expense of serving these institutions."

28. Unfortunately, we can say little about cherry-picking by faculty members at
client universities (as opposed to by the universities themselves) without collecting
considerably more data that would enable us to identify the characteristics of all patents held by these individual faculty members based on searching for their names in
the records of the U.S. Patent and Trademark Office.

29. Although withholding of valuable inventions by clients is never mentioned as a
possible cause of the lack of profitability of the institutional patent program during the
numerous discussions of this problem in the annual reports of the 1950s and 1960s, the
issue is discussed frequently in the corporation's annual reports during the 1970s.

30. As a further check on the degree to which clients were cherry-picking, we compared the quality of the Research Corporation's patents and the independent patents
by client universities by using the number of subsequent citations to a patent as a proxy
for the quality of the patent. For each of the six years discussed above, we regressed the
number of citations received after its issue by a patent on technological field dummies
and a dummy variable indicating whether the patent was assigned to the Research Corporation or to one of its client universities. In none of the years was the coefficient on
the "assignee" dummy statistically significant at conventional levels. Indeed, the only
year at which the coefficient was significant even at the 15 percent level is 1975; in that
year the sign is negative, suggesting that clients' patents were of higher "quality" than
those assigned to the Research Corporation. The results of this analysis suggest little evidence of systematic cherry-picking behavior before the mid-1970s, consistent with the
discussion above.

31. Among the other alternatives considered but not adopted in 1979 was restriction
of the invention administration program to a limited set of technological fields. This

proposal, which reflected a loss of confidence in the feasibility of cost reductions 203
through a technologically diversified patent licensing program, was not adopted because "it would mean losing contact with other disciplines and narrowing our interface
within the scientific community" (Research Corporation, 1979, p. 83).

32. The Corporation's 1964 *Annual Report* (p. 46) noted that "the program of more
frequent visits to institutions with which Research Corporation has patent agreements,
begun in 1963, was continued throughout 1964 and at an expanded pace in the latter
months of the year as the result of institutions accepting the foundation's offer of assistance in matters relating to the new Government patent policies."

33. "Our staff members have been making themselves freely available to these administrators during the year, and have undertaken to establish mutually helpful relationships with as many of these key research administrators as possible" (1967 *Annual
Report*, p. 9).

34. Entry into patenting during the 1970s was dominated by institutions that were
not active Research Corporation clients or that were not Research Corporation clients,
that is, those with little or no history of patenting. This characteristic of entrant institutions once again suggests that increased interinstitutional dispersion of funding,
rather than cherry-picking, inefficiencies at the corporation, or increased enthusiasm
for patenting, drove institutional entry into this activity during the 1970s.

35. With this point in mind, it is interesting to note that the survey of university licensing officers in Jensen and Thursby (2001) reported that "revenue" was rated as "ex-
tremely important" by nearly 75 percent of the respondents, ranking as the most important objective of university licensing offices in their survey.

CHAPTER 5

1. See, for example, Bush (1943) and Bush's testimony on the Kilgore bill, portions
of which are reprinted in U.S. Department of Justice (1947). Most of the debate over
this issue occurred during congressional hearings on Kilgore's proposal for postwar science policy. Although Bush actively opposed the provisions in the Kilgore bill that
would give title to the government, his own proposal for postwar science policy (outlined in *Science: The Endless Frontier*) avoided specifics, recommending only that "the
public interest will normally be adequately protected if the Government receives a
royalty-free license," that is, if contractors retain title ("Letter of Transmittal" in Bush,
1945). Although the disagreements during the Bush-Kilgore debates centered on the effects of government patent policy on private contractors, Bush also supported patenting by university researchers, as we noted in Chapter 2.

2. NASA administrator T. Keith Glennan, commenting on the differences between
NASA and DOD policies, observed that "two such contradictory patent policies, followed by government agencies working in closely related fields of research and development, can be detrimental to the kind of cooperation that we must have from industry" ("Glennan Asks Review of NASA Patent Policy," 1959, p. 33).

3. Memorandum and Statement of Government Patent Policy, 28 *Federal Register*
10,943–46 (1963); Memorandum and Statement of Government Patent Policy, 36 *Federal Register* 16,886 (1971).

4. See also National Science Board (2002), Table 4-3. Universities and colleges (excluding federally funded R&D Centers) performed 6 percent of federally funded R&D in 1953, the first year for which the National Science Foundation has published data. This share had grown to more than 33 percent of federal R&D spending by 2000.

5. President Kennedy's 1963 "Memorandum on Government Patent Policy" had charged the FCST with analyzing the effects of different patent policies on utilization and commercialization of government funded research.

6. The firms screened these compounds for potential biological activity.

7. HEW had instituted an IPA program in 1953, and eighteen universities had negotiated IPAs with the agency by 1958. But after 1958, no additional requests for IPAs were approved by HEW because "opinions of responsible agency officials differed concerning the value of such agreements" (GAO, 1968, p. 24). Pharmaceutical companies also complained that these IPAs were ambiguous about the scope of exclusive rights that licensees could retain.

8. The purpose of the HEW review was "to make sure that assignment of patent rights to universities and research institutes did not stifle competition in the private sector in those cases where competition could bring the fruits of research to the public faster and more economically," according to the testimony of Comptroller General Elmer Staats during the Bayh-Dole hearings (U.S. Senate Committee on the Judiciary, 1979a, p. 37).

9. A patent attorney formerly employed by Purdue University, Norman Latker, was also the chief architect of the changes in HEW's patent policies in 1968 and was fired from HEW after denouncing the agency's subsequent review of these policies. He returned to the HEW's patent office in 1978, after his dismissal was overturned by a civil service review board on procedural grounds. Reporting on these events in *Science*, Broad (1979a, p. 476) noted: "The reinstatement is timely. Support is now building for the Bayh-Dole patent bill, and Latker's return to the HEW is seen by many university researchers and patent transfer fans, to whom Latker is something of a hero, as a shot in the arm for their cause."

10. Identical legislation (H.R. 2414) was introduced in the House of Representatives by Rep. Peter Rodino (D-N.J.) in 1979.

11. Another IPA restriction dropped in the Dole-Bayh bill was the requirement that grantees and contractors try first to offer nonexclusive licenses. According to an anonymous aide to Senator Bayh who was quoted by Henig (1979, p. 281), "'It's too hard and inefficient a process. Universities don't have the financial capability to beat the bushes and try to find someone who is willing to accept a license on a nonexclusive basis.'"

12. A contemporary account noted that limiting the bill to universities and small businesses was "a tactical exclusion taken to ensure liberal support" (Henig, 1979, p. 282). A Senate aide commented, "We'd like to extend [the policy] to everybody . . . but if we did the bill would never have a chance of passing" (Broad, 1979b, p. 474). The original bill also included several provisions designed to defuse criticism that it would lead to "profiteering" at the expense of the public interest, including a recoupment provision requiring that institutions pay back a share of licensing income or sales to funding agencies. The final version of the Bayh-Dole Act eliminated this provision "because

NOTES TO CHAPTER 5

there was no agreement on whether the funds would be returned to the agencies or to general revenue, or how the collection and auditing functions would be conducted" and "fears that the costs of the infrastructure required to administer such a program would exceed the amounts collected." See *http://www.nih.gov/news/070101wyden.htm*.

13. For example, Dole opened the Senate Judiciary Committee's hearings on the bill by observing that "the damaging impact of the Federal patent policy on the economy is dramatic. That we have lost our leadership role to Japan in the field of electronics and shipbuilding is no accident" (U.S. Senate Committee on the Judiciary, 1979a, p. 28).

14. See Harold Bremer, "Public Patents, Public Benefits?" submitted with his testimony during the Senate Judiciary Committee's Bayh-Dole Hearings (U.S. Senate Committee on the Judiciary, 1979a).

15. See, for example, the opening statements by Senators Bayh, Dole, and Orrin Hatch (R-Ut.), as well as the testimony by Elmer Staats, Walter Syniuta, and Betsy Ancker-Johnson (U.S. Senate Committee on the Judiciary, 1979a).

16. See, for example, the testimony by Hector Deluca, Frederick Andrews, and Harold Bremer during the Senate Judiciary Committee's Bayh-Dole Hearings (U.S. Senate Committee on the Judiciary, 1979a).

17. The Senate Judiciary Committee's report on S. 414 noted: "A number of witnesses also pointed out to the committee that when government agencies retain title to inventions made by nonprofit organizations or small business contractors there is absolutely no incentive for the inventor to remain involved in the possible development of the patentable discovery. Virtually all experts in the innovation process stress very strongly that such involvement by the inventor is absolutely essential, especially when the invention was made under basic research where it is invariably in the embryonic stage of development" (U.S. Senate Committee on the Judiciary, 1979b, p. 22).

18. Much of the floor debate in both chambers focused on whether large businesses should be allowed to retain rights to patents resulting from federal contracts. Rep. Robert Kastenmeier (D-Wis.), a supporter of extending rights to large business contractors, noted that "rather than hold hostage [the] non-controversial areas [that is, allowing universities and small businesses to retain title], I think we have no real option but to move forward with this [the bill as amended] and send it to the White House" (U.S. House of Representatives, 1980, p. 30560.) The original bill passed by the House (H.R. 6933) contained the same provisions as the Senate bill introduced by Senators Bayh and Dole but also allowed large firms to obtain "field of use" exclusive licenses for inventions developed with government funds. Senate amendments to this bill eliminated that provision, and the House subsequently passed a bill identical to that passed by the Senate.

19. A journalist covering the hearings observed that "although the Dole-Bayh bill is receiving nearly unprecedented support, some congressional aides point out that it still leaves unanswered fundamental questions about patents in general and patents on university campuses in particular" (Henig, 1979, p. 284).

20. For details, see the Council on Government Relations (1999).

21. Memorandum to the Heads of Executive Departments and Agencies: Government Patent Policy, Pub. Papers 252 (February 18, 1983); Executive Order 12591 (4/10/87); codified at 3 C.F.R. 221.

22. Trademark Clarification Act of 1984, PL 98-620. Among other things, this amendment also allowed contractors at Government Owned, Contractor Operated Labs (GOCOs) to retain title to federally funded inventions.

23. According to Katz and Ordover (1990), at least fourteen congressional bills passed during the 1980s focused on strengthening domestic and international protection for intellectual property rights, and the Court of Appeals for the Federal Circuit, created in 1982, has upheld patent rights in roughly 80 percent of the cases argued before it, a considerable increase from the pre-1982 rate of 30 percent for the federal bench.

24. "Regulatory reform in the United States in the early 1980s, such as the Bayh-Dole Act, have [sic] significantly increased the contribution of scientific institutions to innovation. There is evidence that this is one of the factors contributing to the pick-up of US growth performance" (OECD, 2000, p. 77).

25. "In 1980, the enactment of the Bayh-Dole Act (Public Law 98-620) culminated years of work to develop incentives for laboratory discoveries to make their way to the marketplace promptly, with all the attendant benefits for public welfare and economic growth that result from those innovations. Before Bayh-Dole, the federal government had accumulated 30,000 patents, of which only 5% had been licensed and even fewer had found their way into commercial products. Today under Bayh-Dole more than 200 universities are engaged in technology transfer, adding more than $21 billion each year to the economy" (Hasselmo, 1999, p. 3).

26. "In the 1970s, the government discovered the inventions that resulted from public funding were not reaching the marketplace because no one would make the additional investment to turn basic research into marketable products. That finding resulted in the Bayh-Dole Act, passed in 1980. It enabled universities, small companies, and nonprofit organizations to commercialize the results of federally funded research. The results of Bayh-Dole have been significant. Before 1981, fewer than 250 patents were issued to universities each year. A decade later universities were averaging approximately 1,000 patents a year" (Dickinson, 2000, p. 2).

27. "The Bayh-Dole Act turned out to be the Viagra for campus innovation. Universities that would previously have let their intellectual property lie fallow began filing for and getting patents at unprecedented rates. Coupled with other legal economic and political developments that also spurred patenting and licensing, the results seems nothing less than a major boon to national economic growth" (Zacks, 2000).

CHAPTER 6

1. According to a recent ranking of academic institutions by licensing revenues by the Association of University Technology Managers (AUTM), Columbia University, the UC system, and Stanford University were the first, second, and fifth leading institutions, earning $90.5 million, $76.4 million, and $37.9 million, respectively. Florida State University and Yale University were ranked third and fourth, receiving $54.1 and $38.5 million, respectively (AUTM, 2000, p. 97; all figures in 1996 dollars).

2. According to a March 10, 1975, letter from UC president Charles J. Hitch to Governor Edmund G. Brown Jr. (University of California Office of the President, Office of

Technology Transfer Archives), "The possibility of developing a formal patent policy and program was first considered in the University in the Thirties. But the idea did not achieve full impetus until the war years when the Federal Government began to sponsor research in the University on a large scale and inventions began to be made under research contracts."

3. The "Patent Board" was a committee of UC faculty and administrators charged with oversight of the Patent Office. As revised in 1973, the "University Policy Regarding Patents" states that "an agreement to assign inventions and patents to The Regents of the University of California, except those resulting from permissible consulting activities without use of University facilities, shall be mandatory for all employees, academic and nonacademic." The policy statement goes on to emphasize that "the Regents is [sic] adverse to seeking protective patents and will not seek such patents unless the discoverer or inventor can demonstrate that the securing of the patent is important to the University." This latter sentiment notwithstanding, UC administrators were actively seeking patent protection for faculty inventions by the mid-1970s, as the historical data of the Office of Technology Transfer show.

4. These "independent" licensing offices, which continue to pay a portion of their revenues to the state government, are in charge of invention disclosures (along with any revenues or expenses associated with these disclosures) occurring after their foundation. The UC Office of Technology Transfer, however, continues to collect and report data on disclosures, patents, and licenses from all UC campuses.

5. Almost simultaneously with this shift in university patent policy, an internal study by the OTL Advisory Board in 1993 recommended that "OTL need not be constrained by the principle of 'preference for non-exclusive licensing'" (Stanford University Office of Technology Licensing, 1994b, p. 2).

6. Reflecting faculty sensitivity over assignment to the university of all ownership of all copyrighted material produced under university sponsorship, Stanford's OTL exempted ownership of "books, articles, popular nonfiction, novels, poems, musical compositions, or other works of artistic imagination which are not institutional works" from the policy governing software (Stanford University Office of Technology Licensing, 1994b, p. 1).

7. Figure 6.7 excludes licenses for the Cohen-Boyer patents, which were managed by Stanford's OTL on behalf of the UC system and Stanford University. Strictly speaking, since the revenues from these licenses are split between the UC system and Stanford University, the licenses also should be allocated between the two institutions. Exclusion of this heavily licensed invention thus understates the growth in the biomedical share of Stanford and UC licensing agreements during the 1980s in Figure 6.7.

8. Some indication of the relative magnitudes of licensing revenues from these "site licenses," which for some years were administered by the OTL Software Distribution Center, is given by the following data cited in the 1988–89 report of the OTL, which separated software licensing revenues into those derived from "direct software distribution through OTL's Software Distribution Center ($453,581 from 515 use licenses) and from royalties paid by commercial distributors ($420,000 from 40 distribution licenses to software firms, computer companies, and publishers)" (Stanford University Office of Technology Licensing, 1990, p. 4). Unfortunately, we have been

208   unable thus far to consistently separate software licenses between these two channels of distribution.

9. Portions of this section are based on Crow et al. (1998).

10. Biotechnology inventions accounted for 45 percent of the biomedical inventions that resulted in patents and nearly 70 percent of the biomedical inventions that were licensed.

11. Columbia also experienced growth in the number of licenses for software inventions during the 1980s (a measure that heavily weights inventions licensed on a nonexclusive basis). Software licenses account for well over 50 percent of Columbia licensing agreements after 1988; the majority of these licenses (420 of a total of 648) were associated with one software invention. In addition, and similar to the situation at Stanford University (see below), more than 300 of the 420 licensees for this software invention were academic institutions.

12. In order to deal with the problems of "truncation bias" while accommodating the fact that our data end in 1997, we have imposed a six-year "trailing window" on our invention disclosures. In other words, the analysis includes issued patents or licenses only if these events occur within six years after the date of disclosure of the invention. This convention is used to avoid unfairly biasing the indicators of "productivity" in favor of older disclosures, which have much longer time periods during which to produce patents or licenses.

13. As we noted earlier, a large percentage of Stanford's software licenses cover low-royalty "site licenses" at other academic institutions, which may well raise the shares of Stanford disclosures that yield licensing income without necessarily having a significant effect on overall licensing income. In addition, the Stanford invention disclosures and licensing data contain a large number of agreements covering "clones" of various pieces of genetic material — such agreements are less common in the Columbia or UC data for the period covered by this analysis. These licenses are somewhat more formal than Materials Transfer Agreements and often involve the payment of modest licensing fees. But as with the Stanford software licenses, including these agreements in our data increases the share of disclosures that are licensed or that yield licensing income without having much effect on overall licensing income.

14. See the case study of Cohen-Boyer in the National Research Council workshop, *Intellectual Property Rights and Research Tools in Molecular Biology* (National Research Council, 1997).

15. Data on Stanford patent applications are unavailable, and we therefore are able to compute measures using patent applications only for the University of California. Because the analysis reported in Table 6.3 examines two earlier time periods than Table 6.2, we used a longer, eight-year "trailing window" (see Note 12; we include only issued patents or license agreements within eight years following the invention disclosures) to compare the yield and productivity of Stanford and UC patenting and licensing before and after Bayh-Dole.

16. Since the UC disclosure and licensing data largely exclude software inventions, the most nearly comparable Stanford data are those excluding software inventions and licenses.

17. The data on Stanford licenses are incomplete, as was noted earlier. Moreover,

the licensing income data are reported on a fiscal year basis and license agreements on a calendar year basis, making it difficult to reconcile these data. We have attempted to adjust the licensing income and agreements data to address this incompatibility, but the data for Stanford in the last line of Table 6.3 should be treated with caution.

18. This share is essentially stable, however, when software inventions are added to the sample, reflecting the inclusion within the Stanford software licensing data of numerous academic "site licenses," each of which produced a small but positive licensing income.

19. For example, average income per license may have increased in the second period, although the skewed distribution of the licensing income of both the Stanford and UC technology transfer offices means that any such changes are likely to be small. See Sampat and Ziedonis (2003) for an analysis of the relationship between the level of licensing revenues at the University of California and Columbia and the characteristics of these universities' licensed patents.

20. This third subset of our data is intended to separate those faculty disclosures that occurred before Bayh-Dole could affect the content of academic research but whose commercial promotion by universities (that is, through filing patent applications and seeking licensees) occurred after the effective date of the Act. Unfortunately, the small size of this sample of patents reduces the power and significance of our tests of statistical significance for any differences among the characteristics of the three subsets of patents.

21. Our control samples are constructed differently from those of Henderson, Jaffe, and Trajtenberg (1995, 1998a). They used as their control sample a 1 percent random sample of all U.S. patents granted during the time period covered by their university patent sample. In contrast, our control sample matches each university patent with a nonuniversity patent from the same patent class with an application date at or near the date of application for the university patent.

22. Our definition of biomedical patent classes is based on Technology Assessment and Forecast reports published by the U.S. Patent and Trademark Office that identify three-digit patent classes and subclasses related to medical and biomedical technologies. For a more detailed description of this taxonomy, see Ziedonis (2001).

23. In another analysis not reported because of space limitations, we subdivided the post-1981 period into three subperiods of equal length in order to test for more significant reductions in the importance of Stanford and UC patents during the late 1980s. Henderson, Jaffe, and Trajtenberg (1998a) find that the greatest reduction in importance in their sample of academic patents, especially those assigned to the leading academic patenters, occurs late in the 1980s. Our tests for differences in the means of the university and control patent samples, however, reveal no significant differences.

24. Interestingly, the corrected results reported in the errata appendix to Trajtenberg, Henderson, and Jaffe (1997) find that the importance (measured in terms of the number of forward citations) of academic patents, relative to those from corporate inventors, declines between 1975 and 1980, before the Bayh-Dole Act. This finding is broadly consistent with our conclusion that Bayh-Dole per se had little measurable effect on the relative importance of academic and nonacademic patents.

25. Any such effect was significant during only the early years of Columbia's

patenting and licensing activities, since by 1986–90 the share of disclosures resulting in issued patents and the share of disclosures that result in licenses yielding positive royalty income are fairly similar at Columbia, the University of California, and Stanford, as we noted earlier in this chapter.

26. We also examined the number of UC and Stanford patents from all three subperiods that yielded no citations during the six years following their issue in an effort to replicate the analysis in Henderson, Jaffe, and Trajtenberg (1998a) of "losers." Here, too, we find no consistent trend. "Zero-citation patents" account for 22 percent and 18 percent, respectively, of the UC and Stanford patents for period 1 in Tables 6.5 and 6.6; 16 percent and 0 percent of the UC and Stanford patents in period 2; and 11 percent and 8 percent of the UC and Stanford patents in period 3.

27. We also tested, but do not report results, for the significance of year-specific effects on the relative importance of these academic and nonacademic patents, using a negative binomial specification. We find no significant decline in the importance of these three universities' patents relative to nonacademic patents during the post-1980 period.

28. Stanford's "middle period" biomedical patents also display a lower mean generality score than do their control patents, and UC nonbiomedical patents applied for and issued before 1981 also exhibit slightly lower mean "generality scores" than do their respective control samples.

29. Sampat, Mowery, and Ziedonis (2003) empirically analyze the effects of truncation bias on measures of change in university patent quality after Bayh-Dole.

CHAPTER 7

1. As we pointed out in Note 21 in the previous chapter, the patent control samples used in our analysis are constructed differently from those of Henderson, Jaffe, and Trajtenberg (1995, 1998a).

2. Our construction of the academic patent dataset yields a small number of observations for 1992, and we accordingly omit this year from the results reported in Tables 7.2–4.

3. Specifically, we estimate a "double" tobit model with an lower limit of zero and an upper limit of 1.

4. We also ran probit regressions that examined the number of patents assigned to universities in these three groups that received no citations in the first six years following their issue. Henderson, Jaffe, and Trajtenberg (1998a,b) use this "zero-citation" measure as another measure of change in the characteristics of university patents. The results of these probit regressions were broadly similar to those reported in Tables 7.2–4.

5. Our findings of differences in significance in importance and generality among the "high-intensity" incumbent, "low-intensity" incumbent, and "entrant" subsamples and their respective control groups could be affected by differences in standard errors due to the various sizes of the three subsamples. To check the robustness of our results, we conducted but do not report similar regressions combining all three subsamples and obtained broadly similar results to those reported in Tables 7.2–4.

NOTES TO CHAPTER 7

6. Our matching algorithm used to generate the control sample generated the same control patent for 307 university patents. We thus have 10,574 different control patents matched with our 10,881 university patents.

7. Lanjouw and Schankerman (1998) suggest that five-year citation windows are sufficient to construct meaningful measures of a patent's "importance."

8. We also conducted Poisson regressions but tested for and found evidence of overdispersion, suggesting that the negative binomial model is more appropriate.

9. We also conducted but do not report probit regressions comparing the probability that an academic and nonacademic patent is ever cited within five years of issue using the same university and control group samples. Point estimates of the coefficients for ENT_{8183} and ENT_{8486} in this analysis imply a marginal effect of about -0.05 (that is, entrants' patents applied for during 1981–83 and 1984–86 were approximately 5 percent less likely to be cited at all than were incumbents' patents).

10. Unreported probit regression results for biomedical patents indicate that entrants' patents applied for during 1984–86 were significantly less likely (at the 5 percent level) to be cited than were incumbents' patents. This difference was not statistically significant, however, for entrant-university and incumbent-university patents applied for during 1981–83.

11. In unreported probit regressions for nonbiomedical patents, entrants' patents applied for during 1981–83 are significantly less likely to be cited at all than are the similar patents of incumbent universities (at the 5 percent level), but this differential becomes smaller and statistically insignificant for patents applied for during 1984–86.

12. Improvement in entrants' patent importance could reflect changes in funding patterns. For example, if the average importance of patents in an institution's patent portfolio is correlated with the size of its research budget, increases in their research budgets could lead to an improvement in the importance of entrant universities' patents in the absence of "learning." There is little empirical support for this hypothesis, and we do not test it here. Nevertheless, Geiger and Feller (1995) found evidence of increased interinstitutional dispersion in federal funding of university research during the 1980s, and higher dispersion may well have benefited universities with less pre-1980 experience in patenting. Geiger and Feller (1995) found that growth during the 1980s in funding dispersion was greatest in biomedicine, a field in which we find little evidence of improvement in the importance of entrants' patents. Although it merits additional analysis, this evidence provides little support for a "dispersion hypothesis" in explaining the increased measured importance of entrant universities' patents during the late 1980s.

13. In separate regressions (not reported), we analyze the average importance of an institution's patents at time t as a function of cumulative patenting experience for the entire 1975–92 period. These regressions did not reveal a relationship between cumulative patenting and patent importance.

14. Michael Crow, personal communication, September 28, 2000.

15. We also conducted but do not report the results of regression specifications using interaction terms for individual application years and patent technology classes. These regressions produced results similar to those from regressions where application

212   years were aggregated into three-year intervals. The first application year dummy and first patent class dummy were omitted to avoid perfect multicollinearity.

CHAPTER 8

1. Similar results are reported in Thursby and Thursby (2002), based on a survey of 112 firms that licensed university inventions between 1993 and 1997.

2. Two important publications describing the process were Wigler et al. (1977) and Wigler et al. (1979).

3. Since Columbia did not have a technology transfer office in early 1980, the General Counsel's office handled all potentially patentable inventions disclosed to the university.

4. Columbia's low royalty rates for a key "research process" patent resemble the licensing policies followed by Stanford in its licensing of the Cohen-Boyer patents developed by researchers at the University of California and Stanford University.

5. Niels Reimers, the first head of Stanford's Office of Technology Transfer and manager of the licensure of Cohen-Boyer, subsequently noted, "[W]hether we licensed it or not, commercialization of recombinant DNA was going forward. As I mentioned, a nonexclusive licensing program, at its heart, is really a tax . . . [b]ut it's always nice to say 'technology transfer'" (Reimers, 1998).

6. Materials similar to GaN that are based on aluminum and indium have similar properties and are now used in many of the same applications listed above as a result of the research effort discussed below. Although we focus on GaN, research in this area included research on a class of related semiconductors that included these cousins, namely Class III-V.

7. Blue GaN LEDs had been produced previously—Pankove himself had developed a prototype earlier. But Nakamura's prototype is widely credited as the first GaN LED with significant commercial potential.

8. "GaN-related patents" were selected through a text-based search for "gallium nitride" or "GaN" in the title or abstract of all U.S. patents issuing during 1972–98.

9. Akasaki's patents issued in 1983 and 1984 are largely based on his work at Matsushita, since the patents were applied for during the same year Akasaki accepted his university position.

10. The other university patent issuing during 1983–94 was assigned to Harvard University and covered a thin film process that could be used for GaN as well as other Class III-V compounds.

11. Another significant instance of industrial knowledge flowing into academia occurred in 2000, when Nakamura accepted a position at UC Santa Barbara.

12. In 2002, responsibility for the distribution of the Ames Tests assays was shifted to Xenometrix, the start-up firm that commercialized the Ames II Tests. Xenometrix has maintained the original UC distribution policies for these Ames Tests, policies that in many respects resemble the Materials Transfer Agreements widely used by academic and industrial research laboratories.

13. *http://ist-socrates.berkeley.edu/mutagen/salmut_facil_core.html.*

14. Gene profiling is the process of collecting information on gene activity after ex-

posure to another organism, a chemical, or an environmental change.

15. The *Wall Street Journal* announced after the publication of the paper by Ortho scientists that "a sixth scientific group has entered the already crowded field vying to develop [CD4]" (Chase, 1988). As was the case in the GaN study, the large number of published scientific papers from industrial scientists in this field illustrates the importance of knowledge flows from industrial research to academic institutions.

16. Referring to Upjohn's licensure from the NIH of the competing CD4 treatment (CD4–PE), the *Antiviral Agents Bulletin* observed that "it is interesting to note that Upjohn has licensed this patent application for CD4, although a patent claiming the entire CD4 gene and active portions has been issued to Columbia . . . [i]t appears that Columbia could claim infringement or otherwise try to induce Upjohn to take a license on its CD4 patent, should its CD4-PE show sufficient clinical and commercial potential" ("CD4-PE40 Exotoxin Conjugate in Trials; Other CD4 Conjugates in Development," 1992, p. 69).

17. A 1995 article observed that "although other, much larger companies have pursued development of CD4-based therapeutics, none appear to have active development efforts in this area, and it is somewhat surprising that so few organizations are pursuing development of CD4-based therapeutics" ("Progenics Developing CD4-IgG2 for HIV-Infection," 1995, p. 166).

18. Interest within the research and industrial communities in soluble CD4–based treatments remained high, because antiretroviral drugs have side effects that many patients cannot tolerate, and a growing share of HIV patients have developed resistance to such drugs.

19. Two of the licensees sold their soluble CD4 preparations to other researchers, accounting for the sales-based royalties. In addition to these sales-based royalties, Columbia collected at least $2 million in up-front payments, milestone payments, and legal reimbursements from the licensees.

20. Nonetheless, interviews with licensing officers suggest that very few university inventions face such strong demand from prospective licensees that the officer can select from among several "applicants" for a license in a given field of use.

21. The substantial flow of scientific papers from industrial scientists in AIDS research that was noted earlier also supports this characterization of the firms engaged in commercial development of the soluble CD4 invention.

CHAPTER 9

1. Indeed, Howard Bremer, former patent counsel for the Wisconsin Alumni Research Foundation (WARF) and president of the Association of University Technology Managers (AUTM) during 1978–79, acknowledged in a statement celebrating the "technology transfer harvest" following Bayh-Dole that the growth of patenting of federally funded academic research began not with Bayh-Dole but with the NSF and HEW Institutional Patent Agreements (IPAs) in the 1960s and 1970s, and he notes that "in fact, that law is often looked upon as a codification of the terms and provisions of the IPAs" (Bremer, 2001).

2. In June 1998, a report of the NIH Working Group on Research Tools raised con-

214   cerns about difficulties scientists and institutions faced in getting access to patented biomedical research tools developed with federal funds. In response to these concerns, in the "Technology Transfer Commercialization Act of 2000," Congress added a "technical amendment" to Bayh-Dole, noting that federally funded inventions should be licensed "without unduly encumbering future research and development" (Roumel, 2003). The effects of this change in the language of the Bayh-Dole Act on academic patenting and licensing practices remain unclear.

3. Walsh, Arora, and Cohen (2003) argue that the reliance by academic researchers and research administrators on a de facto research exemption from infringement suits has been an important "working solution" to problems arising from the potential assertion by patentholders of rights over research materials, tools, and similar inputs for the scientific research process. The authors conclude that the *Madey v. Duke* decision, if not reversed judicially or legislatively, "could well chill some of the 'offending' biomedical research that is conducted in university settings" (p. 56).

REFERENCES

Agrawal, A., and R. Henderson. 2002. "Putting Patents in Context: Exploring Knowledge Transfer from MIT." *Management Science* 48: 44–60.

American Association for the Advancement of Science (AAAS). 1934. *The Protection by Patents of Scientific Discoveries: Report of the Committee on Patents, Copyrights, and Trademarks.* New York: Science Press.

Apple, R. D. 1989. "Patenting University Research." *Isis* 80: 375–94.

——— 1996. *Vitamania: Vitamins in American Culture.* New Brunswick, N.J.: Rutgers University Press.

Arrow, K. 1962. "Economic Welfare and the Allocation of Resources for Invention." In R. R. Nelson, ed., *The Rate and Direction of Inventive Activity.* Princeton, N.J.: Princeton University Press.

Association of University Technology Managers (AUTM). 1994. *The AUTM Licensing Survey: Executive Summary and Selected Data, Fiscal Years 1993, 1992, and 1991.* Norwalk, Conn.: AUTM.

——— 1996. *AUTM Licensing Survey 1996, Survey Summary.* Norwalk, Conn.: AUTM.

——— 1998. *AUTM Licensing Survey 1998, Survey Summary.* Norwalk, Conn.: AUTM.

——— 2000. *The AUTM Licensing Survey: FY 1999.* Norwalk, Conn.: AUTM.

"Axel Patent Claims Mammalian Cell Transfer." *McGraw Hill's Biotechnology Newswatch* 3 (1983): 5.

Barrett, P. 1980. "Harvard Fears Congress May Not Pass Patent Bill." *Harvard Crimson,* October 7.

Ben-David, J., 1968. *Fundamental Research and the Universities.* Paris: OECD.

Blum, F. 2000. Telephone interview.

Blumenthal, D., E. Campbell, M. Anderson, N. Causino, and K. Louis. 1997. "Withholding Research Results in Academic Life Science: Evidence from a National Survey of Faculty." *Journal of the American Medical Association* 277: 1224–29.

216   Blumenthal, D., S. Epstein, and J. Maxwell. 1986. "Commercializing University Research: Lessons from the History of the Wisconsin Alumni Research Foundation." *New England Journal of Medicine* 314: 1621–26.

Bok, D. *Beyond the Ivory Tower.* 1982. Cambridge: Harvard University Press.

Bremer, H. 2001. "The First Two Decades of the Bayh-Dole Act as Public Policy." Presentation to the National Association of State Universities and Land Grant Colleges. Available from World Wide Web: http://www.nasulgc.org/COTT/Bayh -Dohl/Bremer_speech.htm.

Broad, W. 1979a. "Patent Bill Returns Bright Idea to Inventor." *Science* 205: 473–76.

——— 1979b. "Whistle Blower Reinstated at HEW." *Science* 205: 476.

Bryson, E. 1984. "Frederick E. Terman: Educator and Mentor." *IEEE Spectrum* (March): 71–73.

Burn, B. B., P. G. Altbach, C. Kerr, and J. A. Perkins. 1971. *Higher Education in Nine Countries.* New York: McGraw-Hill.

Bush, V. 1943. "The Kilgore Bill." *Science* 98: 571–77.

——— 1945. *Science: The Endless Frontier.* Washington, D.C.: U.S. Government Printing Office.

Cameron, F. 1993. *Cottrell: Samaritan of Science.* Tucson, Az.: Research Corporation.

Campbell, E. G., B. R. Clarridge, M. Gokhale, L. Birenbaum, S. Hilgartner, N. A. Holtzman, and D. Blumenthal. 2002. "Data Withholding in Academic Genetics: Evidence from a National Survey." *Journal of the American Medical Association* 287: 473–80.

Camras, C. B., and L. Z. Bito. 1981. "Reduction of Intraocular Pressure in Normal and Glaucomatous Primate (Aotus Trivirgatus) Eyes by Topically Applied Prostaglandin F2 Alpha." *Current Eye Research* 1: 205–9.

Camras, C. B., L. Z. Bito, and K. E. Eakins. 1977. "Reduction of Intraocular Pressure by Prostaglandins Applied Topically to the Eyes Of Conscious Rabbits." *Investigative Ophthalmology and Visual Science* 16: 1125–34.

Carnegie Commission on Higher Education. 1973. *A Classification of Institutions of Higher Education: A Technical Report.* Berkeley, Calif.: Carnegie Commission on Higher Education.

——— 1993. *A Classification of Institutions of Higher Education; A Technical Report.* Berkeley, Calif.: Carnegie Commission on Higher Education.

Caves, R., H. Crookell, and P. Killing. 1983. "The Imperfect Market for Technology Licenses." *Oxford Bulletin of Economics and Statistics* 45: 249–67.

"CD4-PE40 Exotoxin Conjugate in Trials; Other CD4 Conjugates in Development." *Antiviral Agents Bulletin* (March 1992): 69.

Chase, M. 1988. "Group Enters Field Studying CD4 for AIDS." *Wall Street Journal,* June 3.

Chiang, H. 1997. "Court Reinstates Royalty Award to UC Professors." *San Francisco Chronicle,* December 2.

Cohen, W. M., R. Florida, and R. Goe. 1994. "University-Industry Research Centers in the United States." Pittsburgh: Center for Economic Development, Carnegie-Mellon University.

Cohen, W. M., R. Florida, L. Randazzese, and J. Walsh. 1998. "Industry and the Academy: Uneasy Partners in the Cause of Technological Advance." In R. Noll, ed., *Challenges to the Research University*. Washington, D.C.: Brookings Institution.

Cohen, W. M., and D. A. Levinthal. 1990. "Absorptive Capacity: A New Perspective on Learning and Innovation." *Administrative Science Quarterly* 35: 128–52.

Cohen, W. M., R. R. Nelson, and J. P. Walsh. 2002. "Links and Impacts: The Influence of Public Research on Industrial R&D." *Management Science* 48: 1–23.

"Columbia Innovation Enterprise: A Special Report." *Reporter* 7 (1996).

"Columbia University rDNA Patent Licensing." *Blue Sheet* 27 (1984): 3–4.

Colyvas, J., M. Crow, A. Gelijns, R. Mazzoleni, R. R. Nelson, N. Rosenberg, and B. N. Sampat. 2002. "How Do University Inventions Get into Practice?" *Management Science* 48: 61–72.

Committee on Uniform Patent Policies in Land Grant and Engineering Experiment Stations. 1922. "Report of the Committee on Uniform Patent Policies." *Proceedings of the Association of Land Grant Colleges and Universities*: 283–84.

Cottrell, F. 1911. "The Electrical Precipitation of Suspended Particles." *Journal of Industrial and Engineering Chemistry* 3: 542–50.

——— 1912. "The Research Corporation, an Experiment in the Public Administration of Patent Rights." *Journal of Industrial and Engineering Chemistry* 4: 864–67.

——— 1932. "Patent Experience of the Research Corporation." *Transactions of the American Institute of Chemical Engineers* 26: 222–25.

——— 1937. "The Social Responsibility of the Engineer." *Journal of the Western Society of Engineers* 42: 65–77.

Council on Government Relations. 1999. *The Bayh-Dole Act: A Guide to the Law and Implementing Regulations*. Available from World Wide Web: http://www.cogr.edu/bayh-dole.htm.

Crow, M. M., A. C. Gelijns, R. R. Nelson, H. J. Raider, and B. N. Sampat. 1998. "Recent Changes in University-Industry Research Interactions: A Preliminary Analysis of Causes and Effects." Unpublished working paper, School of International and Public Affairs, Columbia University, New York.

Dasgupta, P., and P. David. 1994. "Towards a New Economics of Science." *Research Policy* 23: 487–521.

David, P. A., and D. Foray. 1995. "Accessing and Expanding the Science and Technology Knowledge Base." *STI Review* 16: 13–68.

David, P. A., D. C. Mowery, and W. E. Steinmueller. 1992. "Analyzing the Economic Payoffs from Basic Research." *Economics of Innovation and New Technology* 2: 73–90.

Davis, E. W. 1964. *Pioneering with Taconite*. St. Paul: Minnesota Historical Society.

DenBaars, S. 2000. Personal interview.

Department of Health and Human Services. 2001. *NIH Response to the Conference Report Request for a Plan to Ensure Taxpayers' Interests Are Protected*. Bethesda, Md.: National Institutes of Health. Available from World Wide Web: http://www.nih.gov/news/070101wyden.htm.

Dickinson, Q. Todd. 2000. "Reconciling Research and the Patent System." *Issues in Science and Technology* 16: 27–31.

"Dr. Cottrell and the Research Corporation." *Scientific Monthly* 22 (1926): 181–86.

218

Dreyfuss, R. 2003. "Varying the Course in Patenting Genetic Material: A Counter-Proposal to Richard Epstein's *Steady Course.*" New York University School of Law, Public Law and Legal Theory Research Paper Series, Research Paper No. 59.

Eisenberg, R. S. 1996. "Public Research and Private Development: Patents and Technology Transfer in Government-Sponsored Research." *Virginia Law Review* 82: 1663–1727.

———. 2001. "Bargaining over the Transfer of Proprietary Research Tools: Is This Market Emerging or Failing?" In D. L. Zimmerman, R. C. Dreyfuss, and H. First, eds., *Expanding the Bounds of Intellectual Property: Innovation Policy for the Knowledge Society.* New York: Oxford University Press.

Eskridge, N. 1978. "Dole Blasts HEW for 'Stonewalling' Patent Applications." *Bioscience* 28: 605–6.

Etzkowitz, H. 1994. "Knowledge as Property: The Massachusetts Institute of Technology and the Debate of Academic Patent Policy." *Minerva* 32: 383–421.

Evenson, R. E. 1982. "Agriculture." In R. R. Nelson, ed., *Government and Technical Progress: A Cross-Industry Analysis.* New York: Pergamon.

Executive Office of the President. 1983. "Memorandum to the Heads of Executive Departments and Agencies: Government Patent Policy, February 18, 1983."

Federal Council on Science and Technology (FCST). 1978. *Report on Government Patent Policy, 1973–1976.* Washington, D.C.: U.S. Government Printing Office.

Feldman, M., I. Feller, J. E. L. Bercovitz, and R. Burton. 2002. "Equity and the Technology Transfer Strategies of American Research Universities." *Management Science* 48: 105–21.

Fishman, E. A. 1996. "MIT Patent Policy 1932–1946: Historical Precedents in University-Industry Technology Transfer." Ph.D. diss., University of Pennsylvania.

Flexner, A. 1968 [1930]. *Universities: American, English, German.* London: Oxford University Press.

Foray, D., and A. Kazancigil. 1999. "Science, Economics and Democracy." Management of Social Transformation (MOST) Discussion Paper 42. Prepared for UNESCO World Conference on Science 1999.

Foreman, J. 1988. "Scientists Race to Create AIDS Virus 'Decoy': Crucial Issues Remain, but Interest Is Intense in Using Fake Receptors." *Boston Globe,* January 11.

Fox, J. 1983. "Columbia Awarded Biotechnology Patent." *Science* 221: 933.

Furter, W. F., ed. 1980. *History of Chemical Engineering.* Washington, D.C.: American Chemical Society.

Gee, P. 2001. Personal interview.

Gee, P., D. M. Maron, and B. N. Ames. 1994. "Detection and Classification of Mutagens: A Set of Base-Specific Salmonella Tester Strains." *Proceedings of the National Academy of Sciences* 91: 11606–10.

Geiger, R. 1986. *To Advance Knowledge: The Growth of American Research Universities, 1900–1940.* New York: Oxford University Press.

———. 1993. *Research and Relevant Knowledge: American Research Universities Since World War II.* New York: Oxford University Press.

Geiger, R., and I. Feller. 1995. "The Dispersion of Academic Research in the 1980s." *Journal of Higher Education* 65: 336–60.

Gelijns, A., and N. Rosenberg. 1999. "Diagnostic Devices: An Analysis of Comparative

Advantages." In D. C. Mowery and R. R. Nelson, eds., *Sources of Industrial Leadership*. New York: Cambridge University Press.

Gerth, J., and S. Stolberg. 2000. "Drug Companies Profit from Research Funded by Taxpayers." *New York Times*, April 23.

Gilles, J. 1991. "Research Corporation Technologies Offers Universities 'Critical Mass' of Diverse Expertise." *Technology Access Report*, August: 1+.

"Glennan Asks Review of NASA Patent Policy." 1959. *Aviation Week*, March 30, 33.

Government University Industry Research Roundtable (GUIRR). 1991. *Industrial Perspectives on Innovation and Interactions with Universities*. Washington, D.C.: National Academy Press.

Graham, H. D., and N. Diamond. 1997. *The Rise of American Research Universities*. Baltimore: Johns Hopkins University Press.

Gray, G. 1936. "Science and Profits." *Harpers* 172: 539–49.

Grayson, L. 1977. "A Brief History of Engineering Education in the United States." *Engineering Education* (December): 246–64.

Gregg, A. 1933. "University Patents." *Science* 77: 257–60.

Hall, B. H. 2000. "A Note on the Bias in the Herfindahl Based on Count Data." In A. B. Jaffe and M. Trajtenberg, eds., *Patents, Citations, and Innovations: A Window on the Knowledge Economy*. Cambridge: MIT Press.

Hall, B. H., A. B. Jaffe, and M. Tratjenberg. 2001. "The NBER Patent Citation Data File: Lessons, Insights and Methodological Tools." National Bureau of Economic Research Working Paper 8498.

Harbridge House Inc. 1968a. "Effects of Patent Policy on Government R&D Programs." *Government Patent Policy Study, Final Report*. Vol. 2. Washington, D.C.: Federal Council for Science and Technology.

——— 1968b. "Effects of Government Policy on Commercial Utilization and Business Competition." *Government Patent Policy Study, Final Report*. Vol. 4. Washington, D.C.: Federal Council for Science and Technology.

Hasselmo, N. 1999. *Priorities for Federal Innovation Reform*. Washington, D.C.: Association of American Universities.

Heaton, George R., Jr., Christopher T. Hill, and Patrick Windham. 2000. "Policy Innovation: The Initiation and Formation of New Science and Technology Policies in the U.S. During the 1980s." A Report to Japan External Trade Organization New York office and Japan New Energy and Industrial Technology Development Organization, Washington, D.C.

Heilbron, J., and R. Seidel. 1989. *Lawrence and His Laboratory: A History of the Lawrence Berkeley Laboratory*. Berkeley: University of California Press.

Heller, M. A., and R. S. Eisenberg. 1998. "Can Patents Deter Innovation? The Anticommons in Biomedical Research." *Science* 280: 298.

Henderson, R., A. B. Jaffe, and M. Trajtenberg. 1994. "Numbers Up, Quality Down? Trends in University Patenting, 1965–1992." Presented at the CEPR Conference on University Goals, Institutional Mechanisms, and the "Industrial Transferability" of Research, Stanford University, Stanford, California.

——— 1995. "Universities as a Source of Commercial Technology: A Detailed Analysis of University Patenting, 1965–1988." National Bureau of Economic Research Working Paper 5068.

——— 1998a. "Universities as a Source of Commercial Technology: A Detailed Analysis of University Patenting, 1965–88." *Review of Economics and Statistics* 80: 119–27.

——— 1998b. "University Patenting Amid Changing Incentives for Commercialization." In G. Barba Navaretti, P. Dasgupta, K. G. Mäler, and D. Siniscalco, eds., *Creation and Transfer of Knowledge*. New York: Springer.

Henderson, R., L. Orsenigo, and G. Pisano. 1999. "The Pharmaceutical Industry and the Revolution in Molecular Biology: Interactions Among Scientific, Institutional and Organizational Change." In D. C. Mowery and R. R. Nelson, eds., *Sources of Industrial Leadership*. New York: Cambridge University Press.

Henderson, Y. 1933. "Patents Are Ethical." *Science* 77: 324–25.

Henig, R. 1979. "New Patent Policy Bill Gathers Congressional Support." *Bioscience* 29: 281–84.

Hoskins, W., and R. Wiles. 1921. "Promotion of Scientific Research." *Chemical and Metallurgical Engineering* 24: 689–91.

Hounshell, D. A., and J. K. Smith. 1988. *Science and Corporate Strategy*. New York: Cambridge University Press.

"Innovation's Golden Goose." 2002. *Economist* 365: T3.

Jaffe, A. B., M. S. Fogarty, and B. A. Banks. 1998. "Evidence from Patents and Patent Citations on the Impact of NASA and Other Federal Labs on Commercial Innovation." *Journal of Industrial Economics* 46: 183–205.

Jensen, R., and M. Thursby. 2001. "Proofs and Prototypes for Sale: The Licensing of University Inventions." *American Economic Review* 91: 240–58.

Kahaner, D. 1995. "Blue LEDs: Breakthroughs and Implications." Available from World Wide Web: http://www.atip.or.jp/public/atp.reports.95/atip95.59r.html.

Katz, M. L., and J. A. Ordover. 1990. "R&D Competition and Cooperation." *Brookings Papers on Economic Activity: Microeconomics*: 137–92.

Kevles, D. J. 1977. "The National Science Foundation and the Debate over Postwar Research Policy, 1942–45." *Isis* 68: 5–26.

——— 1978. *The Physicists*. New York: Norton.

——— 1990. *Principles and Politics in Federal R&D Policy, 1945–1990: An Appreciation of the Bush Report*. Washington, D.C.: National Science Foundation.

Kitch, E. W. 1977. "The Nature and Function of the Patent System." *Journal of Law and Economics* 20: 265–90.

Kortum, S., and J. Lerner. 1999. "What Is Behind the Recent Surge in Patenting?" *Research Policy* 28: 1–22.

Lamoreaux, N., and K. Sokoloff. 2002. "Intermediaries in the Market for Technology in the United States, 1870–1920." National Bureau of Economic Research Working Paper 9017.

Lanjouw, J. O., and M. Schankerman. 1998. "The Quality of Ideas: Measuring Innovation with Multiple Indicators." National Bureau of Economic Research Working Paper 7375.

Levin, R. C., A. Klevorick, R. R. Nelson, and S. Winter. 1987. "Appropriating the Returns from Industrial Research and Development." *Brookings Papers on Economic Activity* 3: 783–820.

Levine, D. O. 1986. *The American College and the Culture of Aspiration, 1915–1940.* Ithaca, N.Y.: Cornell University Press.

"Licensing Plan For AIDS Drug Draws Fire." 1988. *Seattle Times,* October 25.

Liebeskind, J. 2001. "Risky Business: Universities and Intellectual Property." *Academe* 87. Available from World Wide Web: http://www.aaup.org/publications/Academe/01SO/soo1lie.htm.

Little, A. D. 1933. *Twenty-five Years of Chemical Engineering Progress.* New York: Van Nostrand.

Louis, K., L. Jones, M. Anderson, D. Blumenthal, and E. Campbell. 2001. "Entrepreneurship, Secrecy, and Productivity: A Comparison of Clinical and Non-Clinical Life Sciences Faculty." *Journal of Technology Transfer* 26: 233–45.

Lowe, Robert A. 2001. "The Role and Experience of Start-ups in Commercializing University Inventions: Start-up Licensees at the University of California." In G. Libecap, ed., *Entrepreneurial Inputs and Outcomes.* Amsterdam: JAI Press.

——— 2002. "Entrepreneurship and Information Asymmetry: Theory and Evidence from the University of California." Unpublished working paper, Haas School of Business, University of California–Berkeley.

Maddison, A. 1987. "Growth and Slowdown in Advanced Capitalist Economies: Techniques of Quantitative Assessment." *Journal of Economic Literature* 25: 649–98.

Maddon, P. J., D. R. Littman, M. Godfrey, D. E. Maddon, L. Chess, and R. Axel. 1985. "The Isolation and Nucleotide Sequence of a cDNA Encoding the T Cell Surface Protein T4: A New Member of the Immunoglobulin Gene Family." *Cell* 42: 93–104.

Mansfield, E. 1991. "Academic Research and Industrial Innovations." *Research Policy* 20: 1–12.

Marcy, W. 1978. "Patent Policy at Educational and Nonprofit Scientific Institutions." In W. Marcy, ed., *Patent Policy: Government, Academic, and Industry Concepts.* Washington, D.C.: American Chemical Society.

Marx, J. 1980. "Gene Transfer Moves Ahead." *Science* 210: 1334–36.

Mazzoleni, R., and R. Nelson. 1998. "The Benefits and Costs of Strong Patent Protection: A Contribution to the Current Debate." *Research Policy* 27: 274–84.

McKusick, V. 1948. "A Study of Patent Policies in Educational Institutions, Giving Specific Attention to the Massachusetts Institute of Technology." *Journal of the Franklin Institute* 245: 193–225.

Merges, R., and R. Nelson. 1994. "On Limiting or Encouraging Rivalry in Technical Progress: The Effect of Patent Scope Decisions." *Journal of Economic Behavior and Organization* 25: 1–24.

Merton, R. K. 1973. *The Sociology of Science : Theoretical and Empirical Investigations.* Chicago: University of Chicago Press.

Mishra, U. 2001. Personal interview.

Mowery, D. C. 1981. "The Emergence and Growth of Industrial Research in American Manufacturing, 1899–1945." Ph.D. diss., Stanford University.

——— 1983. "The Relationship Between Intrafirm and Contractual Forms of Industrial Research in American Manufacturing, 1900–1940." *Explorations in Economic History* 20: 351–74.

——— 1999. *The Evolving Structure of University-Industry Collaboration in the United*

States: Three Cases, in Research Teams and Partnerships: Trends in the Chemical Sciences. Washington, D.C.: National Academy Press.

—— 2002. "The Changing Role of Universities in the 21st Century U.S. R&D System." In A. H. Teich, S. D. Nelson, S. J. Lita, eds., *AAAS Science and Technology Policy Handbook.* Washington, D.C.: American Association for the Advancement of Science.

Mowery, D. C., R. R. Nelson, B. N. Sampat, and A. A. Ziedonis. 1999. "The Effects of the Bayh-Dole Act on U.S. University Research and Technology Transfer: An Analysis of Data from Columbia University, the University of California, and Stanford University." In L. Branscomb and R. Florida, eds., *Industrializing Knowledge.* Cambridge: MIT Press.

—— 2001. "The Growth of Patenting and Licensing by U.S. Universities: An Assessment of the Effects of the Bayh-Dole Act of 1980." *Research Policy* 30: 99–119.

Mowery, D. C., and N. Rosenberg. 1993. "The U.S. National Innovation System." In R. R. Nelson, ed., *National Innovation Systems: A Comparative Analysis.* New York: Oxford University Press.

—— 1998. *Paths of Innovation: Technological Change in 20th-Century America.* New York: Cambridge University Press.

Mowery, D. C., and B. N. Sampat. 2001a. "Patenting and Licensing University Inventions: Lessons from the History of the Research Corporation." *Industrial and Corporate Change* 10: 317–55.

—— 2001b. "University Patents, Patent Policies, and Patent Policy Debates, 1925–1980." *Industrial and Corporate Change* 10: 781–814.

Mowery, D. C., B. N. Sampat, and A. A. Ziedonis. 2002. "Learning to Patent: Institutional Experience and the Quality of University Patents." *Management Science* 48: 73–89.

Mowery, D. C., and T. Simcoe. 2002. "The Origins and Evolution of the Internet." In D. Victor, B. Steil, and R. R. Nelson, eds., *Technological Innovation and National Economic Performance.* Princeton, N.J.: Princeton University Press.

Mowery, D. C., and A. A. Ziedonis. 1998. "Market Failure or Market Magic? Structural Change in the U.S. National Innovation System." *STI Review* 22: 101–36.

—— 2001. "The Geographic Reach of Market and Nonmarket Channels of Technology Transfer: Comparing Citations and Licenses of University Patents." National Bureau of Economic Research Working Paper 8568.

Mowery, D. C., and R. R. Nelson, eds. 1999. *Sources Of Industrial Leadership: Studies of Seven Industries.* New York: Cambridge University Press.

National Research Council. 1982. "Research in Europe and the United States." In *Outlook for Science and Technology: The Next Five Years.* San Francisco: W. H. Freeman.

—— 1997. *Intellectual Property Rights and Research Tools in Molecular Biology.* Washington, D.C.: National Academy Press.

National Resources Committee. 1938. *Research—A National Resource.* Vol. 1. Washington, D.C.: U.S. Government Printing Office.

National Science Board. 1996. *Science and Engineering Indicators: 1996.* Washington, D.C.: U.S. Government Printing Office.

—— 2000. *Science and Engineering Indicators: 2000.* Washington, D.C.: U.S. Government Printing Office.

—— 2002. *Science and Engineering Indicators: 2002.* Washington, D.C.: U.S. Government Printing Office.

National Science Foundation. 1958. *Funds for Scientific Activities in the Federal Government: Fiscal Years 1953 and 1954.* Washington, D.C.: U.S. Government Printing Office.

—— 1980. *National Patterns of Science and Technology Resources: 1980.* Washington, D.C.: U.S. Government Printing Office.

—— 1994. *National Patterns of R&D Resources: 1994.* Washington, D.C.: U.S. Government Printing Office.

—— 1996. *National Patterns of R&D Resources: 1996.* Washington, D.C.: U.S. Government Printing Office.

—— 1998. *National Patterns of R&D Resources: 1998.* Washington, D.C.: U.S. Government Printing Office.

—— 2000. *National Patterns of R&D Resources 2000.* Washington, D.C.: U.S. Government Printing Office.

—— 2001. *National Patterns of R&D Resources 2001.* Washington, D.C.: U.S. Government Printing Office.

Nelson, R. R. 1959. "The Simple Economics of Basic Scientific Research." *Journal of Political Economy* 67: 297–306.

—— 1984. *High-Technology Policies: A Five-Nation Comparison.* Washington, D.C.: American Enterprise Institute.

—— 1992. "What Is 'Commercial' and What Is 'Public' About Technology, and What Should Be?" In N. Rosenberg, R. Landau, and D. C. Mowery, eds., *Technology and the Wealth of Nations.* Stanford, Calif.: Stanford University Press.

——, ed. 1982. *Government and Technical Progress: A Cross-Industry Analysis.* New York: Pergamon.

—— 1993. *National Innovation Systems: A Comparative Analysis.* New York: Oxford University Press.

Nelson, R. R., and P. Romer. 1997. "Science, Economic Growth, and Public Policy." In B. L. R. Smith and C. Barfield, eds., *Technology, R&D, and the Economy.* Washington, D.C.: Brookings Institution.

Noble, D. F. 1977. *American by Design.* New York: Knopf.

Office of Technology Transfer. 1997. *Annual Report: University of California Technology Transfer Program.* Oakland: University of California Office of the President.

Okimoto, D., and G. Saxonhouse. 1987. "Technology and the Future of the Economy." In K. Yamamura and Y. Yasuba, eds., *The Political Economy of Japan.* Vol. 1, *The Domestic Transformation.* Stanford, Calif.: Stanford University Press.

Organization for Economic Cooperation and Development (OECD). 2000. *A New Economy?* Paris: OECD.

—— 2002. *Benchmarking Science-Industry Relationships.* Paris: OECD.

Palmer, A. M. 1934. "University Patent Policies and Procedures." *Journal of the Patent Office Society* 16: 96–131.

—— 1947. "Patents and University Research." *Law and Contemporary Problems* 15: 680–94.

224

———— 1948. *Survey of University Patent Policies.* Washington, D.C.: National Research Council.

———— 1949. *University Research and Patent Problems.* Washington, D.C.: National Research Council.

———— 1952. *University Patent Policies and Practices.* Washington, D.C.: National Academy of Sciences–National Research Council.

———— 1955. *Nonprofit Research and Patent Management Organization.* Washington, D.C.: National Academy of Sciences–National Research Council.

———— 1957. *Patents and Nonprofit Research: A Study Prepared for the Subcommittee on Patents, Trademarks, and Copyrights of the U.S. Senate Committee on the Judiciary.* Washington D.C.: U.S. Government Printing Office.

———— 1962. *University Research and Patent Policies, Practices, and Procedures.* Vol. 1. Washington, D.C.: National Academy of Sciences–National Research Council.

Perlman, D. 1987. "Biotech 'Decoy' May Fool AIDS Virus." *San Francisco Chronicle,* December 18.

Potter, A. 1940. "Research and Invention in Engineering Colleges." *Science* 91: 1–7.

"Progenics Developing CD4-IgG2 for HIV-Infection." 1995. *Antiviral Agents Bulletin* (June): 166.

Pugh, E. W. 1984. *Memories That Shaped an Industry: Decisions Leading to IBM System/360.* Cambridge: MIT Press.

Pursell, C. 1979. "Science Agencies in World War II: The OSRD and Its Challengers." In N. Reingold, ed., *The Sciences in the American Context: New Perspectives.* Washington, D.C.: Smithsonian Institution Press.

Rai, A. T., and R. S. Eisenberg. 2001. "The Public and the Private in Biopharmaceutical Research." Presented at the Conference on the Public Domain, Duke University.

———— 2003. "Bayh-Dole Reform and the Progress of Biomedicine." *American Scientist* 91: 52–59.

Reich, L. S. 1985. *The Making of American Industrial Research.* New York: Cambridge University Press.

Reimers, Niels. 1998. "Stanford's Office of Technology Licensing and the Cohen/Boyer Cloning Patents." An oral history conducted in 1997 by Sally Smith Hughes, Regional Oral History Office, The Bancroft Library, University of California, Berkeley. Available from the Online Archive of California, http://ark.cdlib.org/ark:/13030/kt4b69n6sc.

Research Corporation. 1947–87. *Annual Report.* New York and Tucson, Az.: Research Corporation.

———— 1972. *Science, Invention, and Society: The Story of a Unique American Institution.* New York: Research Corporation.

———— 1979. "Report of the Committee on Goals and Objectives." Unpublished MS, Research Corporation Archives, Tucson, Az.

Research Corporation Technologies. 1996. *Annual Report.* Tucson, Az: Research Corporation Technologies.

Rosenberg, N. 1992. "Scientific Instrumentation and University Research." *Research Policy* 21: 381–90.

——— 1998. "Technological Change in Chemicals: The Role of University-Industry Relations." In A. Arora, R. Landau and N. Rosenberg, eds., *Chemicals and Long-Term Economic Growth*. New York: John Wiley.

Rosenberg, N., and R. R. Nelson. 1994. "American Universities and Technical Advance in Industry." *Research Policy* 23: 323–48.

Roumel, T. 2003. "Development of a Policy to Ensure the Sharing of Unique Biomedical Research Resources in the Biomedical Community." In OECD, *Turning Science Into Business: Patenting and Licensing by Public Research Organizations*. Paris: OECD.

Roush, W., E. Marshall, and G. Vogel. 1997. "Publishing Sensitive Data: Who's Calling the Shots?" *Science* 276: 523–26.

Sampat, B., D. C. Mowery, and A. Ziedonis. 2003. "Changes in University Patent Quality After the Bayh-Dole Act: A Re-Examination." *International Journal of Industrial Organization* 21: 1371–90.

Sampat, B. N., and R. R. Nelson. 2002. "The Emergence and Standardization of University Technology Transfer Offices: A Case Study of Institutional Change." *Advances in Strategic Management* 19.

Sampat, B. N., and A. A. Ziedonis. 2003. "Cite-Seeing: Patent Citations and Economic Value." Presented at the Conference on Empirical Economics of Innovation and Patenting, Centre for European Economic Research, Mannheim Germany, March.

Servos, J. W. 1980. "The Industrial Relations of Science: Chemical Engineering at MIT, 1900–1939." *Isis* 71: 531–49.

Sevringhaus, E. L. 1932. "Should Scientific Discoveries Be Patented?" *Science* 75: 233–34.

Shane, S. 2002. "Selling University Technology." *Management Science* 48: 61–72.

Sharp, M. 1989. "European Countries in Science-Based Competition: The Case of Biotechnology." Designated Research Center Discussion Paper 72, Science Policy Research Unit, University of Sussex, Brighton, U.K.

Simon, H. A. 1969. *The Sciences of the Artificial*. Cambridge: MIT Press.

Smith, B. L. R., and J. J. Karlesky. 1977. *The State of Academic Science: The Universities in the Nation's Research Effort*. New York: Change Magazine Press.

Spencer, R. 1939. *University Patent Policies*. Chicago: Northwestern University Law School.

Stanford University Office of Technology Licensing. 1983. *Annual Report*. Stanford, Calif.: Stanford University.

——— 1990. *Annual Report*. Stanford, Calif.: Stanford University.

——— 1992. *1991–92 Annual Report: Office of Technology Licensing*. Stanford, Calif.: Stanford University.

——— 1994a. *Copyrightable Works and Licensing at Stanford*. Stanford, Calif.: Stanford University.

——— 1994b. *Office of Technology Licensing Guidelines for Software Distribution*. Stanford, Calif.: Stanford University.

Stata Corporation. 1999. *Stata Statistical Software: Release 6.0*. College Station, Tex.: Stata Corporation.

226   Stephan, P. E., S. Gurmu, A. J. Sumell, and G. Black. 2002. "Patenting and Publishing: Substitutes or Complements for University Faculty?" Unpublished working paper, Georgia State University, Atlanta.

Stern, N. 1981. *From ENIAC to Univac.* Bedford, Mass.: Digital Press.

Stokes, D. E. 1997. *Pasteur's Quadrant: Basic Science and Technological Innovation.* Washington, D.C.: Brookings Institution.

Swann, J. 1988. *Academic Scientists and the Pharmaceutical Industry: Cooperative Research in Twentieth-Century America.* Baltimore: Johns Hopkins University Press.

Thursby, J., R. Jensen, and M. Thursby. 2001. "Objectives, Characteristics and Outcomes of University Licensing: A Survey of Major U.S. Universities." *Journal of Technology Transfer* 26: 59–72.

Thursby, J., and M. Thursby. 2002. "Who Is Selling the Ivory Tower? Sources of Growth in University Licensing." *Management Science* 48: 90–104.

Tocqueville, A. de. 1990. *Democracy in America,* trans. by P. Bradley. New York: Vintage.

Trajtenberg, M., R. Henderson, and A. B. Jaffe. 1997. "University Versus Corporate Patents: A Window on the Basicness of Inventions." *Economics of Innovation and New Technology* 5: 19–50.

Trow, M. 1979. "Aspects of Diversity in American Higher Education." In H. Gans, ed., *On the Making of Americans.* Philadelphia: University of Pennsylvania Press.

——— 1991. "American Higher Education: 'Exceptional' or Just Different." In B. E. Shafer, ed., *Is America Different? A New Look at American Exceptionalism.* New York: Oxford University Press.

Trune, D., and L. Goslin. 1998. "University Technology Transfer Programs: A Profit/Loss Analysis." *Technological Forecasting and Social Change* 57: 197–204.

Trustees of Columbia University in the City of New York. 1944. "Statement of Research Policy and Patent Procedures." Columbiana Library, "Patents" folder, Columbia University, New York.

U.S. Congress Joint Economic Committee. 1999. *Entrepreneurial Dynamism and the Success of U.S. High-Tech: Joint Economic Committee Staff Report.* Washington, D.C.: U.S. Government Printing Office.

U.S. Department of Health Education and Welfare. 1974. *DHEW Obligations to Institutions of Higher Education and Selected Nonprofit Organizations, FY 1965–1972.* Washington, D.C.: U.S. Department of Health, Education, and Welfare.

U.S. Department of Justice. 1947. *Investigation of Government Patent Practices and Policies: Report and Recommendations of the Attorney General to the President.* Washington, D.C.: U.S. Government Printing Office.

U.S. General Accounting Office (GAO). 1968. *Problem Areas Affecting Usefulness of Results of Government-Sponsored Research in Medicinal Chemistry: A Report to the Congress.* Washington, D.C.: U.S. Government Printing Office.

——— 1995. *University Research: Effects of Indirect Cost Revisions and Options for Future Changes.* Washington, D.C.: U.S. Government Printing Office.

U.S. House of Representatives. 1980. Floor Debate on H.R. 6933. *Congressional Record,* 96th Congress, Second Session, November 21: 30556–60.

U.S. Office of Management and Budget. 1963. "Memorandum and Statement of Government Patent Policy." *Federal Register* 28: 10943–46.   **227**

―――― 1971. "Memorandum and Statement of Government Patent Policy." *Federal Register* 36: 16886.

―――― 1995. *The Budget of the United States Government for Fiscal 1996*. Washington, D.C.: U.S. Government Printing Office.

U.S. Patent and Trademark Office. 1998. *U.S. Colleges and Universities — Utility Patent Grants, 1969–1998*. Washington, D.C.: U.S. Government Printing Office.

U.S. Senate Committee on the Judiciary. 1979a. *S. Rpt. 96-480 Accompanying S. 414, the University and Small Business Patent Procedures Act*. Washington, D.C.: U.S. Government Printing Office.

―――― 1979b. *The University and Small Business Patent Procedures Act: Hearings on S. 414, May 16 and June 6*. Washington, D.C.: U.S. Government Printing Office.

U.S. Senate Subcommittee of the Senate Select Committee on Small Business. 1963. *Economic Aspects of Government Patent Policies*. Washington, D.C.: U.S. Government Printing Office.

Veblen, T. 1918. *The Higher Learning in America: A Memorandum on the Conduct of Universities by Business Men*. New York: W. B. Huesch.

Vincenti, W. 1990. *What Engineers Know and How They Know It*. Baltimore: John Hopkins University Press.

Walsh, J. P., A. Arora, and W. M. Cohen. 2003. "Research Tool Patenting and Licensing and Biomedical Innovation." In W. M. Cohen and S. Merrill, eds., *The Patent System in the Knowledge-Based Economy*. Washington, D.C.: National Academies Press.

Weiner, C. 1986. "Universities, Professors, and Patents: A Continuing Controversy." *Technology Review* 83: 33–43.

Weissman, R. 1989. "Public Finance, Private Gain: The Emerging University-Business-Government Alliance and the New U.S. Technological Order." Undergraduate thesis, Harvard University.

White, H. 1963. *Industrial Electrostatic Precipitation*. Reading, Mass.: Addison-Wesley.

Wigler, M., S. Silverstein, L. S. Lee, A. Pellicer, Y. Cheng, and R. Axel. 1977. "Transfer of Purified Herpes Virus Thymidine Kinase Gene to Cultured Mouse Cells." *Cell* 11: 223–32.

Wigler, M., R. Sweet, G. K. Sim, B. Wold, A. Pellicer, E. Lacy, T. Maniatis, S. Silverstein, and R. Axel. 1979. "Transformation of Mammalian Cells with Genes from Procaryotes and Eucaryotes." *Cell* 16: 777–85.

Wildes, K. L., and N. A. Lindgren. 1985. *A Century of Electrical Engineering and Computer Science at MIT, 1882–1982*. Cambridge: MIT Press.

Williamson, O. E. 1979. "Transaction Cost Economics: The Governance of Contractual Relation." *Journal of Law and Economics* 22: 233–62.

Zacks, R. 2000. "The TR University Research Scorecard 2000." *Technology Review* (July/August): Available from World Wide Web: http://www.technologyreview.com/articles/scorecard0700.asp.

Ziedonis, A. A. 2001. "The Commercialization of University Research: Implications for

228   Firm Strategy and Public Policy." Ph.D. diss., Haas School of Business, University of California–Berkeley.

Zinsser, A. 1927. "Problems of the Bacteriologist in His Relation to Medicine and the Public Health." *Journal of Bacteriology* 13: 147–62.

Zucker, L., M. Darby, and J. Armstrong. 1994. "Inter-Institutional Spillover Effects in the Commercialization of Bioscience." *ISSR Working Papers in Social Science* 6.3.

INDEX